SAINT MARY'S PRESS®

W9-ATO-993

CATHOLIC ETHICS IN TODAY'S WORLD

JOZEF D. ZALOT
BENEDICT GUEVIN, OSB

The publishing team included Leslie M. Ortiz, general editor; and John B. McHugh, director of college publishing; prepress and manufacturing coordinated by the production departments of Saint Mary's Press.

The scriptural quotations in this book are from the New American Bible with Revised New Testament and Revised Psalms (NAB). Copyright © 1991, 1986, and 1970 by the Confraternity of Christian Doctrine, Washington, D.C. Used by the permission of the copyright owner. All rights reserved. No part of the New American Bible may be reproduced in any form without permission in writing from the copyright owner.

Copyright © 2008 by Jozef D. Zalot and Benedict Guevin. All rights reserved. No part of this book may be reproduced by any means without the written permission of the publisher, Saint Mary's Press, Christian Brothers Publications, 702 Terrace Heights, Winona, MN 55987-1318, www.smp.org.

Cover images royalty-free from Shutterstock

Printed in the United States of America

7007

ISBN 978-0-88489-959-4

Library of Congress Cataloging-in-Publication Data

Zalot, Jozef D.
        Catholic ethics in today's world / Jozef D. Zalot , Benedict Guevin.
        p. cm.
ISBN 978-0-88489-959-4 (pbk.)
        1. Christian ethics—Catholic authors. I. Guevin, Benedict. II. Title.
BJ1249.Z35 2008
241'.042—dc22
                                                                2007044944

Contents

INTRODUCTION

What Does the Catholic Church Really Teach?

This question often comes up in theology courses and in parishes across our country. Large numbers of Catholic laity (the non-ordained) are genuinely interested in learning more about their faith and actively seek answers to their questions. They want to know what our Church teaches about the Bible, what it teaches as doctrine, and why our Church follows specific traditional practices. The questions are most often asked in terms of ethics. Today, as individuals, as a nation, and as a world community, we are confronted with many difficult and contentious ethical challenges. We are faced with such social issues as the death penalty, just war, and the forced repayment of foreign debts. We are challenged by ever-present sexual questions and changes in the medical field, including the morality of reproductive technologies and the level of care appropriate for dying patients. Ethical dilemmas are often the most challenging matters of faith for Catholics and non-Catholics alike. That's why they are the focus of this text.

Many Catholics are confused about what the Church does and does not teach, particularly in the area of ethics. There are a number of reasons for this confusion. Official magisterial[1] and bishops' conference statements that address important ethical issues are generally written for scholars, not laypeople. When laypeople try to read these documents they often walk away more confused than when they began.

A second reason for confusion is that the institutional Church generally does not do a good job of articulating what it teaches, and an even worse job of explaining why. Ask a random group of students or parishioners what the Church as a whole teaches about justified war, the death penalty, or removing a comatose patient from life support, and you will likely encounter blank stares. Although most people are aware that the Church opposes nonmarital sexual relations, ask them why it holds this teaching and again you will encounter blank stares. The problem here lies not necessarily with the magisterium, but with Church ministers (ordained and lay) acting on the local level. When was the last time you heard a homily — the Church's primary teaching tool — or attended a parish educational program concerning an ethical issue? If you have, good for you and congratulations to the priest, deacon, or lay minister who offered it! For the rest of us, such opportunities occur rarely if ever. Ordained clergy, in collaboration with their pastoral associates, have a duty to help parishioners know and understand what their Church teaches concerning ethical challenges. To the extent that this is not done, these teachings will remain the Church's "best kept secret."[2]

A third reason for confusion concerns the Church's theologians. The only time that most lay Catholics hear about theologians, particularly moral theologians, is when these individuals publicly dissent from official Church teaching. On the rather rare occasion that occurs, the media jump all over it and often misrepresent the real points of contention at the heart of the disagreement, causing more confusion. And some theologians who write Catholic ethics texts spend a significant amount of time critiquing official Church teaching, sometimes even spending more time on the critique than on the teaching itself. Now it is good that people question official Church teaching. Respectful, critical dialogue is essential to the ongoing tradition of the Church. The problem is that even when this critical questioning is done in a respectful way, it can become a further source of confusion if lay people misunderstand what the Church actually teaches.

A further issue is that those responsible for educating others—school teachers, pastoral associates, and college professors — are sometimes not well trained in Catholic ethics. As a result of their misinterpretation of Church teachings, students and parishioners receive mixed messages, which can lead to greater confusion.

This book seeks to offer a clear, detailed examination of not only what the Church teaches on a range of challenging ethical topics but also why it teaches what it does. We seek to demonstrate that our Church addresses many contemporary social, sexual, and medical challenges and in doing so offers moral principles to help form our consciences. By explaining what the Church teaches and why, we hope to offer some practical suggestions for how people can respond to moral challenges and live out their call to be Christian disciples in the world today.

Some ethicists and moral theologians may complain that this book presents the teachings of the Church uncritically, or that it is too close to the magisterium to be used effectively in an academic or pastoral setting. We strongly disagree. In this text, we wish to offer a baseline, a clear presentation of what the Catholic Church teaches on a particular topic so that people will be able to evaluate the teaching on its own merits and in light of the critique of others. We recognize that faithful Catholics disagree — in fact, even the authors do not completely agree on every topic addressed in this text — and that critical dialogue among different parties can be healthy. We encourage readers to seek out other sources to gain further insight and different perspectives from those presented here. Our text is meant to be a starting point for Catholic-based reflection on contemporary ethical challenges, not the final word.

Structure of this Text

Our first three chapters are foundational in that they provide a basic overview of how one "does" moral reflection. Chapter 1 focuses on what moral theology is and why Christian faith is so important for living the moral life. In chapter 2 we speak about moral acts and how we are called to form our consciences in truth. Chapter 3 introduces the reader to Catholic Social Teaching by providing a historical overview and then explaining the moral principles it upholds.

The remaining chapters focus on specific ethical challenges. Chapters 4 and 5 speak to questions of economic justice, the American corporate world, and the ongoing effects of Western-imposed debt repayment and structural adjustment programs on the people of sub-Saharan Africa. Chapters 6 and 7 discuss the direct taking of human life, exploring the morality of the death penalty and of the Church's traditional call to maintain peace while also detailing specific moral principles to be upheld in war. Chapter 8 focuses on medical ethics and discusses, among other issues, the Church's teachings on embryonic stem cell research and the level of care due to comatose patients. Finally, chapter 9 tackles sexual ethics by discussing the morality of extramarital relations, contraception, and homosexuality.

In contemporary society, the ethical challenges we face in these realms are many and complex. Although a thorough discussion of the issues is impossible in a text such as ours, we hope to lay a solid foundation of understanding on which to build.

ENDNOTES

1 The magisterium, which consists of the pope working in collaboration with the bishops of the world, is the official teaching authority of the Roman Catholic Church. In terms of morality, the magisterium is charged with interpreting God's revelation in light of the many ethical challenges we face and then formulating authoritative responses to them. We will speak more of the magisterium in chapter 2.

2 *Catholic Social Teaching: Our Best Kept Secret* is the title of a book, now in its fourth edition, by Edward P. DeBerri, James E. Hug, Peter J. Henriot, and Michael J. Schultheis (Maryknoll, NY: Orbis, 2003). The text introduces readers to Catholic Social Teaching and provides an overview of numerous nineteenth- and twentieth-century papal and bishops' conference documents.

PART I

FOUNDATIONS

1. THE FOUNDATIONS OF CHRISTIAN MORALITY

You have been told, o man, what is good, and what the Lord requires of you: Only to do the right and to love goodness, and to walk humbly with your God.

— Micah 6:8

To speak intelligently about the many ethical issues we face today, it is important to have a basic familiarity with the foundations of Christian morality. In this chapter we wish to introduce the reader to some of the basic terminology that we will use in this text and demonstrate some of the main sources of moral reflection. This introduction is not exhaustive, but should provide a baseline for understanding Christian morality and how we use it to respond to the many moral decisions we face. We begin by explaining what morality is and why we should study it, then we explain the difference between moral philosophy and moral theology, and finally, we speak to the uniqueness of Christian morality by demonstrating how it is shaped by Scripture and by our understanding of the good.

What Is Morality?

The first step in any study of Christian morality is to understand what is meant by the terms *morality* and *ethics*, for although they are often used interchangeably, they do mean different things. *Morality* refers to the standards or norms that an individual or group holds concerning good and evil as well as what constitutes right and wrong behavior. It concerns the basic moral principles that are considered beneficial for society. *Ethics* is the inquiry into, or the investigation of, the subject matter of morality, or the study of how we are to act in morally good ways. Ethics is the discipline that critically examines the moral standards or norms held by a particular society and then seeks to apply these standards or norms to life. In this sense, the goal of ethics is to develop a body of moral standards on which we can draw to help us respond to the many moral challenges we face.[1]

While morality refers to the standards or norms held by a particular group of people, it is not static. Different cultures have different standards or norms of acceptable behavior as do different religious traditions, social classes, and age groups. It should come as no surprise that the morality of the generation that lived through World War II is different from that of "Generation X."

It is important to note that individuals regularly belong to more than one group and thus they are influenced by more than one set of moral standards. Consider this example. Lisa is an eighteen-year-old American Catholic who is pressured by her friends to try illegal drugs. Her Church teaches that drug use is immoral because it is harmful to her body, a body that has been given and entrusted to her by God. Her community maintains that drug use is illegal; however, its punishment for first-time offenders is relatively light. Her culture teaches that she can take whatever drug she wants as long as she does not hurt herself or anyone else. Given this diversity, which "morality" does Lisa draw upon when making her decision about trying illegal drugs? Which does she choose when the various groups to which she belongs have different standards concerning right and wrong behavior?

As stated above, one of the purposes of ethics is to help us apply moral principles to the specific decisions we must make. When faced with an important ethical issue we draw from the generally accepted moral principles of our church, family, community, culture, and more, to help us decide how to act. These principles inform us of what is expected of us and offer us guidelines for action. Ethics responds to the question, "What should I do?" by identifying the relevant moral principles at stake and then helping us apply them to the specific decision we must make.

In theory ethical reflection is a fairly straightforward endeavor, but in practice it often is not. Sometimes generally accepted moral principles do not clearly apply to the situation in question or competing moral principles are at work. Our situation with Lisa illustrates this well. In making her decision about trying illegal drugs, Lisa first draws upon the moral standards held by her different groups. Following this, she asks, "How do the various moral principles apply, or not apply, to the specific decision I must make?" Lisa must critically evaluate the various principles before her and use them to help her come to a decision about how she will act. Now from the Catholic perspective her Church holds a privileged position, so it is hoped that Lisa will draw more heavily from its moral principles than from those of her community and culture. However, even if Lisa does draw more heavily from the moral standards of her Church, it is important to point out that ethics is not an exact science, it does not always yield black-and-white answers. Ethics often involves a lot of gray area and in fact well-intentioned people can disagree as to what constitutes an appropriate ethical response to a particular moral dilemma. While in this particular case the Church's position is unambiguous — don't take the drugs — sometimes the Church's moral teachings do not provide clear responses to the dilemmas we face. We will deal with a number of these dilemmas throughout this text.

At this point you may be asking yourself, "Why should we study morality?" or, "What can the study of morality add to my life?" Philosopher Louis Pojman says one reason we should study morality is that it helps to keep society from falling apart. Imagine a society where people decide independently what is good and what is evil, where there are no commonly held standards of right and wrong behavior. When good and evil become relative, morality becomes a free-for-all and society cannot survive. Studying morality also helps us to lessen human suffering and promote human flourishing; it allows us to resolve conflicts of interest in just, orderly ways; and it allows us to assign praise, reward, blame, and punishment for our actions. In fact, a general sense of morality that is written and codified in laws is an essential foundation for any functional society.[2]

Theologian Richard Gula agrees with Pojman but adds that the study of morality helps us to develop what he terms an "ethic of doing" and an "ethic of being." An ethic of *doing* focuses on one's actions: "What should I do in this particular situation?" An ethic of *being* focuses on the kind of person I am, or am seeking to become, through my moral decisions. The question we must all ask ourselves is, what kind of person do I want to be? Do I want to be known as a good person or an evil person? To become a good person I must consistently make good moral choices and, generally speaking, to make consistently good moral choices I must be a good person. However, the opposite is also true. If I am not a good moral person I cannot consistently make good moral choices and, generally speaking, I cannot make consistently good moral choices if I am not a good person. The ethic of being moves well beyond my external actions and deals with my character. It continually asks, "Through my moral decisions, what kind of person am I now and what kind of person am I striving to become?"[3]

Four important points must be kept in mind within any discussion of morality. The first concerns personal responsibility. Too often today we hear people saying, "It's not my fault that this happened!" "Yes, officer, I crashed my car into that tree, but it wasn't my fault because the bartender should have refused to serve me any more drinks." This excuse may sound trite, but we hear variations of it every day. Personal responsibility means that it was not the bartender's or anyone else's fault that I did something wrong and must now face the consequences of my actions. Personal responsibility means that I am ultimately accountable for the actions I perform. As long as I perform the act with full knowledge and freedom (an act of the will), responsibility for it lies with me.

The second point is that morality is "housed" in the human will. Morality implies choices, the choices we make each day to do good or evil. Human beings have free will — although some philosophers and social scientists try to dispute this. We have the ability to freely choose what we wish to do and not do. We are not forced to act in specific ways. In fact, if we did not have free will we could never be held responsible for our actions. Thus morality is inextricably related to our ability to make free choices.

Third, our moral decisions and actions have consequences. When we perform an action we set into motion a chain of events. For example, if I were to decide to have sexual relations with someone I have just met at a party, what are the possible consequences? First of all, the next morning I will probably feel guilty for having violated the sixth commandment as well as for having used the other person as an object of my own sexual gratification. Other consequences may come to light later such as an unwanted pregnancy, a sexually transmitted disease, a reputation for being promiscuous, or alienation or depression. Things happen as a result of the moral decisions we make. The consequences of our actions can be profound or minute, they can be foreseen or not. A general rule of thumb is that the more serious the action, the more serious the consequences.

A final point is that morality has a communal dimension, meaning that in addition to affecting ourselves, our moral decisions can often have profound effects on others. An extreme example of this is the 9/11 hijackers. For the hijackers themselves the personal consequences of their actions came to an abrupt end when their airplanes hit the World Trade Center, the Pentagon, and a field in western Pennsylvania. However, the consequences of their decisions have been experienced by millions of other people around the world. Over three thousand people died on that day, the families of those killed were forced to deal with the loss of loved ones, the governments of Afghanistan and Iraq were toppled, and the war on terrorism continues in various locations around the world. The point is that our moral decisions have consequences that affect not only our own lives but the lives of many others as well.

Thus far we have been speaking about morality in general. However, because this is a Christian ethics text, we must address the question, what difference does faith make in terms of living a moral life? We begin to answer this question by distinguishing between moral philosophy and moral theology.

Moral Philosophy and Moral Theology

Louis Pojman defines moral philosophy as a systematic endeavor to understand moral concepts and to justify moral principles and theories. It analyzes concepts such as "right," "wrong," "permissible," "ought," "good," and "evil," each within its moral context. Moral philosophy investigates which values and virtues are central for the overall good of society, and it seeks to establish principles of right behavior that act as moral guides for both individuals and groups.[4] From the philosophical perspective, the foundation of morality is human reason. Human reason can be defined in different ways, but generally it refers to our capacity to acquire intellectual knowledge, to contemplate or critically evaluate decisions, to foresee possible consequences of our actions, and to formulate particular judgments and conclusions. Most people possess the capacity to reason and thus have the ability to engage in moral reflection and discern varying levels of moral truth.

Keep in mind that in its strictest sense, moral philosophy has no reference to God. The reason for this is fairly simple: one cannot prove through reason that God exists so one cannot appeal to God as a source of moral knowledge. In making this point, however, we should clarify that not every moral philosopher rejects the existence of God. Many are faith-filled believers. Nevertheless, moral philosophy is primarily concerned with what our ability to reason tells us is right and wrong.

Moral theology is somewhat different. *Theology* is made up of the Greek words "theo," which refers to God, and "logy," which means "speaking of" or "the study of." Theology, therefore, means "speaking of" or studying God and what God has revealed to humanity. Moral theology is a subcategory of theology as a whole, referring to the study of what God reveals to humanity about how to live a moral life. A common misconception about moral theology is that it has no place for moral philosophy. Some Christian denominations hold that because of Adam's sin (the Fall), humanity is so completely corrupt that we cannot know any moral truth through our capacity to reason. Catholic moral theology rejects this claim. It is true that humanity is wounded as a result of its sinfulness, but it is not completely corrupt. The Roman Catholic Church holds that some moral truth can be known through reason apart from religious faith. In fact, as we will see in chapter 2, Catholic moral theology incorporates human reason as an essential element in the formation of conscience.

Although human reason is an important source of moral knowledge, it is not the only one. For Catholics, and for Christianity as a whole, the primary source of moral knowledge is divine revelation. *Divine revelation* refers to the truth that we believe God has revealed to us, the truth that God wants us to know. From the Catholic perspective, divine revelation comes to us in two forms: Scripture and the Tradition of the Church. This brings up another point of contention between the various Christian churches: although all Christian denominations hold that God reveals divine truth through Scripture (the Hebrew [Old] and Christian [New] Testaments), some hold that this truth is revealed only by this means. The Catholic Church, along with the Eastern Orthodox and many Protestant churches, teaches that God can and does reveal truth by other means. God's revelation continues to this day, as evidenced by the fact that we hold many truths that are not explicitly stated in Scripture — yet are based on and consistent with Scripture. We call this ongoing revelation *Tradition.*

In regard to moral theology, divine revelation specifically refers to what God teaches about correct human behavior. Through faith we recognize God's revelation in Scripture and Tradition, believe in it, and seek to act in accord with it in our lives. Here we see the relationship between faith and reason: Catholic moral theology holds that faith always informs reason. We use our capacity to reason in making moral decisions, but our reason is always informed by the truth that we believe God has revealed to us. The Church often uses the phrase, "Reason informed by faith." This captures the relationship perfectly, as does St. Anselm's dictum, "Faith seeking understanding." Pope John Paul II summarizes this relationship by describing moral theology as "a science which accepts and examines Divine Revelation while at the same time responding to the demands of human reason."[5] In other words, moral theology takes our ability to reason and forms it in light of what we believe God has revealed to us about correct, or moral, behavior.

Some clarification is in order here. Moral theology is a generic term that does not refer to any specific tradition or form of religious expression. A Christian is one who confesses that Jesus Christ is the Son of God who became a human being, lived among us, taught us, redeemed us through his suffering and death, rose from the dead, and will ultimately return to judge us. Moral theology from the Christian perspective, therefore, refers to how our faith in Jesus Christ influences the way we live. For Jews, moral theology refers to how faith in God as expressed in the Hebrew Scriptures and the Talmud influences the way to live. For Muslims, moral theology refers to how one's faith in Allah (God) as expressed through Allah's revelation to Muhammad in the Koran influences how to live. Thus the study of moral theology is not limited to Christians. The focus of this text, however, is Christian — and in particular, Catholic — moral theology.

Does Being a Christian Make a Difference?

If moral theology can be practiced by any believer in God or the divine, what makes Christian moral theology unique? Does being a Christian affect the way we understand morality and apply it in our lives? Should it? In this section we examine two sources that demonstrate the uniqueness of Christian moral theology. These sources are Scripture and the Christian understanding of the good.

Scripture

The primary reason Christian moral theology is unique is that it is founded in the teachings of Jesus Christ. Christ came into the world, in part, to teach us how to live a moral life. Jesus was Jewish, and he was influenced by the moral teachings of the Hebrew Scriptures. So we will begin by briefly looking at some of what the Hebrew Scriptures teach concerning correct moral behavior.

The most important and well-known moral teaching of the Hebrew Scriptures is the Ten Commandments. In the Book of Exodus, God delivers the Israelites from slavery in Egypt and enters into a covenant with them, promising that they will be his "special possession" as long as they remain faithful to him (Exod. 19:3 – 8). As the sign of what is expected of them in this covenantal relationship, God gives them the Ten Commandments (20:1–17). The first three focus on the peoples' relationship with God:

1. I, the LORD, am your God. . . . You shall not have other gods besides me.
2. You shall not take the name of the LORD, your God, in vain.
3. Keep holy the Sabbath day.

These first three commandments remind the Israelites — and Christians — that God is God. At the time the commandments were given, the Israelites were living among peoples who worshipped pagan idols; they needed to be reminded to offer unwavering faith and obedience to God. This message still rings true for us today. In light of our culture's almost incessant messages that happiness can be found in wealth, power, good looks, or material possessions, these first three commandments remind us that God must always remain the primary focus of our lives.

The remaining commandments deal with the Israelites' relationships with one another:

4. Honor your father and your mother.
5. You shall not kill.
6. You shall not commit adultery.
7. You shall not steal.
8. You shall not bear false witness against your neighbor.
9. You shall not covet your neighbor's house.
10. You shall not covet your neighbor's wife.

These commandments, as well the subsequent "Covenant Code" laid out in Exodus, reflect God's great concern for the overall well-being of the Israelite people. These commandments deal with how the people are to live together as members of the covenant community. They place a high value on human life and are applicable to all members of society, no matter what one's position in it.[6] These commandments, given to the Israelites over three thousand years ago, are just as relevant for our world today. Walk into a school and you will witness the effects of a lack of respect for parents and those in positions of authority. Turn on the television and you will see murder, sexual transgression, theft, lying, and covetousness—just on the evening news! The Ten Commandments do not cover every moral dilemma we face in our lives, but they do provide a starting point for moral reflection and a foundation for living a moral life. It is no coincidence that the *Catechism of the Catholic Church*, "Part Three: Life in Christ," uses the Ten Commandments as the outline for its extended discussion of morality.[7]

The Book of Deuteronomy goes on to spell out in detail the Israelites' moral duties toward both God and one another in much more detail. After recalling the covenant and restating the Ten Commandments (Deut. 5:1–21), Deuteronomy proceeds to extended discussions of specific moral (and other) issues. For example, it warns against giving in to the lure of riches (8:17–20). It explains how we should tithe our possessions in gratefulness to God and forgive the monetary debts owed by others (14:22–29 and 15:1–11). It further demands fair treatment of all people in business dealings (24:10–15 and 25:13–16).

Although the basic teachings of Exodus and Deuteronomy are similar, the tone of Deuteronomy is somewhat different in that it focuses much more on love. The Israelite people are called to act morally not simply out of obedience to God but as a positive response to God's love for them. This theme is exemplified in Deuteronomy 6:4–5: "Hear, O Israel! The LORD is our God, the LORD alone! Therefore, *you shall love the LORD, your God,* with all your heart, and with all your soul, and with all your strength" (emphasis added). The understanding within Deuteronomy is that God does not give moral laws simply for the sake of giving moral laws. God gives these laws because, as the people's God, he knows what is in their best interests. In other words, it is for both their individual and communal good that the people abide by the rules of conduct that God has proclaimed. Thus for Deuteronomy, following moral rules is the people's proper response to the love that God continually offers to them.[8]

This theme of love so evident in the Book of Deuteronomy also serves as the foundation for Jesus' moral teachings in the Christian Scriptures. When asked which is the greatest of the commandments, Jesus responds: "You shall love the Lord, your God, with all your heart, with all your soul, and with all your mind. . . . You shall love your neighbor as yourself" (Matt. 22:37–39).[9] By quoting the first part of this teaching from the Book of Deuteronomy, Jesus upholds the moral teachings of the Hebrew Scriptures. Remember, Jesus did not come to abolish the law (Matt. 5:17–18), but to fulfill it. By restating the Hebrew Scripture obligation to love God and commit ourselves completely to him, Jesus reemphasizes both the importance of covenant membership and living lives worthy of what this covenant entails.

The second part of Jesus' teaching, "You shall love your neighbor as yourself," also has roots in the Hebrew Scriptures. These same words are found within the Holiness Code of the Book of Leviticus (19:18) where the Israelite people are again being instructed about living in relationship with one another. Jesus uses this exhortation from Leviticus to help explain the "Great Commandment" and then throughout the rest of the Gospels offers us examples of how we can embody it in our lives. For example, when people press him as to exactly who is the neighbor they ought to love, Jesus teaches them the parable of the good Samaritan (Luke 10:29–37). In the Sermon on the Mount he teaches his followers, "Love your enemies, and pray for those who persecute you" (Matt. 5:44. See also Luke 6: 27–36). At the Last Supper, he demonstrates his love through his extended prayer for his disciples (John 14:15 – 21 and 17:1– 26) as well as the washing of their feet (John 13:1–17). The question for us is, what does Jesus mean when he says we are to love one another? In the Christian sense, love means consistently willing the good of the other. If we truly love our neighbor we will their good in every circumstance—just as we will the good of ourselves—and do whatever we can to help them achieve it. This understanding of love is so important to Jesus' message that St. Paul reiterates it:

> Owe nothing to anyone, except to love one another; for the one who loves another has fulfilled the law [of Moses]. The Commandments . . . are summed up in this saying, "You shall love your neighbor as yourself." Love does no evil to the neighbor; hence, love is the fulfillment of the law. (Rom. 13:8 –10)[10]

A second great theme of Jesus' moral teaching is his compassion for the poor and powerless. Throughout the Gospels we see Jesus ministering to and even socializing with those whom the community rejects. He focuses his greatest attention on lepers, tax collectors, people possessed by demons, and even prostitutes: all to the consternation of the religious authorities. Jesus is teaching that the Kingdom of God is open to all people; therefore we have a moral duty to love *all* our brothers and sisters by doing what we can to help them in their need. Perhaps the most striking example of this moral theme is found in Matthew 25:31– 46, the story of the Last Judgment. In this story, Jesus informs the sheep that they will enter the Kingdom of heaven because they fed Jesus when he was hungry, gave him drink when he was thirsty, clothed him when he was naked, welcomed him when he was a stranger, cared for him when he was ill, and visited him when he was in prison. When these people ask when they did these things, Jesus replies, "Whatever you did for one of these least brothers of mine, you did for me." Conversely, the goats are sent off to eternal punishment because they did not feed, offer drink, clothe, welcome, care for, or visit Jesus in his time of need. When these people ask him when they failed to do these things, Jesus responds, "What you did not do for one of these least ones, you did not do for me."

In addition to these general themes of love and compassion, Jesus offers specific ways we can all strive to live a better moral life. In the Beatitudes of Matthew's Gospel (5:3 –12), he teaches, "Blessed are the poor in spirit, for theirs is the kingdom of heaven." This beatitude is not praising those who have little faith, but those who recognize their complete dependence on God. These people recognize that everything comes from God; they are grateful to God for what they have been given and are willing to share their gifts with others.[11] Further beatitudes are also important for living a Christian moral life. We are "blessed" when we are meek (humble), when we hunger and thirst for justice, when we show mercy to others, when we are clean of heart, and when we act as peacemakers in our world. As with the Ten Commandments, the Beatitudes do not always offer practical, concrete suggestions for how we are to act in specific situations, but they do represent virtues that all Christians are called to emulate in their lives.[12]

This summary is not a comprehensive explanation of the moral teachings we find in Scripture, but gives us a sense of the sort of actions God calls us to perform and the type of person God calls us to be. In the second part of this section we change gears and speak about the Christian understanding of the good and what this understanding means in terms of living a moral life.

The Good

The primary goal of any moral system, whether philosophical or theological, is discerning the good. For Christians, the good is God, understood as Father, Son, and Holy Spirit. Anything in the created order that we deem to be good is good only in relation to God or as a reflection or mediation of God's own goodness. Stated differently, goodness is not an attribute or characteristic of God; God *is* goodness. God is good in God's own self and all goodness existing in creation has its origin and ultimate fulfillment in God. In practical terms, this means that the good we do in our lives is really not of ourselves, but is a reflection of the goodness that is God.[13]

From the Christian perspective, God offers each person the unconditional gift of God's goodness (we could also call this love or grace). One of the great truths and challenges of Christianity is that whether one is Christian or not, God loves all people equally and unconditionally. God wants nothing more from us than to accept him and ultimately exist in full communion with him for all eternity. Thus God continually offers his gifts of goodness, love, and grace to all people no matter what they believe or what they may have done in their lives. However, God also gives us the gift of free will. God does not force us to accept this goodness; we can accept or reject it. When we accept this goodness and act accordingly, it is reflected through our actions for all to see. Take the example of Mother Teresa. Most people would agree that Mother Teresa was a good person. She dedicated her life to providing material and spiritual comfort to the destitute of Calcutta and was known around the world for her charity. However, Mother Teresa was not good in and of herself. The work she did with the poor, as well as the effect this work had on others, was a reflection of the goodness that God had offered to her. She experienced God's goodness, committed herself to acting upon it, and through her many charitable deeds provided a model of true Christian living for millions of people around the world.

Unfortunately, there is always the other side of the story. Just because God offers us the gift of his own goodness does not mean that we always act in morally good ways. The reason for this is, once again, free will. We have the opportunity to reject God's goodness and act in ways that are contrary to what God intends for us. Adolf Hitler, for example, used his free will to reject God and God's goodness. Hitler recognized some other "good" in his life and chose to pursue that instead. This rejection of God and God's goodness is what we term "evil." Evil, in the theological sense, is the absence of good. It is rejection of what God has revealed to be good. It is rejection of God.

Mother Teresa and Adolph Hitler demonstrate fairly clear examples of accepting or rejecting God's goodness, but it is important for us to recognize that we too both accept and reject this goodness in our own lives. Most of us can think of examples of good that we have done: volunteering for a community service project, comforting a neighbor in need, helping an old lady across the street. Christians recognize that the good we do in these situations is not really of us, but of God. God is working through us to achieve a good end. We simply choose to participate with God and in doing so reflect God's goodness through our action. Consequently, we should think twice before patting ourselves on the back after doing a good deed. There is nothing wrong with feeling a sense of satisfaction for having done something good, but we must always keep in mind that the source of this good deed is God, not us. Conversely, we can also think of times when we have done evil in our lives: ignoring others in need, deceiving others for our own gain, or abusing alcohol, drugs, or our sexuality. When we commit evil acts or sin, we are rejecting God's goodness. In fact, sin is what results when *we* — not God — determine the good in a particular situation. All humans sin. We all reject God at various points throughout our lives. Therefore, before condemning anyone else for their evil actions, we need to look at ourselves. The evil we commit continually reminds us of our rejection of God and God's goodness in our lives.

With this understanding of God's goodness, we can now speak of the importance that it maintains for our moral lives, assuming of course that we accept it. Belief in God as good and as the source of all goodness offers the Christian a reason to be moral; we ought to be moral because God's goodness both enables and requires us to be responsible for the goodness of the world. This concept is easier to grasp than it sounds. The key to understanding what it means to live a Christian moral life lies precisely in this question: "What is God enabling and requiring me to be and do?" If God enables me with the gifts, talents, or abilities to become a specific kind of person, then I have a moral duty to become that person (ethic of being). If God enables me with the gifts, talents, or abilities to do a specific thing, then I am morally required to do this thing (ethic of doing). In other words, enabling and requiring are intimately connected; you cannot have one without the other. Because God authorizes and requires morality in this way, we can say that our moral responsibilities are not only to ourselves, to other people, or to the demands of rationality; they are first and foremost responsibilities to God. Actions are judged to be moral not simply because they bring "good" to ourselves and others, but because they are properly responsive to what God enables and requires of us. Likewise, actions are judged immoral not simply because they cause harm to ourselves and others, but because they are not properly responsive to what God enables and requires of us in our lives.[14]

Let's clarify here: God does not require the impossible. God enables each of us with specific gifts, talents, and abilities and then requires us to use them to reflect his goodness in the world. However, we are not morally required to do things for which we have not been enabled. If we have not been enabled with the gifts, talents, or abilities to become a specific kind of person, then God cannot require us to become that person. Again, enabling and requiring are intimately connected: God requires of us that for which we have been enabled, but does not require that for which we have not.

With this perspective in mind, the Christian moral life can be properly understood as our response to God's offer of love. Through faith, we recognize God's offer of love through Jesus Christ and the Holy Spirit as an open invitation to live a life of good, to live a life of God. Our free response to this invitation is the moral life. The purpose of Christian moral theology, then, is to demonstrate how belief in Jesus Christ makes a difference in the way we live. It seeks to demonstrate the implications of Christian faith for the actions we ought to perform as well as for the kind of person we are striving to become.[15]

Morality, or living a moral life, thus poses profound challenges to the Christian believer. Morality does not mean simply following biblical commandments or Church rules. Morality involves a deep commitment on the part of the believer to discern what God is calling us to both be and do. Moral reflection is not easy; it involves great effort on our part. When faced with an important ethical decision, we must critically examine ourselves and discern, as best we can, how God is calling us to use the gifts, talents, and abilities that we have been given. We must also recognize that throughout our lives we mature and develop as human persons. What we may have thought was a moral response to a specific dilemma when we were a teenager may not seem so clear when we are faced with a similar one twenty years later (and vice versa). And we must remember that all human beings are different. We have been graced by God with different gifts, talents, and abilities, so valid responses to similar moral dilemmas may vary from person to person. Morality, therefore, is not as cut and dried as many people think. It involves a deep commitment on the part of individuals to understand not only God's call in their lives but also themselves as human persons. Morality truly entails a lived response to God's invitation of love.

In sum, Christian morality is intimately related to our beliefs and experiences of God. God is the source and end of all that is good, and therefore we must always view ourselves, others, and the whole of creation in reference to God. In the next chapter we continue by discussing the nature of the moral act and the importance of rightly formed conscience.

Review Questions

1. How are morality and ethics technically different?

2. What philosophical reasons are offered for why we should study morality?

3. What is the difference between an ethic of doing and an ethic of being?

4. What four important points do we need to keep in mind within any discussion of morality?

5. What is moral philosophy? On what is it based?

6. What is moral theology? On what is it based?

7. From the Catholic perspective, what are the two forms of divine revelation, and how are they related?

8. What is the relationship between faith and reason?

9. Why is the theme of love so important in the Scriptures?

10. What does it mean to say that God's goodness both enables and requires us to be responsible for the goodness of the world?

ENDNOTES

1 Manuel Velasquez, *Business Ethics: Concepts and Cases*, 5th ed. (Upper Saddle River, NJ: Pearson, 2002), 7–12, and John Boatright, *The Ethical Conduct of Business*, 5th ed. (Upper Saddle River, NJ: Pearson, 2007), 22–23. In a more specific way, ethics can also be defined as the "rules" or "code of conduct" governing the actions of a particular group of people. For example, if we are speaking about a code of conduct for people working within the health care field, we are speaking of health care or medical ethics. If we are speaking about a code of conduct for those working in the business world, we are speaking of business ethics.

2 Louis Pojman, *Life and Death: Grappling with the Moral Dilemmas of Our Time*, 2nd ed. (Belmont, CA: Wadsworth, 2000), 7.

3 Richard Gula, *Reason Informed by Faith: Foundations of Catholic Morality* (New York: Paulist, 1989), 7–8.

4 Pojman, *Life and Death*, 2.

5 John Paul II, *The Splendor of Truth* (Washington, DC: U. S. Catholic Conference, 1993), no. 29.

6 Roger H. Crook, *An Introduction to Christian Ethics*, 4th ed. (Upper Saddle River, NJ: Prentice Hall, 2002), 68.

7 *Catechism of the Catholic Church* (Vatican City: Libreria Editrice Vaticana, 1994), 498 – 611.

8 *Catholic Bible, Personal Study Edition*, ed. Jean Marie Hiesberger et al. (New York: Oxford University Press, 1995), 87. See also Cooke, *Introduction to Christian Ethics*, 69.

9 See also Mark 12:29 – 31, Luke 10:27 – 28, and John 13:34 – 35.

10 In 1 Cor. 13:4 – 8a,13, Paul further expands upon this understanding of love: "Love is patient, love is kind. It is not jealous, it is not pompous, it is not inflated, it is not rude, it does not seek its own interests, it is not quick-tempered, it does not brood over injury, it does not rejoice over wrongdoing but rejoices with the truth. It bears all things, believes all things, hopes all things, endures all things. Love never fails. . . . So faith, hope, love remain, these three; but the greatest of these is love."

11 Closely related to this, Jesus also teaches that discipleship entails a full commitment to him (Matt. 10:37 – 39 and Luke 14:25 – 33), and that the gaining of wealth, power, or prestige mean nothing if you lose your soul in the process (Matt. 16:25 – 26 and Luke 18:24 – 30).

12 Although in this section we have focused on Jesus' positive moral teachings, we would be remiss if we failed to mention that his moral teachings also decry those who do evil. He states that it would be better for one to have a millstone placed around his neck than to lead another into sin (Mark 9:42 and Luke 17:1 – 2). He castigates the Pharisees for their hypocrisy (Matt. 23:1 – 36, Mark 7:1 – 15, Luke 11:37 – 12:1, and John 9:1 – 41) as well as his own disciples for their desire to be the greatest (Mark 10:35 – 45, Luke 9:46 – 48). He speaks against those who exhibit great pride (Luke 14:7 – 11) and those who seek ever greater wealth (Luke 6:24 – 26 and 12:13 – 15). Finally, he demonstrates his anger against those who turn the Temple, his Father's house, into a marketplace of fraud and greed (Matt. 21:12 – 17, Mark 11:15 – 17, Luke 19:45 – 48, and John 2:13 – 17).

13 Gula, *Reason Informed by Faith*, 43 – 44.

14 Ibid., 44 – 45.

15 Ibid., 6 – 7.

2. THE MORAL ACT AND CONSCIENCE

Caitlin is a senior at a midsize Catholic college. After graduation she plans to go to graduate school to pursue a master's degree in special education. In fact, she has already been accepted to graduate school. On a whim, she decided to take a financial accounting course during her last semester. This has been the hardest course she has ever taken, and she is in real danger of flunking if she does not pass the final exam. She is desperate and is even considering cheating if it will help her pass the final. For all of her academic struggles, Caitlin has never cheated before. But if she flunks this course, she will not graduate, and her plans to pursue a master's degree will have to be put on hold. By cheating, she will pass the course, graduate, go on to graduate school, and do the good work of a special education teacher. No one will know, no one will get hurt, and she promises herself that she will never do it again. Just this once. . . . But it's so unlike her. What should she do?

Caitlin is facing a crisis of conscience not unfamiliar to college students. She knows that cheating is wrong, yet she sees her future and all the good that she could do going up in smoke because of one lousy financial accounting course that is not even a requirement. Her story and the dilemma she faces may conjure up images from our childhood. We see a little devil perched on one shoulder whispering in Caitlin's ear that cheating is not so bad, everybody does it, it's really for a good cause, no one need know, and no

32

one will be hurt by it. On the other shoulder is perched a little angel whispering in her ear that cheating is bad even if everybody else does it, one can never achieve a good end by doing evil, God will know that she's cheated, and the entire class will be hurt by her cheating.

This childhood image is, of course, naïve. But many people evoke this image when asked what conscience is and what role it plays in guiding our moral choices. Even if we don't picture a devil and an angel, we still describe conscience as "the little voice inside us telling what's right or wrong." The image is given credence in the following description of conscience taken from the Second Vatican Council document *Pastoral Constitution on the Church in the Modern World*:

> Deep within his conscience man discovers a law which he has not laid upon himself but which he must obey. Its voice, ever calling him to love and to do what is good and to avoid evil, sounds in his heart at the right moment. . . . For man has in his heart a law inscribed by God. . . . His conscience is man's most secret core and his sanctuary. There he is alone with God whose voice echoes in his depths.[1]

In this document, the Second Vatican Council describes conscience in scriptural terms as the law of God inscribed in the human heart. It is also the voice of God that echoes in our depths. Although this is certainly a beautiful and apt description of conscience with deep biblical roots (see Jer. 31:31–34), we must take care not to misinterpret it, turning conscience into a thing rather than an activity. In Catholic moral theology, conscience refers more technically to (1) the basic principles of practical reason (reason, that is, as concerned with action), (2) the application of these principles to a specific set of circumstances, and (3) our self-evaluation of how we have carried out this application and whether we have lived up to what we have judged we ought to do. Later in this chapter we will consider this description of conscience in more detail, but first we must determine what a moral act is.

The Moral Act

All human beings act, and our actions can be categorized in two ways. A general act refers to actions such as blinking one's eyes or breathing.

Although they are performed by human beings, these kinds of actions are not moral acts. They occur without our willing them or thinking about them. Moral acts, however, are freely chosen acts that come into existence through both reason and the will and, as such, they can be morally evaluated. The question is, how does one evaluate a moral act?

Traditionally, we evaluate moral acts using the three-font principle: the object, the intention, and the circumstances. The object is an action that is rationally chosen by the will and, according to Pope John Paul II, the morality of any human action "depends primarily and fundamentally" on the object.[2] The object of an act is a freely chosen and willed kind of behavior or thought that gives an act its particular moral character. Put another way, "The object is the proximate end of a deliberate decision which determines the act of willing on the part of the acting person."[3] What do we mean by "the proximate end of a deliberate decision"? The answer to this can be found in the intention.

The *intention* is not, as many suppose, the reason we act or our motive for action. Rather, the intention is the choice of the will to do something. For example, my choice to drink a glass of water is my intention. I will to drink the water and I do it. Now one cannot see my willing to drink the glass of water. One only sees the results of my willing to perform this action. The choice of my will to drink the water is my intention. The actual drinking of the water is the object. The intention and the object are so closely connected (the former being the choice; the latter being what I choose to do) that they are sometimes combined under the expression "the intentional act." This intentional act is subject to moral evaluation.

Moral acts do not occur in a vacuum, of course. They always occur within a set of *circumstances*. Circumstances involve questions such as who, what, where, when, why, how, and how much? Circumstances are not negligible features of the moral act. For instance, in order to evaluate a moral act one must know who is acting and what is involved. Was the action performed by a two-year-old? A thirty-year-old? Was the amount stolen two pennies or ten million dollars?

Note that the "why" question appears with the circumstances. The reason for this is that it involves motive. Why did I choose to drink the glass of water? Was I thirsty? Did I have to take a pill? Was it to suppress my appetite so that I would eat less at my next meal? Although the intention or the choice of the will to do something is called the proximate end, the motive is sometimes referred to as the remote or further end. The remote or further end is my reason for choosing to act or think in a certain way. Just as the other circumstantial questions are important for determining the morality of an act, so too is the motive. For example, Mr. Smith has chosen to give fifty million dollars to a children's hospital. Why did he do so? Was it out of generosity? Was it to get his name in the paper? If Mr. Smith chose to give the money out of generosity, then we can say that the object was one of generosity. But if he did so out of the desire for publicity, then the object is no longer generosity but vainglory. Both actions may look the same, but they are quite different. True, the hospital benefits regardless of Mr. Smith's motives, but Mr. Smith will not benefit morally if the gift is given out of a desire for publicity. He has already received his reward.

Another lesson to be learned from this example is that we cannot really know the morality of a human act except from the perspective of the acting person.[4] Only the individual and God can know the object of the act that gives it its moral specificity. When Jesus commands us not to judge lest we be judged, he means this kind of judgment. In other words, as rational human beings we are able to judge actions as objectively right or wrong. But what we cannot judge is the heart of the person who chooses to act.

As we said before, the morality of the human act depends primarily and fundamentally on the object, understood as the intentional act. The will may choose a course of action for the best of motives—stealing to feed the poor, cheating to pass a test—but a fundamental principle of morality is that one may not do evil so that good may come of it. In fact, the *Catechism of the Catholic Church* teaches there are "certain specific kinds of behavior that are always wrong to choose, because choosing them involves a disorder of the will, that is, a moral evil."[5] For an act to be good, all parts of it must be good — the object, the proximate end, the further end, and the circumstances. Only these kinds of actions are in conformity with the good of the person. Conscience is that faculty that guides us to do what is truly good for us. Let us now consider what conscience is and how it helps us live an upright and moral life.

Conscience

In order to speak about conscience, we first need to make a distinction between conscience itself and the judgment of conscience. In his encyclical *Splendor of Truth*, Pope John Paul II wrote "the relationship between man's freedom and God's law is most deeply lived out in the 'heart' of the person, in his moral conscience."[6] Conscience is the place deep in the human heart where we meet God and respond in freedom to his law.

Now, what exactly is God's law and how can we follow it? The Catholic Church teaches that God's law, or the eternal law, is knowable to God alone. However, in order that we can "know" the good and live fulfilling lives, God wills that we know some aspects of this eternal law and apply it in our lives. Thus, God reveals certain elements of the eternal law to us through our capacity to reason. This is the natural law. Natural law is defined as human participation in God's eternal law though our capacity to reason, and it is also understood as the law "written on the human heart" by God.[7] This natural law is "knowable" to all people. Because God works through our capacity to reason, one need not have religious faith to understand it. All people — atheists included — are bound by the natural law.

What then is conscience? Conscience involves us using our capacity to reason in order to respond to God and to God's eternal law. A relationship is at work here: the natural law makes known the objective and universal demands of the moral good, while conscience is the application of this law to a particular case.[8] The *Catechism of the Catholic Church* explains further that "conscience is a judgment of reason whereby the human person recognizes the moral quality of a concrete act that he is going to perform, is in the process of performing, or has already completed."[9]

The Roman Catholic Tradition ascribes three dimensions to conscience: (1) *synderesis*, the basic tendency or capacity within us to do good and avoid evil; (2) *moral science*, the process of discovering the particular good that ought to be done or the evil to be avoided; and (3) *judgment*, the specific judgment of the good that one must do in a particular situation, or has done in a past situation, or will do in the future. Let us examine these three dimensions of conscience in more detail.

Synderesis is the necessary foundation for the exercise of conscience. It is a capacity or tendency with which we are all born. With this capacity, we are capable of choosing good and avoiding evil. Moreover, this capacity to choose good and avoid evil is infallible, i.e., it never errs. We will always and everywhere choose what we perceive to be "good" and avoid what we perceive to be "evil."

Notice that we are saying we invariably choose what we *perceive* to be good, though this choice may not be good in the true sense of the word. For example, Mindy sees herself as fat even though she is not. So what does Mindy do? She can starve herself (anorexia) or binge and purge herself (bulimia). Both behaviors are destructive to her body, and she should avoid them. But Mindy sees anorexia or bulimia as a "good" choice in her misguided pursuit of an unrealistic body shape. In another example, Joshua would like to try out for the varsity football team, but he is too small. So he decides to take steroids to gain size and strength in spite of the bad effects of steroid use on both the body and the mind. In his pursuit of the goal to play varsity football, Joshua sees the steroids as good. Or consider an extreme example: suicide. A person seeking to end his or her life does not view death as an evil to be avoided. Instead, it seems to be a good choice because it provides a means to end unbearable physical or mental pain.

In each of these cases, something that is objectively bad for the person is perceived by that person to be good. Despite the negative consequences of these behaviors, they are seen as good and not evil. In fact, we will never choose what we perceive to be bad for us, we will only choose what we think is good. Clearly our basic capacity or tendency to choose good and avoid evil needs to be formed if we are to make truly good moral choices. This formation is called moral science.

Moral science is the process that shapes, educates, examines, and transforms synderesis. It is the means by which we learn whether a particular choice is, in fact, good or evil. The process we name *moral science* can also be called "the formation of conscience."

The formation of conscience does not take place in a vacuum. Even though we are individuals, we have our feet in a number of worlds. Our native culture, whether it is of the United States or some other land, is not morally neutral. Culture can either form our conscience or deform it. For example, living in the United States with its free market economic structure may, without our even realizing it, shape our attitudes toward money, spending, and gratification. This may make us insensitive to poverty both in our own country and around the world. At the same time, Americans are generous. We spend a lot on ourselves, but we also spend billions of dollars trying to alleviate the plight of others. Thus our consciences can be both deformed and formed by our culture's view of money.

Cultures are not only national in nature. Within each culture there exists any number of subcultures: country clubs, universities, trade unions, political organizations, Goths, and so on. Each of these subcultures is also able to form or deform our view of what is good and evil, and thus our consciences. Likewise families and friends can also play a significant, even primary, role in forming or deforming our consciences. So too can the various branches of learning. Insofar as they strive to uncover truth and what it means to be truly human, the academic disciplines are invaluable tools in the formation of conscience.

As we saw in chapter 1, Christians have another source for forming the conscience, namely the life and teachings of Jesus Christ as revealed in sacred Scripture. In addition to this, Catholics also have recourse to the Church and its magisterium. The magisterium is made up of the pope and the bishops who are in communion with him. Their task, as part of the teaching office of the Church, is to provide the faithful with an authentic interpretation of Scripture and Tradition.[10]

The Second Vatican Council spoke to the importance of the magisterium when it stated:

> In forming their conscience the Christian faithful must give careful attention to the sacred and certain teaching of the Church. For the Catholic Church is by the will of Christ the teacher of truth. Her charge is to announce and teach authentically that truth which is Christ and at the same time with her authority to declare and confirm the principles of the moral order which derive from human nature itself.[11]

Allowing oneself to be guided by God's truth means, among other things, a religious assent to the teachings of the ordinary magisterium — even when a specific teaching has not been infallibly defined.[12] What this means is that Catholics are to give the benefit of the doubt to the truthfulness of the Church's teaching regarding the moral law — particularly when it says that a particular action is intrinsically evil (homicide, genocide, abortion, euthanasia, slavery, prostitution, etc.).[13] The reason for this is that our choice to commit an intrinsically evil act would not only set our freedom in opposition to God's law,[14] but it would also separate our freedom from God's Truth. The point here is that we become authentically free human beings — always choosing to do good while avoiding evil — to the extent that we allow ourselves to be guided by truth.

Cardinal Newman once wrote that "conscience has rights because it has duties."[15] If we have the obligation to follow our conscience, we also have the equally important task of forming it correctly. The formation of conscience certainly involves gaining information, but it also means gaining truthful information. Pope John Paul II spoke to this point when he stated that the "maturity and responsibility" of conscience is measured not by personal autonomy or by a "liberation" of the conscience from God's objective truth. Instead, the true maturity and responsibility of conscience is measured by "an insistent search for truth and by allowing oneself to be guided by that truth in one's actions."[16]

It may seem that the Church's authoritative teaching on moral questions limits our freedom of conscience, but this is not the case. Pope John Paul II affirms that the freedom of conscience "is never freedom 'from' the truth but always and only freedom 'in' the truth." In other words, the magisterium does not formulate moral truth and then impose it on the Christian conscience. Instead, it "brings to light" those truths that conscience should already know. In this sense, the Church and her magisterium are always at the *service of conscience.*[17]

It should be clear by now that the formation of conscience is complicated, not only because of the many competing voices that can inform our conscience, but also because these same voices can pull it in one direction and then the other. So how are we to exercise our judgment of conscience? How are we to do good and avoid evil?

The third dimension of conscience concerns *judgment.* After we have been informed of what is truly "right" through the process of moral science, we must then make a concrete decision about how we will act. Making this judgment of conscience seems easy enough — choose what I know to be morally good — however, this is not always so easy. What if the "correct" course of action is difficult or unpopular? What if I will be ostracized by my friends or ridiculed by society for my beliefs? Knowing what to do can be easy, actually making the judgment to do it often is not.

Judgment concerns the specific determination of the good that I must do in a particular situation, and it concerns past actions as well. As we grow older — and hopefully wiser! — we can look back on our lives and critically evaluate the moral decisions we made in the past. Sometimes when we look back on these decisions we realize that, while at the time we thought we were making a correct moral decision, in reality we were not. Judgment also deals with future decisions. Coupling what we've learned from the past together with what we know today, we can anticipate what a correct moral judgment will be if we are faced with a particular situation in the future. Thus, the judgment of conscience can be defined as the specific determination of the good that I must do in a particular situation, have done in a past situation, or will do in the future.

Another way to understand judgment of conscience is to look at Saint Paul's Letter to the Romans:

> For when the Gentiles who do not have the law by nature observe the prescriptions of the law, they are a law for themselves even though they do not have the law. They show that the demands of the law are written in their hearts, while their conscience also bears witness and their conflicting thoughts accuse or even defend them. (Rom. 2:14–15)

According to Saint Paul, conscience confronts us with the law, understood as Jesus' dual command to love God and neighbor (Matt. 22: 34–40), and it becomes a witness for us as to whether we are faithful to this law. Because its judgments issue from the depth of the human heart, conscience is in fact the only witness to what takes place in the heart. It remains unknown to everyone except the individual and God. In this sense, the judgment of conscience is dialogical in nature. Certainly it is a dialogue within the individual person, but it is also a dialogue between the person and God, the author of the law. When we arrive at a judgment of conscience we do so not alone, but with God's voice calling us to obedience. As such, conscience does not command on its own authority, but rather from the authority of God. This is why the judgment of conscience is morally binding.

It is easy to say, "Let conscience be your guide," but how do we know if our conscience is moving us in the right direction? What if we make a mistake, even a mistake in good faith—are we still morally bound to follow our judgments of conscience? Let us explore these questions in more detail.

The Mistaken Conscience

In the previous section, we noted that *synderesis,* our capacity to do good and to avoid evil, is infallible—at least from the perspective of the person choosing. Not so with conscience. Because of the many competing voices to which we listen to form our conscience, and because of our own sinfulness, we can err in our judgments of conscience. Notice that the role of conscience is *not* to decide what is good or evil. The role of conscience is to bear witness to the authority of the natural law and to the first principle of practical reason: to do good and avoid evil.[18] Just because one's conscience judges a past, present, or future action to be good, it does not make it so. Conscience can be mistaken. In spite of that fact the Church teaches that our conscience is always binding. If we truly believe that the judgment we are making is correct, then we are obligated to follow it. Let us examine how the Church has come to this teaching.

According to Thomas Aquinas, the correct judgment of a rightly formed conscience binds absolutely, without qualification and in all circumstances.[19] For example, if your conscience judges that you should not commit adultery, then you must follow this judgment and not commit adultery. To change your judgment would be, in Aquinas's words, seriously sinful because of the very error of changing such a judgment. Therefore, a correct judgment of conscience that tells you not to commit adultery binds absolutely, without qualification, and in all circumstances.

Difficulties arise, however, when it comes to the binding nature of a mistaken judgment of conscience. Aquinas argues that a mistaken judgment of conscience is still binding, but only conditionally and in a qualified sense. For example, if your judgment of conscience leads you to believe that it is permissible to fornicate, you are obliged to follow this dictate as long as such a judgment remains. To act otherwise, i.e., to act against your judgment, would entail sin. But for Aquinas, a mistaken judgment of conscience does not obligate in every event and circumstance. The reason for this is that with further information (moral science), you may change your understanding of the good to be pursued and the evil to be avoided. When this occurs, you are no longer bound to follow your originally mistaken judgment of conscience. To clarify, consider the following scenario.

Suppose you lived on an island where you were raised to believe that hospitality is expressed, among other ways, by fornicating with guests. Fornication is objectively wrong, but if you believe and judge it to be right, then you are obliged to follow that judgment. Not to do so would entail sin. But suppose some missionaries visited the island, instructed you concerning the "proper" use of sexuality, and you accepted their teaching. Now you have changed your judgment concerning fornication as an expression of hospitality. In this case, (1) you are no longer obliged to follow your previously mistaken judgment, and (2) you can no longer appeal to conscience to do what you had previously thought to be right. You are now obliged, in all events and circumstances, to follow your new, correct judgment of conscience.

Does a mistaken judgment of conscience excuse us from sin? That depends. Moral culpability turns on the issue of ignorance, of which there can be different sorts.[20]

First, there is *antecedent ignorance*, or ignorance that precedes an act of the will and is, therefore, unwilled. As long as such ignorance remains, one is not responsible for the consequences of the action. For example, let us suppose that Bob is target shooting. Unbeknown to him, Jane is near the target. Bob shoots at the target, misses, and the bullet strikes Jane, killing her. Because Bob was ignorant of the presence of Jane near the target, he is not morally responsible for her death.

Second, there is *consequent ignorance*. Consequent ignorance arises when an individual: (1) deliberately chooses to remain ignorant, (2) operates out of inattention, or (3) exhibits *crass ignorance* about obtaining information on matters of fact or of law. Generally speaking, a person is not excused from moral culpability as a result of consequent ignorance. Thus, a person is guilty of moral wrongdoing if he or she deliberately chooses to remain ignorant about a moral teaching, for example failing to learn why the Catholic Church teaches against the use of contraceptives. Individuals are also culpable of moral wrongdoing if they are inattentive to a matter that they should have known, for example driving 60 mph through a 35-mph zone because they did not see the speed limit sign. In addition, individuals are morally responsible for their actions when they demonstrate crass ignorance, such as drinking alcohol simply to get drunk. They are morally responsible because (1) they pretend they do not know their behavior is wrong, or (2) they know their behavior is wrong but they choose to do it anyway. In sum, a mistaken judgment of conscience that proceeds from consequent ignorance is morally culpable. However, as we saw above, individuals can reverse their error since their ignorance is voluntary and can be overcome.

Let us return to the story of Caitlin and the issue of cheating with which this chapter began. Like all of us, Caitlin has the capacity to choose good and avoid evil. She already has a well-formed conscience in that she understands that cheating is wrong and her "inner voice" reminds her of this. However, as well formed as her conscience is, it is temporarily asleep. She is seriously contemplating cheating to graduate and to pursue a worthwhile career. Will she remain true to herself in spite of the danger of failing the course and thus delaying her career plans? Or will she cheat? What do *you* think she will do? What would you do?

Review Questions

1. How is conscience defined in Catholic moral theology?

2. How does a moral act differ from a general act?

3. What is considered in the three-font principle?

4. How are conscience and judgment of conscience different?

5. What is *synderesis*, and how is it related to the formation of conscience?

6. Reflect on some of the subcultures to which you belong. How have these cultures formed your conscience?

7. How do rights and duties relate to conscience?

8. What are the three major factors that aid in the formation of conscience for Catholics?

9. What is the difference between antecedent and consequent ignorance? Are we excused from sin when any of these forms of ignorance are at play?

ENDNOTES

1 *Catechism of the Catholic Church* (*CCC*), 2nd ed. (Rome: Libreria Editrice Vaticana, 1997), 1776, and *Pastoral Constitution on the Church in the Modern World* (1965), 16.

2 John Paul II, *Splendor of Truth* (1993), 78.

3 Ibid., 78.

4 Cf. ibid.

5 *CCC*, 1761.

6 John Paul II, *Splendor of Truth*, 54.

7 See Rom. 2:14–15. The natural law has a varied and rich tradition. Basically the natural law refers to human beings' participation in the eternal law, which is in fact God's law. We know God's law by theoretical or speculative reason. The first principle of reason is the law of noncontradiction: something cannot be and not be at the same time. The first principle of practical reason is to do good and to avoid evil.

8 Cf. John Paul II, *Splendor of Truth*, 59.

9 *CCC*, 1778. Cf. John Paul II, *Splendor of Truth*, 59.

10 *CCC*, 85.

11 Cf. Vatican II, *Declaration on Religious Freedom* (1965), 14.

12 Cf. *CCC*, 892, and Vatican II, *Dogmatic Constitution on the Church* (1964), 25.

13 Cf. Vatican II, *Dogmatic Constitution on the Church* (1964), 27, and John Paul II, *Splendor of Truth*, 81.

14 John Paul II, *Splendor of Truth*, 56.

15 John Henry Newman, *A Letter Addressed to His Grace the Duke of Norfolk: Certain Difficulties Felt by Anglicans in the Catholic Teaching*, uniform ed. (London: Longman, Green and Company, 1868–1881), 2:250. Cited in John Paul II, *Splendor of Truth*, 34.

16 John Paul II, *Splendor of Truth*, 61.

17 Ibid., 64.

18 Cf. John Paul II, *Splendor of Truth*, 57-58.

19 Cf. *On Truth*, q. 17, art. 4, reply.

20 Cf. *ST* I–II, q. 6, a. 8. I have taken these distinctions from *Summa Theologiae*, volume 17, appendix 15: "Conscience," 182–83.

3. CATHOLIC SOCIAL TEACHING: AN INTRODUCTION

Action on behalf of justice and participation in the transformation of the world fully appear to us as a constitutive dimension of the preaching of the Gospel, or, in other words, of the Church's mission for the redemption of the human race and its liberation from every oppressive situation.

— International Synod of Bishops, *Justice in the World* (1971)

In this chapter we explore the social teachings of the Catholic Church. In their 1998 *Sharing Catholic Social Teaching: Challenges and Directions*, the United States Catholic bishops deplored the fact that most American Catholics are ignorant that our Church has a well-developed body of teachings concerning important social issues that are essential to the way we live out our Christian faith. The bishops call upon Catholic educators to incorporate these teachings into all educational programs, including college courses and adult faith-enrichment programs.[1] This book is a contribution to this effort. Here we introduce readers to Catholic Social Teaching (CST) by explaining what it is and where it came from, identifying its main principles, and demonstrating why it is foundational for us. We must understand what CST is before we can apply it to the specific ethical issues discussed in the remainder of the text.

Catholic Social Teaching: What Is It and Where Does It Come From?

Catholic Social Teaching refers to the substantial body of writings that the Catholic Church maintains concerning important social, economic, and political issues. These writings come from various popes and bishops' conferences, both on the national and international levels. Their purpose is to demonstrate how we are called to live our Christian faith in the world. Just a few examples of these writings include Pope Leo XIII, *On the Condition of Labor (Rerum Novarum)* (1891); Pope Pius XI, *After Forty Years* (1931); Pope John XXIII, *Christianity and Social Progress* (1961) and *Peace on Earth* (1963); the Second Vatican Council, *Pastoral Constitution on the Church in the Modern World* (1965); Pope Paul VI, *On the Development of Peoples* (1967) and *A Call to Action* (1971); the International Synod of Bishops, *Justice in the World* (1971); and John Paul II, *On Human Work* (1981), *On Social Concern* (1987), and *On the Hundredth Anniversary of Rerum Novarum* (1991). The United States Catholic bishops have also written a number of documents addressing social concerns pertinent to our nation. These include their *Statement on Capital Punishment* (1980), *Economic Justice for All* (1986), *The Challenge of Peace* (1983), and *The Harvest of Justice Is Sown in Peace* (1993). The overall point of these writings is to demonstrate the communal dimension of Christian faith. Faith does not concern solely our individual or private relationship with God, it also concerns our relationships with others and how we are called to work for the common good of all. As we move through the following chapters we will make reference to the documents listed above as well as to other, lesser-known writings from around the world.

Unfortunately, as the United States bishops lament in *Sharing Catholic Social Teaching*, most American Catholics are unaware that these writings even exist — they are often called the Church's best-kept secret. Those who are aware of these teachings often mistakenly believe that CST began with Leo XIII's *On the Condition of Labor* (1891). Actually, CST traces its roots back to the Bible — both the Hebrew (Old Testament) and Christian (New Testament) Scriptures — and the writings of the early church fathers. Owing to space constraints, we must limit ourselves to only a few examples.

Scripture

In the Hebrew Scriptures, the law of Moses clearly indicates how the Israelite community should treat its poor and defenseless:

> When you reap the harvest of your land, you shall not be so thorough that you reap the field to its very edge, nor shall you glean the stray ears of grain. Likewise, you shall not pick your vineyard bare, nor gather up the grapes that have fallen. These things you shall leave for the poor and the alien. (Lev. 19:9–10. See also Deut. 24:19–22)

> If you lend money to one of your poor neighbors among my people, you shall not act like an extortioner toward him by demanding interest from him. If you take your neighbor's cloak as a pledge, you shall return it to him before sunset; for this cloak of his is the only covering he has for his body. What else has he to sleep in? (Exod. 22:24–26. See also Deut. 24:10–15)

Either implicitly or explicitly, the operating terms in these and other related passages are *mispat* and *sedaqah*, generally translated "justice" and "righteousness." Together, *mispat* and *sedaqah* connote a sense of communal peace and harmony, virtues that were supposed to characterize the Israelites' relationship with God and with one another. We explore the understanding of justice more thoroughly in chapter 7 when we speak of war and peace, but for now suffice it to say that justice and righteousness "consist in avoiding violence, fraud and any other actions that destroy communal life" while at the same time "pursuing that which sustains the life of the community."[2]

The Hebrew Scriptures also demonstrate what happens when justice and righteousness are lacking. Numerous prophets unequivocally convey God's displeasure toward the wealthy and ruling elites who shamelessly exploit the lower classes of Israelite society.

> Hear this, you who trample upon the needy and destroy the poor of the land! "When will the new moon be over," you ask, "that we may sell our grain, and the sabbath, that we may display the wheat? We will diminish the ephah, add to the shekel, and fix our scales for cheating! We will buy the lowly man for silver, and the poor man for a pair of sandals; even the refuse of the wheat we will sell!"

The LORD has sworn by the pride of Jacob: Never will I forget a thing they have done! (Amos 8:4 – 7)

Woe to those who plan iniquity, and work out evil on their couches; In the morning light they accomplish it when it lies within their power. They covet fields, and seize them; houses, and they take them; They cheat an owner of his house, a man of his inheritance. Therefore thus says the LORD: Behold, I am planning against this race an evil from which you shall not withdraw your necks. (Micah 2:1– 3)

Through numerous prophetic passages, the Hebrew Scriptures clearly teach that God expects the people to act justly in their dealings with one another. For the Israelites as well as for us today, practicing justice is essential for anyone who claims membership in the "people of God."

In the Christian Scriptures (New Testament), Jesus also offers numerous teachings that deal directly with how we are to live in right relationship with both God and one another. In Luke's Gospel Jesus begins his public ministry by quoting the prophet Isaiah:

The Spirit of the Lord is upon me, because he has anointed me to bring glad tidings to the poor. He has sent me to proclaim liberty to captives and recovery of sight to the blind, to let the oppressed go free, and to proclaim a year acceptable to the Lord. (Luke 4:18 –19; cf. Isa. 61:1– 2)

Jesus identifies himself with the outcasts of society throughout the Gospels. He ministers to and heals the poor, the blind, the lame, and sinners, and calls each of us to do the same (see Luke 14:12 –14,21). Jesus teaches his disciples to model their lives on the Beatitudes (Matt. 5:3 –12 and Luke 6:20 – 26), to give alms to the poor (Matt. 6:2), and always to act toward others as we would have them act toward us (Matt. 7:12). He demonstrates how we should be willing to help our neighbor in need through the parable of the good Samaritan (Luke 10:25 – 37). He shows the importance of serving others through the washing of the disciples' feet (John 13:1–20). He also teaches how we should forgive one another through the parable of the prodigal son (Luke 15:11– 32) and the story of the woman caught in adultery (John 8:1–11).

On a more negative note, Jesus warns against the trappings of wealth and power (Matt. 19:16-30; Mark 10:17– 22) and denounces the scribes and Pharisees for these faults (Matt. 23:1–11). Similar stark warnings against both the lure and effect of riches can be seen in the parable of the rich fool (Luke 12:13–21), the parable of the rich man and Lazarus (Luke 16:19–31), and in Jesus' teaching that "it is easier for a camel to pass through the eye of a needle than for a rich man to enter the kingdom of God" (Luke 18:25; Mark 10:23–25). Through the parable of the talents (Matt. 25:14–30), Jesus admonishes his followers to be careful stewards of the gifts God has entrusted to them, and through the story of the Last Judgment (Matt. 25:31–46), he warns that our eternal fate will be determined, in part, on how we aid our brothers and sisters in need.

These are but a few of the many passages from both the Hebrew and Christian Scriptures that deal with social relations, but in them we recognize two great values that have particular relevance for us today. The first is that one's faith is not simply a private affair between oneself and God. Through the law of Moses, the Israelite people's faith in God is translated into the various customs and regulations that both guide communal life and protect the dignity of society's most vulnerable members. The message of the Christian Scriptures is essentially the same. Jesus does not teach, heal, and forgive simply because he is a nice guy; he does so to demonstrate his solidarity with the poor, powerless, and outcasts of society. This is the type of solidarity that we are called to exemplify.

The second value revealed through these scriptural passages is a vision of what we might term a *contrast society*. This contrast society is not characterized by pride, greed, and the unrestrained pursuit of power; instead, it is one where people recognize that their individual goods are intertwined with the good of the community and that the needs of the poor and powerless become the "touchstone of right relationship with God."[3] This vision is part and parcel of the Hebrew people's notion of communal living. It is also implicit in Jesus' call — particularly through the Beatitudes — to live a countercultural life. Today, as in biblical times, we tend to measure worth by how much wealth one possesses or how much power one wields in society. The scriptural message demonstrates the exact opposite. True human worth rests with the fact that we are created in the image and likeness of God, and true human power is exercised through the practice of love, justice, and service. CST is built upon this three-part foundation, which is clearly revealed to us through Scripture.

Early Church Fathers

In addition to Scripture, contributions from the third- and fourth-century Church fathers also serve as an important foundation for modern-day CST. The early Fathers are particularly concerned about people's attachment to their material possessions and what they do with them. Clement of Alexandria urges Christians to recognize that their possessions are gifts from God, given for their benefit and the benefit of others. In other words, the possession of material wealth has a social dimension. Clement further asserts that possessions are to be employed for "divine and noble" purposes and that our ability to "suffer loss cheerfully" shows whether we are the master of our possessions or their slave.[4]

Origen and Cyprian take an even more critical approach. Origen calls upon the wealthy of his time to examine themselves in light of how they both view and employ their possessions.

> Let each one of us now examine himself and silently and in his own heart decide which is the flame of love that chiefly and above all else is afire within him, which is the passion that he finds he cherishes more keenly than all others. You must yourselves pass judgment on the point and weigh these things in the scales of your conscience; *whatever it is that weighs the heaviest in the balance of your affection, that for you is God.* But I fear that with very many the love of gold will turn the scale, that down will come the weight of covetousness lying heavy in the balance.[5]

Cyprian, the third-century bishop of Carthage, speaks forcefully against the "unbounded self-interest" within his own community:

> [The rich and powerful] add forests to forests and, excluding the poor from their neighborhood, stretch out their fields far and wide into the space without limits, possess immense heaps of silver and gold and mighty sums of money, either in built up riches or in buried stores. . . . Their possession amounts to this only, that they can keep others from possessing it.[6]

> The deep and profound darkness of avarice has blinded your carnal heart. You are the captive and slave of your money; you are tied

by the chains and bonds of avarice, and you whom Christ has freed are bound anew![7]

Both Origen and Cyprian offer unambiguous challenges to the wealthy members of their communities. The unbridled pursuit of wealth was these people's god, and their use of wealth exacerbated inequalities within the community. One also recognizes, particularly within Cyprian, the warnings of Amos and Micah, who condemn the wealthy for their exploitation of the poor, and Jesus' warning that a disordered attachment to possessions leads to condemnation and death.

It might seem from these examples that the early Church fathers generally opposed wealth per se, but this is not necessarily the case. Gregory of Nyssa, among others, holds that individuals maintain the right to own property, although that right is not absolute. People can lawfully possess property (land, money, and other material wealth) and use it to fulfill the goods they recognize in their lives; however, one cannot do with this property whatever one wants. Gregory explains this point by stating that the right to ownership must "yield" to the needs of one's brothers and sisters, which means that in times of great need, the wealthy have a moral obligation to use their wealth to support the entire community, particularly the poor.[8] Ambrose of Milan similarly distinguishes between avarice and the rightful possession of wealth. Rightful possession means that one's wealth should be used to meet the needs of those who cannot provide for themselves and for the betterment of the community as a whole. *Avarice*, on the other hand, is the term used to describe an individual's excessive desire for wealth. Ambrose and Cyprian unequivocally condemn avarice as the vice of those who live ostentatiously in their greed and who exploit the poor for their own gain.[9] For Gregory of Nyssa and Ambrose of Milan, the problem is not wealth in itself but its use. Material wealth can be good as long as one recognizes that its source is God and that its purpose is to help establish justice within the community. Material wealth is not good when it is pursued at the expense of others or when it is viewed as an end in itself.

A number of important conclusions can be drawn from this brief overview of the early Church fathers. First, Christians are called to renounce wealth and power as the ultimate values in their lives. CST has always maintained that true human fulfillment is not found in what we have, but in who we are. As such, we are called to seek happiness not in external goods, but in the love of both God and neighbor. A second, closely related conclusion is that all material goods are bestowed by God for the benefit of all. Although each person has a right to own property, each person also has a duty to share his or her possessions in times of great need. Third, although nothing is inherently wrong with the possession of material goods, problems inevitably arise in terms of their use.[10] Although there is nothing wrong with the desire to live comfortably, we are not to covet the goods of our neighbors or view wealth as the barometer of anyone's worth. The point here is that we must not view wealth as an end in itself but as a means to achieve some greater good in society. John Chrysostom, another Church father, sums up the proper attitude that Christians should have toward material wealth:

> I am often reproached for continually attacking the rich. Yes, because the rich are continually attacking the poor. But those I attack are not the rich as such, only those who misuse their wealth. I point out consistently that those I accuse are not the rich, but the rapacious; wealth is one thing, covetousness another. Learn to distinguish.[11]

While the foundations of CST are rooted in Scripture and the writings of the early Church Fathers, many other historical figures have contributed to its development as well. Medieval scholars such as Thomas Aquinas echoed and expanded upon these foundations by placing the scriptural and early Church teachings in dialogue with secular philosophy. Aquinas wrote extensively about the virtue of justice in his *Summa Theologiae*, and he offered in-depth discussions on a variety of social issues that still confront us.[12] In the nineteenth century, Pope Leo XII further contributed to the development of CST by committing the Church to the care of all people (but "especially the poor") through almsgiving, supporting a variety of service organizations, and establishing hospitals for the poor and homes for orphans.[13] During the nineteenth and early twentieth centuries, Bishop Wilhelm Emmanuel von Kettler (Germany) and laymen Léon Harmel, Albert de Mun, and René de La Tour du Pin (France) championed the rights of workers and, in their own ways, set the stage for Pope Leo XIII's

On the Condition of Labor (1891), the encyclical that marked the beginning of modern CST.[14]

The Principles of Catholic Social Teaching

Now that we understand what CST is and where it comes from, we can discuss why the Church considers it so important. Many wonder, "Why should we look to the Catholic Church when debating present-day social issues? What does it have to offer?" The answer is that within CST there is a set of moral principles that provide a foundation for making social policy decisions. These principles follow directly from the foundations presented in the previous section. It is important to clarify, however, that the principles of CST are not laws or commandments that inform us exactly what we should or should not do in a particular situation. Instead, the principles are meant to offer a framework for making moral decisions concerning how we live in society as well as how we formulate public policy. In short, the principles of CST offer a moral guide for how we can live out our Christian faith in the world. Let us explore these principles in more detail.[15]

Human Dignity

The first principle of CST is human dignity. The Catholic Church teaches that because all people are created in the image and likeness of God, and because God became human through the person of Jesus Christ, each individual maintains an inherent dignity and an infinite worth. Human dignity upholds the sacredness of human life at all stages, from conception until the moment of natural death. Although many Church teachings (at least those that get the most press) tend to focus on issues involving the beginning of life (abortion) and the end of life (euthanasia), we must remember that human life is sacred at all moments, as expressed in the quote from the International Synod of Bishops at the beginning of this chapter. Practically speaking, human dignity means that all people must be afforded basic human rights and must always be treated with respect. We cannot view others as objects: we cannot exploit them, treat them as a means to our own end, or ignore the consequences of our actions on them. When faced with a decision that will affect others, we must always ask ourselves, "Do our decisions respect others as persons in themselves?"

Community

The next two principles are closely interrelated. The principle of community teaches that we humans are one family and we need one another. Physically we are dependent upon one another to meet our basic material needs. Socially we develop and fulfill ourselves only in relationship with others. The principle underscores the fact that we are not the isolated individualists that our culture tells us we are. The principle of community has a theological basis as well. Jesus taught his followers that we are to love God with our whole heart, mind, soul, and strength; and that we are to love our neighbors as ourselves (Mark 12:30–31). God offers the perfect model of this principle through the Trinity. Christians profess belief in God as Father, Son, and Holy Spirit; the "community" that exists within God models how we are called to live in communion with one another.

Common Good

The principle of community leads directly to the principle of the common good. This principle teaches that because all people live, work, and fulfill themselves in community with one another, we must look to fulfill not only our individual good, but work to build a society that benefits all people. The Second Vatican Council defines the common good as "the sum of those conditions of social life which allow social groups and their individual members relatively thorough and ready access to their fulfillment."[16] Stated differently, the common good is a social order where all individuals have the opportunity to meet their basic needs, interact with others, and ultimately fulfill themselves as human persons. The common good is not, as some have charged, another term for socialism. It simply means that society has the moral obligation to provide the conditions through which its members can develop themselves to their full potential. By developing themselves to their full potential, these individuals then contribute to the overall good of society. It is for this reason that CST maintains that the common good is not opposed to individual good. The two are, in fact, complementary.

Participation

Building directly off the principles of community and the common good are the principles of participation and subsidiarity. The principle of participation states that at all levels of society people have the right to participate in the decision-making process concerning issues that affect them directly. An excellent example of this is the Revolutionary War slogan, "No taxation without representation," which points to the injustice of forcing people to obey laws that they had no voice enacting. Participation is vitally important because it is the community's primary means of self-determination. By participating in political and other processes, the community decides for itself who will govern, how it will provide necessary services (education, fire protection, etc.), and how its resources will be allocated. Self-determination is most often exercised through voting.

Subsidiarity

The principle of subsidiarity states that as much as possible, public policy decisions should be made on the local level. The basis of this principle is that the people who have the best knowledge of what needs to be done in a particular location are those who actually live there. For example, in order to address the issue of rising crime rates in Cincinnati, Ohio, the policy makers should be people who actually reside in Cincinnati. National or international bodies should not interfere with a local situation if the local community can handle it on its own. Higher authorities can step in if the local community cannot adequately address the situation, but these higher authorities cannot change or nullify the decisions of a local community without a compelling reason.

Preferential Option for the Poor

The sixth principle of CST is preferential option for the poor. The rationale for this principle is that as Jesus and the prophets championed the cause of the poor (both materially and spiritually), so also we are called to do the same. The Second Vatican Council made this point clear in the opening line from its *Pastoral Constitution on the Church in the Modern World*:

> The joys and hopes, the grief and anguish of the people of our time, especially those who are poor or afflicted, are the joys and hopes, the grief and anguish of the followers of Christ as well.[17]

This insight developed into a fuller recognition of the Church's vocation to stand with the poor as well as its duty to evaluate economic, political, and social activity from the perspective of society's most vulnerable. The United States bishops underscored this insight twenty years later in *Economic Justice for All* by claiming that the poor "have the single most urgent economic claim on a nation." The bishops further argued that economic policy decisions must be judged on what they do "for the poor, to the poor, and what they enable the poor to do for themselves." For the bishops, the "fundamental moral criterion" of any economic policy is that it be done "at the service of all people, especially the poor."[18]

Stewardship

The seventh principle of CST is stewardship. As we saw with the Church fathers, the Catholic Church has traditionally upheld the right of individuals to own property. Reasons for this include that private property functions to meet basic needs (food, clothing, shelter, etc.) and that we are more diligent with our own property than with property commonly held. The Church teaches, however, that we must view our property as a means to self-fulfillment, not as an end in itself. That is, we must not allow the pursuit of material wealth to become the primary driving force in our lives. Money is important, but only to the extent that it provides the means to live a genuinely fulfilling life. We are not to orient our lives to gaining more.

This understanding of the correct use of private property gives rise to the principle of stewardship. Many people equate stewardship with caretaking, but it means much more than this. Caretaking simply means watching over something — such as a house or a child — for another during the other's absence. Stewardship means accepting full responsibility for that which is in your care. If a situation arises where an important decision has to be made, the steward has the full responsibility to act and, in turn, will be held accountable for the decision that he or she makes. This understanding of stewardship has profound implications for how we live. As the earth and everything contained in it are gifts from God, we have a moral obligation to use these gifts responsibly. One way to do this is by using our property for the benefit of others in times of great need. We saw an excellent example of this in the hours following the 9/11 attacks: store owners in lower Manhattan gave away food and drink to those in need. When we see others in great need, we are called to do the same.

Stewardship also has important environmental implications. Genesis, chapter 1 states that God has given humanity dominion over the earth. God has made us stewards of the created order and has given us the privilege of using the world's resources to improve upon human life. However, along with this privilege comes responsibility. We are called to recognize the created order as a good in itself and then act accordingly. This means that we must use resources prudently by cutting waste and overconsumption, and not harm the environment unnecessarily through pollution or other means.

Solidarity

Finally, the principles of human dignity, community, common good, participation, subsidiarity, option for the poor, and stewardship all culminate in the principle of solidarity. What exactly is solidarity? In the aftermath of a natural disaster, we see images on television of people who have lost everything and our immediate response is one of compassion. As implied by its etymology, *com-passion* entails a response of "feeling with" the other and a spontaneous desire to let the other know that she or he is not alone. Solidarity involves compassion, but is more than that. Solidarity involves the conscious decision to form community with the one for whom you have compassion, the one who is suffering. Solidarity takes place when one recognizes another's need and then commits oneself to action with the intent of either making some positive change in the suffering person's life or assuring that this person's situation will improve in the long run. Solidarity also involves a sense of mutuality, a two-way relationship with both sides giving and receiving. Those who offer assistance begin to realize that their giving actually fosters their own growth. Those who receive assistance discover that their plight can serve to open people's eyes to the suffering of others around the world.[19]

Solidarity entails being in relationship with others. It is not feeling sorry for another or being charitable to another out of a sense of pity. Solidarity entails the recognition that we are one human family. We are responsible for the well-being of all, and we cannot turn our backs on one another or become isolationists in the face of global difficulties. The late Pope John Paul II expressed this in his own definition of solidarity:

> [Solidarity] then is not a feeling of vague compassion or shallow distress at the misfortunes of so many people, both near and far. On the contrary, it is *a firm and persevering determination to commit oneself to the common good*; that is to say to the good of all and of each individual, because we are all really responsible for all.[20]

The Strengths of Catholic Social Teaching

Now let us briefly consider the three reasons we use CST as the foundation for discussing contemporary moral issues. First, CST is grounded in practical reality. CST does not arise from speculative theology or from technical theological arguments, but from the reality of people's lives. Pope Leo XIII wrote *On the Condition of Labor* in 1891 from the perspective of what was happening in Europe at the time, most notably the effects of the Industrial Revolution and the rise of Marxist socialism. Subsequent papal and bishops' conference documents have done the same. John XXIII's *Peace on Earth* examined challenges to world peace within the context of the Cold War, Vatican II's *Pastoral Constitution on the Church in the Modern World* aimed to update the Church in light of changes in society in the 1960s, and John Paul II's *On the Hundredth Anniversary* spoke about the emerging world reality following the fall of the Soviet Union. While always maintaining continuity with previous writings, these and other CST documents addressed issues specific to the authors' own audiences. The authors, speaking in the "here and now," sought to articulate the Church's response to important social issues as they actually existed. Similarly, the principles of CST do not exist in a vacuum. Although one can understand them abstractly, as they were presented in the previous section, they only take on their true moral character when applied in real situations.

A second reason we use CST is that its principles apply to all people, not just Catholics. The principles apply universally because they can be understood both philosophically (through human reason) and theologically (through God's revelation). The principle of human dignity illustrates this point clearly. From a philosophical perspective, we humans maintain dignity because of our free will and our capacity to reason. We are the only animal that possesses these characteristics, and we are the only earthly beings that can make moral choices. For these reasons, philosophers (among others) hold that humans possess an inherent dignity simply by virtue of the fact that we are persons. This recognition is explicitly stated in Article I of the United Nations' *Universal Declaration of Human Rights*, which maintains that because all humans "are endowed with reason and conscience," all human persons are "equal in dignity and rights."[21]

Catholic theology certainly incorporates this philosophical perspective, but expands it by teaching that human dignity is rooted in the fact that we are created in the image and likeness of God. Being created in God's image and likeness is an honor bestowed on humans alone, an honor that demonstrates just how precious and valuable human life really is. Catholic theology also holds that humans maintain an inherent dignity through the incarnation of Jesus Christ. Through Christ, God chose to become human to teach us, heal us, and ultimately redeem us through his Passion and death. Christ, by deigning to become a human being and doing all the things he did for us, demonstrates how profoundly significant human life is.

The same philosophical-theological foundations are true with the other principles as well. Because each has both a philosophical and theological basis, they speak to, and are morally binding upon, all people regardless of their religious affiliation. Because of this reality, many post–Vatican II documents are addressed not only to Catholics but to all people "of good will."

A third reason we focus on CST is that it does not tell people exactly how they should act in a particular situation. Notwithstanding its statements concerning reproductive ethics, the Church does not usually propose single, concrete teachings on social issues. This means that faithful Catholics — and non-Catholics — can disagree as to how the principles of CST should be applied in specific situations. The reason for this is that the Church recognizes three distinct levels in its social teachings, each of which demands a different level of assent. The highest level is that of universal moral principles, those that require the assent of, and are morally binding upon, all people. The next level is formal Church teaching, which is binding on Catholics only. The third level is the application of the universal principles to specific ethical situations, an application that involves "prudential judgments . . . that can change or which can be interpreted differently by people of good will."[22]

This is actually simpler than it sounds. The Church is saying that the principles of CST are morally binding on all people in a general sense, but they can be concretely applied in different ways. For example, all people are morally bound to uphold the principle of human dignity, but how do we apply this principle in terms of a specific issue such as welfare reform? Since the late 1990s, many states have revised their welfare programs by limiting the time recipients can receive benefits as well as requiring them to get a job, start a job-training program, or perform public service. Some argue that welfare reform programs violate the principle of human dignity because they remove necessary services such as food stamps, housing subsidies, and medical care from needy women and children. Others counter by asking how dignity is fostered when recipients receive benefits without being required to do anything in return or without being provided any incentive to improve their condition in life? The morality of welfare reform is an open question (and will not be addressed in this text). The point here is that the principles of CST offer a moral framework within which specific policy decisions concerning welfare reform must be made, yet the principles do not tell us exactly how we should act. People "of good will" can and do apply human dignity differently with respect to welfare reform, and they often come up with different — but moral — solutions. The Church recognizes that moral certainty is much easier to achieve at a general level than when it comes to specifics. As such, in the areas of economics, politics, and the other social sciences, the Church yields the practical application of its principles to the expertise of those working in the field.[23]

With this general introduction, we can now begin to apply the principles of CST to various social issues facing our nation. In the following chapters, we explore the Church's teachings concerning a number of different issues, including corporate ethics, the forced imposition of debt repayment and structural adjustment policies, the death penalty, and just war. While these are not the only ethical issues facing our nation today, they are important questions that demand an informed moral response from us all.

Review Questions

1. What is Catholic Social Teaching? What is its overall point? Why is it often referred to as the Church's "best-kept secret"?

2. What are *mispat* and *sedaqah*? Why are they important for understanding the message of the Hebrew Scriptures?

3. What are the two "great values" concerning social life that we learn from the Hebrew and Christian Scriptures? What relevance do these values have for us today?

4. What do Clement of Alexandria, Origen, and Cyprian of Carthage teach about material possessions? What do Gregory of Nyssa and Ambrose of Milan teach about material possessions?

5. What conclusions can be drawn from the early Church fathers?

6. If the principles of CST are not commandments—in that they do not tell us exactly how to act in a specific situation—what is their purpose?

7. What is the principle of human dignity? What is its theological basis? What does this principle mean in practice?

8. What is the principle of community? What is its theological foundation?

9. What is the principle of the common good? How is it defined by the Second Vatican Council?

10. What are the principles of participation and subsidiarity? What do these principles mean in practice?

11. What is the principle of preferential option for the poor? What is its theological basis? How do the United States bishops say it must be applied in terms of economic policy decisions?

12. Why does the Catholic Church uphold the right to own property? What cautions come with the exercise of this right?

13. What is the principle of stewardship? What makes stewardship distinct from caretaking?

14. What is the principle of solidarity? What does it mean in practice? How does John Paul II define solidarity?

15. What does it mean to say that CST is grounded in practical reality?

16. Why are the principles of CST morally binding on all people and not just Catholics?

17. Why does CST not tell us exactly how we should act in a given situation?

ENDNOTES

1 United States Conference of Catholic Bishops (USCC), *Sharing Catholic Social Teaching: Challenges and Reflections* (Washington, DC: USCC, 1998).

2 John R. Donahue, SJ, "The Bible and Catholic Social Teaching: Will This Engagement Lead to Marriage?" in *Modern Catholic Social Teaching: Commentaries and Interpretations*, ed. Kenneth Himes, OFM, et al. (Washington, DC: Georgetown University Press, 2004), 14. Donahue notes that the terms *mispat* and *sedaqah*, or variations of them, appear over nine hundred times in Scripture.

3 Ibid., 21. The two "great values" are taken from this text.

4 Clement of Alexandria, *Quis dives salvetur*, cited in William Walsh, SJ, and John Langan, SJ, "Patristic Social Consciousness—The Church and the Poor," in *The Faith That Does Justice* (New York: Paulist Press, 1977), 120.

5 Origen, *Homily on the Book of Judges* 2.3, cited in Walsh and Langan, "Patristic Social Consciousness," 121–22 (emphasis added).

6 Cyprian of Carthage, *To Donatus* 12, cited in Walsh and Langan, "Patristic Social Consciousness," 122.

7 Cyprian of Carthage, *On Works and Almsgiving* 13, cited in Walsh and Langan, "Patristic Social Consciousness," 124.

8 Gregory of Nyssa, *Love of the Poor* 66, cited in Walsh and Langan, "Patristic Social Consciousness," 127.

9 Ambrose of Milan, *Naboth* 1, cited in Walsh and Langan, "Patristic Social Consciousness," 128.

10 These are the conclusions of Walsh and Langan, "Patristic Social Consciousness," 146–47.

11 John Chrysostom, *Fall of Eutropius* 2.3, cited in Walsh and Langan, "Patristic Social Consciousness," 128.

12 See Aquinas, *Summa Theologiae*, II – II, qs. 57–79.

13 Leo XII, *Charitate Christi*, 18, cited in Michael Schuck, *That They Be One: The Social Teachings of the Papal Encyclicals* 1740 –1989 (Washington, DC: Georgetown University Press, 1991), 29 – 30.

14 See Paul Misner, *Social Catholicism in Europe: From the Onset of Industrialization to the First World War* (New York: Crossroad, 1991).

15 These principles, as well as a comprehensive explanation of the Church's social teachings, can be found in the Pontifical Commission for Justice and Peace, *Compendium of the Social Doctrine of the Church* (Vatican City: Libreria Editrice Vaticana, 2004).

16 Second Vatican Council, *Pastoral Constitution on the Church in the Modern World*, in *Catholic Social Thought: The Documentary Heritage* (Maryknoll, NY: Orbis Books, 1995), no. 26.1.

17 *Pastoral Constitution on the Church in the Modern World*, no. 1.

18 USCC, *Economic Justice for All: Tenth Anniversary Edition* (Washington, DC: USCC, 1997), nos. 24, 86, 88.

19 Marie Giblin, "What Catholics Should Know about Solidarity," *Catholic Update* (June 2007): 1– 4.

20 John Paul II, "On Social Concern," in *Catholic Social Thought*, no. 38 (emphasis in the original).

21 See Article I of the United Nations' *Universal Declaration of Human Rights* (1948). In its introduction (preamble), the *Declaration* also states, "Recognition of the inherent dignity and of the equal and inalienable rights of all members of the human family is the foundation of freedom, justice and peace in the world."

22 United States Catholic bishops, *The Challenge of Peace: God's Promise and Our Response*, in *Catholic Social Thought*, no. 10. See also *Economic Justice for All*, nos. 134 – 35.

23 The United States bishops make this point clear in *Economic Justice for All*: "In our letter, we write as pastors, not public officials. We speak as moral teachers, not economic technicians. We seek not to make some political or ideological point but to lift up the human and ethical dimensions of economic life, aspects too often neglected in public discussion" (no. 7). For further discussion on the gradations of authority in Catholic Social Teaching, see Richard Gaillardetz, "The Ecclesial Foundations of Modern Catholic Social Teaching," in *Modern Catholic Social Teaching: Commentaries and Interpretations*, ed. Kenneth Himes et al. (Washington, DC: Georgetown University Press, 2005), 89 – 90.

PART II

CONSIDERING ETHICS IN TODAY'S WORLD

4. BUSINESS ETHICS AND THE AMERICAN CORPORATION

On March 3, 1974, a Turkish Airlines DC-10 took off from Paris heading for London with 348 people on board. Shortly after takeoff, the left rear cargo door suddenly blew off and sent the aircraft into a dive from which the pilots could not recover. Within minutes, the plane crashed into a dense forest and all aboard were killed. The subsequent accident investigation revealed that the main cause of the disaster was a faulty design in the cargo door latching system, and that the aircraft's manufacturer, McDonnell Douglas, was fully aware of this design fault well in advance of the Paris accident, but for monetary and "rush to delivery" reasons, it chose to do nothing about it. Unfortunately, situations like this are not unheard of in the American corporate world. During the early to mid-1970s, the Ford Motor Company manufactured its Pinto automobile line with gas tanks that tended to rupture during low- and moderate-speed rear-end collisions. Through lawsuits brought by the victims of these collisions, it was revealed that Ford was aware of safety problems with the gas tanks, but determined through a cost-benefit analysis that it would be less expensive to pay damages to injured parties than to redesign or retrofit the gas tanks with a protective safety bladder.

Economic ethics is a large topic that encompasses many different issues and points of view. In the next two chapters, we consider economic issues that present important ethical challenges for American Catholics today. In this chapter, we focus on business ethics and in particular on how Catholic Social Teaching (CST) calls corporations to act ethically. In the next chapter, we examine how Western-imposed debt repayment and structural adjustment policies have impacted the people of sub-Saharan Africa. The overall purpose of these chapters is to demonstrate that Catholic Social Teaching offers us an important moral guide for living out our Christian vocation in the economic realm.

Business Ethics and Catholic Social Teaching

Business ethics is an important topic in our nation today, particularly in light of past financial scandals surrounding Enron, WorldCom, Tyco, and numerous other corporations. Each of these corporations knowingly violated accepted norms and financial practices, resulting in the disappearance of millions of dollars of investor funds, the loss of thousands of jobs, and arguably undermining United States financial markets. Because the lives of millions of people are affected by the actions of corporations — or of individuals acting in the corporate name — corporate behavior has profound ethical implications for us all.

Traditionally the study of business ethics has been viewed as a branch of applied philosophy. In recent years, however, Christian social ethicists have begun to address the topic and have demonstrated that the Christian tradition has much to add to the field.

Corporations and business entities play an important and necessary role in American economic life. They provide jobs, create the capital necessary for future growth, and are at the forefront of technological advances. However, to be truly beneficial to society, corporations must operate within a basic moral framework. Christianity teaches that, as the author of creation, God is Lord over the world and everything in it. As such, God's moral law extends to the entire created order, including the realm of business. The bishops of the Second Vatican Council affirmed this teaching in their *Pastoral Constitution on the Church in the Modern World*, stating that it was a mistake to think that religion consisted solely in "acts of worship," or that earthly concerns could be "altogether divorced from the religious life." The Council claimed that the contradiction between the faith that people profess and the way they live was one of the most serious errors facing our world.[1]

The United States Catholic bishops expanded upon these teachings in their 1986 pastoral *Economic Justice for All*. In this document they surveyed the American economy and offered practical suggestions for how it could allow for greater justice and benefits for all people, explicitly linking faith with business.

> Our faith is not just a weekend obligation, a mystery to be cel- ebrated around the altar on Sunday. It is a pervasive reality to be practiced every day in homes, offices, factories, schools, and businesses across our land. We cannot separate what we believe from how we act in the marketplace and the broader community, for this is where we make our primary contribution to the pursuit of economic justice.[2]

The moral precepts recognized by the Church apply to actions performed in the corporate name in the same way they apply to those per- formed in the individual's private life. There is no distinction between the two. This means that business people are not immune from the duty to act ethically. They cannot commit an act they know to be morally wrong and claim "that's just business." With this foundational lesson in mind, let's explore how principles of CST relate to business ethics.

Principles of Catholic Social Teaching for Business Ethics

Human Dignity

As noted, Catholicism teaches that all human beings are created in the image and likeness of God and have infinite worth. Each individual main- tains an inherent dignity by virtue of the fact that he or she is a person. Perhaps the most important implication of this principle for business ethics is that the primary goal of any business enterprise should be the well-being of the human person, not the pursuit of profit. This undoubtedly sounds strange in our culture, particularly to corporate shareholders, but it is the foundation for any Catholic business ethic. Profit is necessary for the business's continued operation, and there is nothing intrinsically wrong with earning a profit. However, profit is a means to an end, not an end in itself. The moral justification for business involves the contribution it makes to human flourishing, how its activity corresponds with God's plan for creation, and how it unfolds God's Kingdom on earth.[3] The ultimate goal of business is meeting the needs of people, not accumulating profit. Business exists to serve people, not the other way around.[4]

Pope Leo XIII spoke to the importance of recognizing human dignity in business in his encyclical *On the Condition of Labor* (1891). According to the pope, "Each requires the other; capital (understood as owners) cannot do without labor nor labor without capital." Here, he recognized the truth that for any business entity to succeed there needs to be mutual cooperation between ownership and labor. Workers have an obligation to honor agreements with owners, and owners have an obligation to respect their workers, recognize the inherent dignity of their labor, and not "look upon them merely as so much muscle or physical power." The pope continued with a stern warning to the business owner:

> His great and principal obligation is to give to everyone that which is just . . . [and he] should remember this — that to exercise pressure for the sake of gain upon the indigent and destitute, and to make one's profit out of the need of another, is condemned by all laws, human and divine.[5]

Leo XIII's call for mutual respect between ownership and labor was made during the Industrial Revolution, but it is vitally important for us today. This call to mutual respect can be extended to include not only corporate executives and their employees, but customers, shareholders, suppliers, subcontractors, and any other stakeholder in the corporation. Each must be treated with dignity and respect. The United States bishops also underscored this teaching in *Economic Justice for All* when they claimed that every economic decision and institution "must be judged in light of whether it protects or undermines the dignity of the human person."[6]

Arguably the most visible area where American corporations can uphold human dignity is by promoting just working conditions. CST maintains that human work has an inherent dignity for three primary reasons. First, work is the principal means by which we satisfy our material needs. The food we eat, the clothes we wear, and the homes we live in are provided by the wages we earn from our work. Second, work is a means for us to participate with God in the continual re-creation of the world. Catholicism teaches that God endows each of us with particular talents, which we must use to improve the condition of human life. Third, CST maintains the dignity of work because individuals "become who they are," in part, through their work activity. Most often we concentrate on the objective aspect of work: how much we produce, how much we sell, how many hours we bill. However, our work profoundly affects who we are as people. This is the subjective aspect of work. Pope John Paul II spoke to this aspect in his encyclical *On Human Work* (1981):

> [The human] is a person, that is to say, a subjective being capable of acting in a planned and rational way, capable of deciding about himself, and with a tendency to self-realization. As *a person, man is therefore the subject of work.* As a person he works . . . [and] these actions must all serve to realize his humanity. [7]

The pope continued by claiming that as work intimately involves the individual's self-worth, self-expression, and self-fulfillment, the value of human work rests with the person who performs it. Human work maintains an inherent dignity and must never be viewed as a commodity that can be bought and sold.

This understanding of work's inherent dignity has a number of important implications for American corporations. First, it means that corporations have a moral obligation to pay employees a just or living wage, one that is sufficient to meet the basic needs of the employee's family and to allow for future investment. Our nation's current federal minimum wage is hardly sufficient to allow an individual, much less a family, to live a dignified life. Determining a just wage involves many factors, including the nature of the job, the firm's capabilities, the local cost of living, the fairness of wage negotiations, and the rate of pay within the industry itself.[8] Corporations must be aware of what a living wage is in their local area and offer commensurate salaries.

Corporations also need to reevaluate their levels of executive compensation. No one begrudges an executive for earning a salary greater than that of a line production worker, but the discrepancies we see today raise serious questions of justice. Corporations also need to look at their outsourcing policies. There may be nothing inherently wrong with shifting production or support facilities to a developing nation, but ethical questions do surround the reasons for doing so. Do companies relocate to foreign nations or contract with foreign producers because they honestly want to offer the people living in these nations a better standard of living, or are they doing it simply to take advantage of lower labor costs and increase their own profits?

Wages and wage-related issues are critical concerns, but they do not exhaust a corporation's ethical obligations concerning the dignity of labor. CST maintains that corporations should offer employees health care and disability benefits as well as a retirement or pension program. To increase the employee's stake in the company's success, corporations should, when possible, establish stock purchase or profit-sharing programs. Corporations could also show greater respect for families by offering cafeteria benefits plans and allowing for flexible hours, parental leave, and work-from-home programs. In addition, corporations must establish fair hiring and promotion policies that do not discriminate on the basis of gender, race, age, ethnicity, sexual orientation, or religious belief. They must establish clear policies of employee governance and procedures for employee grievance. They must also refuse to do business with companies that knowingly violate human rights, such as companies that employ child or slave labor, or that fail to address dangerous working conditions.

One final way that CST seeks to uphold the dignity of labor is through its support of labor unions. Since even before Pope Leo XIII's *On the Condition of Labor*, the Catholic Church has upheld the right of every worker to join a union, as well as the duty of ownership and management to recognize and respect this right. Leo XIII, writing within the context of the Industrial Revolution, praised the founding of labor associations that sought to protect the rights of workers and promote their well-being. According to the pope, workers maintained a "natural right" to join these associations, and they could not be prevented by anyone from becoming members of them. Pope John Paul II picked up on this "right to association" in his 1981 encyclical *On Human Work*, in which he claimed that labor unions constitute an "indispensable element of the social life" of today's industrialized world. Unions act as a "mouthpiece for social justice" in that their primary purpose is to uphold workers' rights vis-à-vis those who own and control the means of production. In this sense, active union membership actually demonstrates a "prudent concern for the common good." The United States

Catholic bishops echoed both Leo XIII and John Paul II by reiterating in *Economic Justice for All* that the Church "fully supports" the right of workers to join a union, and it vigorously opposes any effort at union busting or otherwise denying workers their right to association. The bishops also claimed that workers may legitimately resort to calling a strike when they see this as the only remaining means of justice available to them.

Although the Catholic Church has historically supported the rights of individual workers as well as the labor movement as a whole, this support is not without its limits. CST maintains that union members have important moral duties as well. Workers must use their collective power for the common good of society as a whole, not simply for their own individual goods or the good of the union itself. Workers must exercise their right to strike only for "extreme" reasons, they must never abuse this right under some "external" political motivation, and they must never resort to violence. Finally, union leaders have a particular responsibility to exercise proper stewardship of the union's resources as well as to uphold the good name of the entire union movement.[9]

Community and the Common Good

The principles of community and the common good are vital for business ethics, as is evident in both papal and bishops' conference statements. Pope John XXIII, recognizing the rapid growth of corporations in his *Christianity and Social Progress* (1961), insisted that regardless of their size, corporations must offer workers the opportunity to purchase shares of stock. His rationale centered on the principle of community. By offering workers the opportunity of ownership, businesses would "assume the character of true human fellowship whose spirit suffuses the dealings, activities and standing of all its members." He underscored this point later in the encyclical by citing the Church's traditional teaching that the human person is the "foundation, cause, and end of all social institutions."[10] In addition to being an economic entity whose purpose is to earn a profit, the business enterprise is a social entity composed of human persons who interact and cooperate with one another to ensure its successful operation. Thirty years later, in *On the Hundredth Anniversary of Rerum Novarum* (1991), Pope John Paul II echoed his predecessor by stating that a business must not be viewed solely as a "society of capital goods." Instead, it must be viewed as a "society of persons" within which individuals "participate in different ways and with specific responsibilities" to achieve an overall good.[11]

The United States Catholic bishops invoked the principle of the common good in *Economic Justice for All*. Speaking specifically to the business enterprise, they maintained that the degree to which economic activity fulfills the demands of justice is contingent upon how its resources are managed by owners, managers, and "investors of financial capital." Business and entrepreneurial freedom must always be protected, but incumbent with this freedom is the duty to respect both the norms of justice and the societal common good.[12] The bishops offered further observations: workers must exercise their right to strike only for "extreme" reasons, they must never abuse this right under some "external" political motivation, and they must never resort to violence.

> Persons in management face many hard choices each day, choices on which the well-being of many others depends. Commitment to the public good and not simply the private good of their firms is at the heart of what it means to call their work a vocation, and not simply a career or job.[13]

Two important points within this quotation have a direct bearing on present-day study of business ethics. First, the bishops recognized that corporate executives face difficult ethical decisions and that correct responses are not always clear. Corporate decisions, like individual decisions, can sometimes fall into a moral gray area. Nevertheless, the bishops warned that as corporate decisions affect many people, executives must always take these people's well-being into consideration when deciding how to act.

Second, the bishops' call for a commitment to the common good contributes to the ongoing debate between shareholder and stakeholder theory. Briefly, shareholder theory maintains that because the shareholders actually own a corporation, management's primary responsibility is to them. Their interests must be considered above any other concern. The rationale for this theory is that corporate managers have a fiduciary responsibility to increase shareholder wealth, a responsibility that provides the framework for any corporate decision. Stakeholder theory, on the other hand, recognizes that many constituencies are affected by a corporation's actions. Some, such as employees, customers, suppliers, and subcontractors, have a direct interest in the corporation's success because they depend upon it for their well-being. Other constituencies, like the local community, are less directly affected by a corporation's actions. Nevertheless, the corporation interacts with many constituencies; in fact, much of its success depends on how it manages the claims that each constituency makes. Stakeholder theory maintains that corporations have important moral duties to many groups of people, not just shareholders.[14]

The United States bishops' call for a "commitment to the common good" favors the stakeholder position. We saw in chapter 1 that actions always have consequences, and that individuals are responsible for the consequences of their moral decisions. The same is true for a corporation. When confronted with an ethical decision, corporate managers must not consider solely the good of the firm or its shareholders. They have a moral obligation to determine, to the best of their ability, how the consequences of their decision will affect the wider community. The United States bishops made this point:

> In U. S. law, the primary responsibility of managers is to exercise prudent judgment in the interests of a profitable return to investors. But morally, this legal responsibility may be exercised only within the bounds of justice to employees, customers, suppliers, and the local community.[15]

It is important to note that the bishops maintain that management has duties toward shareholders and that the shareholders' good is essential for the well-being of the corporation. Nevertheless, the bishops stress that justice to other constituents overrides the primacy of the shareholders' claim. To hold that a corporation has an overriding, or even absolute, moral duty to one preferential group not only violates the principle of the common good, but it potentially can have disastrous effects on the lives of real people. We will see examples of such effects in the case studies at the end of the chapter. Now that we have seen how the principles of community and the common good can be applied generally in the corporate world, how do we apply them concretely? Aaron Feuerstein, owner of Malden Mills in Lawrence, Massachusetts, gained international attention in the aftermath of a devastating fire at his textile manufacturing plant in the winter of 1995. Following the fire, his advisors strongly suggested that he collect the insurance money (approximately three hundred million dollars) and either retire or relocate the plant overseas where labor costs would be much lower. Feuerstein refused to do either. Instead, he announced that Malden Mills would be rebuilt and that all 3,100 employees would continue to receive their salaries and benefits in the short term, even if there was no work for them to do. When asked why he made this decision, Feuerstein explained:

> Corporate responsibility to me means, yes, you must . . . take care of the shareholder, but that is not your exclusive responsibility. The CEO has responsibility to his workers, both white collar and blue collar, and he has responsibility to his community and city. And he has to be wise enough to balance out these various responsibilities and . . . to act justly for the shareholder as well as the worker.[16]

Clearly, Aaron Feuerstein upheld the principles of community and the common good in his decisions concerning Malden Mills. His first concern was for his employees, not himself, and he did what he could to assure that their needs would be met. He also upheld the good of Lawrence, a struggling, working-class city near Boston that would have suffered greatly if Malden Mills had closed. Contrast this with executives like Kenneth Lay (Enron), Dennis Kozlowski (Tyco), and Bernie Ebbers (WorldCom), who failed to recognize these principles. By falsifying financial records, embezzling corporate funds for personal use, and misleading both shareholders and government oversight agencies, these CEOs focused on their own "good," with destructive and demoralizing consequences. A commitment to the public good means that corporate decision makers have a moral obligation to determine how a specific action will affect not only their firm and its shareholders but also the wider society as a whole. Granted, this is not always an easy thing to do. However, as with human dignity, regard for community and the societal common good are essential elements of any Catholic business ethic.

Stewardship

The fourth principle of CST important for business ethics is stewardship. In chapter 3, we spoke about proper stewardship of the resources (or property) that have been entrusted to us by God. In *Economic Justice for All*, the

United States bishops applied this teaching to corporate management by stating that business and finance have a moral duty to be "faithful trustees" of the resources placed at their disposal. Citing Thomas Aquinas's *Summa Theologiae* and Pope Paul VI's *On the Development of Peoples* (1967), they argued that as no one owns resources absolutely, no one can control their use without regard for the needs of others. In light of this, they decried the practice of reaping short-term profits at the expense of long-term growth, as this tends to stunt the production of necessary goods and services. They also cautioned managers that "resources created by human industry" do not belong to the corporation alone, because in gaining these resources the corporation benefited from the earlier progress of others. For this reason, technological advance and innovation must not be regarded as the exclusive property of the corporation, but always should be used to benefit society as a whole.[17]

The principle of stewardship also applies to business in terms of environmental issues, particularly pollution and the use of natural resources. Historically, businesses that have polluted have done so primarily for economic reasons, as it is less costly to release pollutants into the environment than it is to deal with them in other ways. Contributing to this was the belief that the environment's carrying capacity is so large that each firm's contribution of pollution is relatively insignificant, and the assumption that the environment is a "free good" that can be used without reimbursing anyone for its use.[18] Today, with scientific studies indicating that human activity is at least contributing to global warming, companies are under greater pressure, both legally and morally, to minimize their effects on the environment.

CST has relatively few documents focusing specifically on the environment. However, the teachings that do exist are crystal clear. In his message from the 1990 World Day of Peace, Pope John Paul II held that as the earth was created by God and that God deemed it to be good (Genesis, chapter 1), the created order has intrinsic value. In other words, the earth and all of the created order are good in and of themselves. Scripture also teaches that God created the earth for humanity and entrusted it to our care. God gave us dominion over the earth, which means that we are fully responsible for how we treat it and for how we use its abundance. In light of these teachings, we are called to be proper stewards of the created order in everything, including our business activities.[19] In making this claim, however, we must be careful not to confuse dominion with domination. Dominion does not mean we have a "divine grant" over creation to exploit it in any way we choose; that would be domination. Dominion means that our actions must always be in accord with what God values concerning the created order as well as with God's ultimate will for it.[20]

Based on these scriptural teachings, CST maintains that environmental degradation in any form constitutes a moral crisis for the entire human community. John Paul II specifically identified industrial waste, the burning of fossil fuels, and the use of herbicides, coolants, and other propellants as environmental risks that demand greater care from those who use them. He stated that many of the environmental problems we face today are the direct result of business activities in which individual economic interests have taken priority over the common good.[21] The United States bishops identified many of these same factors in their pastoral *Renewing the Earth* (1991), but added that solutions to the problems caused by pollution will require greater scientific research and technological innovation. The bishops claimed that when we employ appropriate technology in response to environmental issues, we display "respect for creation and reverence for the Creator." As such, they challenged business leaders to make environmental protection a "central concern" of their activities and to collaborate for the common protection of the earth.[22]

In addition to pollution, environmental stewardship also involves our use of the world's resources. We are inundated today with claims that world oil supplies are finite, and without proper conservation we will deplete them by the end of this century. Other nonrenewable resources such as fresh water supplies, forests, and topsoil raise similar concerns. Philosopher John Rawls has argued that as a matter of justice, we have a moral obligation not to deprive future generations of the resources we enjoy today. As such, we must determine a "just savings schedule" that balances how much of the world's resources we should set aside for our descendants against what we were entitled to claim of our predecessors. In other words, justice demands that we hand over to our children a situation no worse than that which we received from our parents.[23]

CST speaks to the issue of environmental depletion by calling on both individuals and businesses to evaluate critically the amount of resources they consume. John Paul II maintained that ecological problems cannot begin to be solved until the vices of consumerism and instant gratification are replaced by the virtues of simplicity, moderation, and self-sacrifice.[24] In other words, we must abandon our desire to *have more* and instead seek to *be more* with what we already possess. The United States bishops concurred, arguing that first-world consumption is the single greatest source of environmental degradation. As a matter of highest priority, we have a moral obligation to address our wasteful and often destructive habits of consumption.[25] Businesses must also act as stewards of creation in all their operations. This includes foregoing short-term profits to reduce environmental harm, using resources prudently, cutting waste wherever possible, researching the use of renewable energy sources, and developing products that significantly cut our consumption of nonrenewable resources.

Option for the Poor

The fifth principle, option for the poor, means that we have a moral obligation to evaluate all economic and social activity from the perspective of society's least advantaged. In terms of business ethics, this means that corporations have a moral duty to do what they reasonably can to meet the needs of the most vulnerable members of the community. Corporations are called to produce quality goods and services that meet authentic human needs. They are called, when appropriate, to offer opportunities for at-risk individuals through job training or apprenticeship programs. They are called, when appropriate, to locate in low-income areas and, if possible, not to abandon these areas when profits are marginal. They are called to help the poor in securing loans for educational advancement or for starting new businesses. They are also called to enter into partnerships with organizations that work to alleviate poverty and suffering, and to donate money or products to worthy causes in times of need.

Option for the poor also means that corporations must evaluate their operations in terms of how they affect the poor. More often than not, factories and other production facilities are located in lower-income areas. The noise, pollution, and other byproducts of the production process most directly affect those who live in close proximity to the plants. Some corporations view the workforce as expendable in the sense that because many people are willing to work for low wages, the corporation can pay little and offer few benefits to their employees. Other corporations exploit the poor through their stated business practices. Examples of this include check-cashing or paycheck-loan stores that charge inflated "fees" for their services, and credit card companies that target individuals with poor credit and then charge them exorbitant rates of interest. No one begrudges corporations and businesses for earning a profit, but these entities must continually evaluate their activities to assure that their success is not enhanced through the exploitation of others, particularly the poor.

The option for the poor operates on an international level as well. Corporations must evaluate the impact of their operations on people and cultures around the world. As noted in chapter 3, ever-increasing globalization demonstrates just how interconnected we are. Decisions and actions in the United States affect people around the world and vice versa. Most people would agree that the developing world is in desperate need of Western corporate investment, yet how should this investment be implemented? Option for the poor offers one perspective by maintaining that the primary focus of any investment should be the people themselves. Western corporations must adopt an attitude of cooperation with people in the developing world, not one of paternalism. In establishing new business entities, they must first recognize the needs of the local populations and assure that their own objectives do not frustrate those of the local communities. This means that the products or services produced must conform to local needs and that operations must serve the good of the local communities. To the greatest extent possible, managerial and staff positions in these new businesses must be offered to locals, and the workers must be offered shares of ownership. These opportunities afford individuals a personal stake in the corporation's success and also offer them a greater incentive to work toward its overall good. In addition, corporations must not turn a blind eye to human-rights violations. They should critically evaluate whether it is in the best interest of the local population to do business in nations where human rights are not respected. We must note that each of the issues we have mentioned here is complex, and there is not one, overarching response to them. Corporations can and do act in various ways based on local circumstances; option for the poor offers a moral framework within which the specific, local decisions must be made.[26]

Solidarity

The final principle of CST that is relevant for the study of business ethics is solidarity, or the "firm and preserving determination to commit oneself to the common good."[27] Solidarity is essential to any Catholic business ethic because it incorporates the principles of human dignity, community, common good, stewardship, and option for the poor, and it challenges us to both internalize these principles and manifest them in our actions. It demands that we willingly and consistently make choices to protect and promote the interests of others, not just our own. To function ethically, any human organization, including the corporation, must manifest and actively promote this virtue.

With this understanding of solidarity in mind, we argue that for any corporate action to be considered ethical, those who are charged with its planning, formulation, and execution must look beyond the fiduciary responsibility they have to their shareholders and judge to the best of their ability how the proposed action will both respect the dignity of others and promote the societal common good. Stated differently, corporate actions must be expressions of social solidarity. We recognize that this statement is controversial, yet we believe it provides the foundation for business ethics as a whole. Yes, corporate managers have a fiduciary responsibility to their shareholders and, generally speaking, they must safeguard their interests. However, when the decision in question involves harmful consequences to others, the primacy of the shareholder argument cannot be upheld. Fiduciary responsibility cannot supersede a corporation's moral duty to protect stakeholders from being adversely affected by its actions.

Today corporations wield tremendous economic and political power. The question for corporate executives is, "How will this power be used?" Will it be used solely for the "good" of the corporation and its shareholders, or will it be used for the good of society as a whole? We recognize once again that no individual acting in the corporate name can foresee all possible consequences of an ethical decision, but it is entirely possible, if not morally imperative, to include solidarity and the other CST principles in corporate decision-making processes. Had this been done, perhaps thousands of Enron jobs and stock portfolios might have been saved and the lives of those flying on the ill-fated DC-10 or riding in defective Pintos might not have been lost.

Catholic Social Teaching and Business Ethics: The Cases

We stated in chapter 3 that CST does not exist in a vacuum. For the principles to demonstrate their true ethical character, they need to be applied in real situations. We will now apply CST to three actual cases to demonstrate what happens when a corporation does, or does not, uphold the Church's moral principles in its actions.

The DC-10

During the early 1970s, the American commercial aircraft industry was extremely competitive. McDonnell Douglas competed with Boeing and Lockheed to design and build a new generation of aircraft for our nation's emerging airline industry. The DC-10 competed directly with Lockheed's L-1011 for the 250+-seat, short- to medium-haul market, and the stakes were high. The manufacturer that brought its product to the market first would generate significantly greater sales, and many characterized this as a battle that neither could afford to lose. Throughout the design and testing process of the DC-10, concerns were raised over the aircraft's cargo door latching system. McDonnell Douglas had contracted with General Dynamics' Convair Division to design the aircraft's fuselage and doors. Because the cargo doors opened outward and had to withstand the force of cabin pressurization in flight, Convair engineers proposed an industry-accepted hydraulic system. To reduce weight and because of a request from one of its customers (American Airlines), McDonnell Douglas decided instead to use an electrical system. Convair engineers expressed concerns that the electrical system was inadequate and repeatedly advised McDonnell Douglas that the already proven hydraulic system was necessary for safety. Engineers even sent an analysis to McDonnell Douglas outlining nine different scenarios where the proposed electrical latching system could fail in flight, resulting in the loss of the aircraft. Concerning one of these scenarios, the Convair engineers wrote:

> Door will close and latch but will not safely lock. Indicator light will indicate normal position. Door will open in flight—

resulting in sudden decompression and possibly structural failure of the floor.[28]

Despite these warnings from Convair, McDonnell Douglas went ahead with its own design. Problems with the cargo doors began to surface almost immediately. During a May 1970 ground pressurization test, a cargo door actually blew off. This was a significant event not only because the electrical system had failed but because the resulting rapid decompression had also caused the main cabin floor to collapse. The in-flight control systems in the DC-10 are located under the main cabin floor, so if a collapse were to occur, it could sever these systems, leading to a complete loss of control of the aircraft. McDonnell Douglas attributed this ground test failure to human error. In 1971, the Dutch equivalent of the United States Federal Aviation Administration (FAA) issued a report that also expressed concerns about the possibility of a cabin floor collapse. The Dutch government had planned to purchase the DC-10 for its national fleet but was concerned with the likelihood that a rapid decompression could sever the aircraft's control systems. McDonnell Douglas made some modifications to the latching system, but did not make all the design changes for which the Convair engineers had been calling. The company's position was that the chances of an in-flight failure were remote, and an extensive redesign was not warranted.

On July 29, 1971, the FAA certified the DC-10 and it went into passenger service. In June of 1972 the cargo door of an American Airlines DC-10 blew off over Windsor, Canada, shortly after takeoff from Detroit. Fortunately, the aircraft carried only a light passenger load so although the cabin floor partially collapsed, the pilots were able to maintain control and land the plane with only minor injuries to passengers and crew. The incident investigation revealed that a pressurization vent on the cargo door (one of McDonnell Douglas's modifications) had not been closed properly; in fact the door had been jammed shut by a baggage handler at the Detroit airport. The FAA threatened to issue a public Airworthiness Directive concerning the DC-10, which would have made the safety concerns public knowledge and would have effectively grounded the aircraft until changes were made. McDonnell Douglas was able to get this directive rescinded after promising the FAA that it would issue private "service bulletins" to its airline customers.

Following the Windsor incident, numerous engineers repeated their concerns about the cargo door latching system and warned that a similar failure could happen again. Dan Applegate, director of product engineering at Convair, sent a lengthy memo to his superiors stating, in part, that the fundamental safety of the latching system had been "progressively down-graded" since the beginning of the DC-10 project. The DC-10 "demonstrated an inherent susceptibility to catastrophic failure," and McDonnell Douglas had taken a "hard line" in regard to "change cost negotiations." Applegate also expressed fears that the cabin floor would collapse during a rapid decompression and called on Convair to press McDonnell Douglas to make fundamental design changes in the aircraft, changes that he admitted would cost significant time and money and would likely have "disastrous effects" on DC-10 sales. Nevertheless, he believed these changes needed to be made and concluded his report by stating, "It seems to me inevitable that, in the twenty years ahead of us, DC-10 cargo doors will come open, and I would expect this to usually result in the loss of the airplane."[29]

Applegate's fears were confirmed outside Paris in the spring of 1974. A fully loaded Turkish Airlines flight had taken off from Paris and was climbing to 11,500 feet when the left rear cargo door blew out. The resulting decompression ejected several passengers and partially collapsed the cabin floor, severely impairing the in-flight control systems. For seventy-seven seconds the crew tried to correct the aircraft's dive, but without the ability to control the plane they were unsuccessful. The DC-10, traveling at 430 knots, slammed into a forest near Ermenonville, France, and all aboard were killed instantly. One month later, French investigators confirmed what McDonnell Douglas had feared most. The primary cause of the DC-10 crash was a faulty cargo door.

The Ford Pinto

The Ford Motor Company was facing difficult challenges in the automobile market during the late 1960s and early 1970s. Due to rising gas prices and increased competition from Japanese and German manufacturers, Ford decided to build a car using the "Rule of 2000." This car was to weigh no more than two thousand pounds (for gas efficiency) and cost no more than two thousand dollars (to remain competitive). It also needed to be designed and produced quickly. The result was the Ford Pinto.[30]

Early prototypes of the Pinto revealed at least four major design flaws. The first was that the Pinto's gas tank was placed between the rear axle and the rear bumper, allowing for more trunk room, but leaving only nine to ten inches of "crush space" in the event of an accident. In other comparable vehicles, the gas tanks were located *over* the rear axle. Second, the rear bumper was designed to reduce weight and cost, but it was little more than a chrome strip that offered far less protection than the bumper on any other American-produced automobile. Third, the Pinto lacked reinforcing pieces or "hat sections" in its rear end. Hat sections made the car more crush resistant in crashes and were standard equipment on Ford vehicles manufactured overseas. Finally, the Pinto's differential (a series of gears that allows a set of wheels to rotate at different speeds) had a line of exposed bolt heads. In a rear-end collision where the gas tank was driven forward, these bolt heads could rupture the tank, causing highly flammable gasoline to spill and catch fire. Crash tests confirmed each of these problems, and existing video demonstrates that in some low-to-medium-speed rear-end collisions the automobiles were engulfed in flames. Underlying each of these problems was the fact that the Pinto was designed and produced quickly. The normal design and production period for a new vehicle at the time was forty-three months. The design and production period for the Pinto lasted only twenty-five months.

When confronted with these problems, Ford executives essentially did nothing. This despite the fact that executives had the crash-test results, numerous reports from their own engineers, and the findings from a late-1960s UCLA study (that Ford itself helped to finance), which concluded that "fuel tanks should *not* be located directly adjacent to the rear bumper or behind the rear wheels adjacent to the fender sheet metal as this location exposes them to rupture at low speeds of impact."[31] The company also had crash-test data from other subcompact cars (including competing models) whose gas tanks were placed over the rear axle, vehicles that performed significantly better than did the Pinto.

Ford executives did, however, perform a cost-benefit analysis to determine whether they should make design changes to the Pinto before it went to market. Companies use cost-benefit analyses to determine whether the cost they must bear for a proposed project actually justifies the projected benefit the project will bring. It is a means to determine the most economical course of action. Following is a summary of the cost-benefit analysis purportedly used by Ford in its decision not to redesign or retrofit the Pinto's gas tank as well as the gas tanks on similarly designed vehicles.

Cost to Ford of performing repairs:

Sales: 11 million cars, 1.5 million light trucks

Unit Cost: $11 per car, $11 per truck

Total Cost: 11,000,000 x ($11) + 1,500,000 x ($11) = $137.5 million

---

Benefit to Ford of not making repairs:

Savings: 180 burn deaths, 180 serious burn injuries, 2100 burned vehicles

Unit Cost: $200,000 per death, $67,000 per injury, $700 per vehicle

Total Benefit: 180 x ($200,000) + 180 x ($67,000) + 2100 x ($700) = $49.5 million

---

Ford determined that it would cost $11 per vehicle to redesign or retrofit the automobiles. In all, it would have cost the company $137.5 million. If the company did nothing, it estimated that it would cost $49.5 million to settle death, injury, and property damage claims. The "cost" of fixing the vehicles was significantly greater than the "benefit" of not fixing them. What troubled many people about Ford's use of a cost-benefit analysis in this case was the monetary figure it placed on human life. Using figures from a 1972 National Highway Traffic Safety Administration (NHTSA) study, Ford estimated that a human life was worth $200,750, and this was the figure it used to determine the per-person benefit of not redesigning its automobiles. We should note that there is some disagreement as to how much of a direct impact this cost-benefit analysis had on Ford's decision not to redesign the Pinto and other models. There is no clear public evidence that Ford executives made their decision based on this analysis, although at least one former high-ranking manager at the company testified that they did. Regardless of whether its result was the definitive factor in their decision, the cost-benefit analysis demonstrated that from a purely financial perspective it made sense for Ford to do nothing about the Pinto's design problems, and that is exactly what the company chose to do.[32]

The Pinto hit the retail market in the fall of 1970 and was an immediate success. Thousands were sold as customers sought an inexpensive but reliable mode of transportation. However, almost immediately reports rolled in of people dying or becoming permanently injured as a result of fires that broke out following rear-end collisions. Records are unclear and the numbers are disputed, so we do not know exactly how many people were killed or injured as a result of the Pinto's design flaws. Estimates range from twenty-three, the number offered by Ford, to as high as nine hundred. Examination of NHTSA reports during the late 1970s indicated that at least twenty-seven people had been killed and at least twenty-four seriously wounded from fires resulting from low-speed collisions; however, the examiners readily admitted that the numbers were probably much higher. What is certain is that a significant number of people were killed or injured in Pinto fires, and Ford has paid dearly for it. For example, in 1972 the company was ordered to pay Richard Grimshaw, a teenager who was permanently disfigured from burns sustained in a Pinto rear-end collision, $2.5 million in compensatory and $125 million in punitive damages (the punitive damages were later reduced to $3.5 million). It was also ordered to pay $559,600 to the estate of Lilly Grey, a driver who died as a result of the burns she sustained. Overall, between 1971 and 1978, approximately fifty lawsuits were brought against Ford stemming from Pinto rear-end collisions, costing the company tens of millions of dollars in damages and legal fees.

In May 1978, the NHTSA announced that its own tests had revealed a safety defect in the Pinto's fuel system. Ford responded one month later by recalling all Pintos manufactured between 1971 and 1976 and installing necessary safety features. The recall affected approximately 1.5 million cars and was estimated to have cost the company between $20 and $40 million. As the result of damages, legal fees, recalls, and lost sales due to negative press, the defective Pinto eventually cost Ford significantly more than its original $49.5 million "benefit" of not making repairs.

The DC-10 and Pinto cases demonstrate the impact that corporate decisions can have on peoples' lives. Each case raises numerous ethical questions, but perhaps the most important is, if we had been executives at McDonnell Douglas or Ford, would we have acted differently? We had an obligation to act in the interests of the corporation as well as a fiduciary responsibility to our shareholders. We were engaged in high-stakes competition and were, as many believed, fighting for our company's survival. We certainly did not intend to injure people with our products nor design them to fail in the ways that they did. However, how should we have balanced our responsibilities to our company with a prudent concern for public safety?

Building upon what we know so far, we turn to the principles of CST. The first and most important principle is human dignity. Human dignity demands that we recognize the other as a person created in the image and likeness of God, possessing infinite value and worth. Particularly in terms of product safety, it demands that a manufacturer do everything it reasonably can to protect the user of its product from harm. Based on the sheer volume of literature available concerning the DC-10 and Pinto, we can say that executives at McDonnell Douglas and Ford blatantly disregarded this principle in their actions. Through their actions—or more precisely, their inactions—these executives demonstrated that they valued the success of their company over the health and well-being of their customers.

We recognize that corporate decisions often contain unforeseen contingencies, and corporate agents cannot be held morally accountable for things of which they were not aware. However, with the DC-10 and Pinto, this was not the case. When presented with credible information concerning the cargo door latching system, upper management at McDonnell Douglas failed to act on it in a comprehensive way. Granted, the latching system was probably one of a number of issues that arose during the DC-10's design and manufacturing process, but with the numerous warnings, the failed ground test, and the "incident" over Windsor, company executives had to know there was a serious problem with their plane. The fact that what actually happened to the ill-fated Turkish Airlines flight—rapid decompression, partial floor collapse, and loss of control—was predicted by Convair engineers only adds to the executives' culpability. The same is true with Ford. Ford's own engineers knew there were serious design flaws with the Pinto, and these concerns were forwarded to upper management along with the appropriate supporting evidence. Some members of upper management simply ignored these concerns while others apparently chose not to act on them based on the results of the cost-benefit analysis. Once again, high level executives at both McDonnell Douglas and Ford made decisions based not on the intrinsic value of those who would be using their products, but on the corporate bottom line. They knew, or should have known, that people's lives would be imperiled if they did not fix the known defects, yet they failed to take appropriate action. As a rule, corporate executives must consider the potential effects that their decisions will have on the people who they (the executives) reasonably foresee will be affected by the decisions.[33] If they fail to do this, their actions cannot be morally justified.

Two further, closely related CST principles that are highly relevant for the DC-10 and Pinto cases are the common good and solidarity. The principle of the common good states that when faced with a decision that will affect other people, we have a duty to act in ways that benefit society as a whole, even if that runs contrary to our own "good." The principle of solidarity, in turn, calls us to willingly and consistently commit ourselves to acting for the common good. Based again on the sheer volume of literature concerning these cases, it is clear that McDonnell Douglas and Ford failed to uphold these moral principles. Philosopher Peter French has argued that, while not intending their planes to crash, McDonnell Douglas was willing to manufacture an aircraft that it knew to be defective, and it was also willing to allow a harmful outcome to occur as a result of policies and procedures that the company itself had put into place. McDonnell Douglas willingly marketed a plane that it knew had a higher than normal probability of in-flight failure.[34] Similarly, Ford did not intend to build a car that would burst into flames, but it did willingly manufacture and sell a vehicle that it knew to be defective, and its own internal policies and procedures allowed this to happen. We stated earlier that disastrous results can occur when a corporation pursues its own "good" at the expense of the health and well-being of its stakeholders. The DC-10 and Pinto cases clearly bear this out. Corporations have a moral duty to determine to the best of their ability how their decisions will affect the wider community and then commit themselves to acting in the interest of the societal good.

Thankfully, not all corporations act unethically. It is important to remember that many American corporations are seeking to do the "right thing." We conclude our chapter with one example.

Tylenol

In 1982, seven people in the Chicago area died after taking cyanide-laced Extra-Strength Tylenol® capsules. The perpetrator, who has never been caught, removed the capsules from stores, injected them with cyanide, and then repackaged and returned them to store shelves without leaving any evidence of tampering. The capsules were manufactured by McNeil Consumer Products, a subsidiary of Johnson & Johnson, and were among the company's most important and profitable products. At the time of the poisonings, Extra-Strength Tylenol had a 35 percent market share, its total sales were $350 million per year, and it accounted for 17 percent of Johnson & Johnson's overall profits.[35]

When the deaths became public, Johnson & Johnson executives were faced with a daunting decision. One option was to recall all Extra-Strength Tylenol capsules and risk losing both market share and millions of dollars in sales, a decision that would place the company in serious financial peril. The other option was to leave the capsules in stores and risk the deaths of even more people. The executives acted quickly. Within days, they recalled all capsules from retail stores, approximately 31 million bottles with an estimated value of over $100 million. They then halted the production and advertising of Tylenol and warned the public not to consume any product that had already been purchased. These decisions were extremely costly for Johnson & Johnson as Tylenol's market share fell to below 7 percent.

Johnson & Johnson executives then sought to remedy the situation. They cooperated with the Chicago Police, the FBI, and the Food and Drug Administration to aid in the search for the perpetrator as well as prevent further tampering. They announced that consumers could exchange their previously purchased Tylenol capsules for a free bottle of Tylenol tablets. They later ran advertisements asking the public to trust in Tylenol again and gave away coupons for $2.50 off a bottle of tablets. They also redesigned the capsules' packaging to be more tamper-resistant by gluing shut the outer box, covering the bottle's cap and neck with a tight plastic seal, and covering the bottle's opening with an inner foil seal. The newly designed packaging cost Johnson & Johnson 2.4 cents per unit, an expense the company was more than willing to absorb, and allowed Tylenol to be back on store shelves just ten weeks after the initial recall.

The response of the Johnson & Johnson executives was in keeping with the company's *Credo*, which states, in part, "We believe our first responsibility is to the doctors, nurses and patients, to mothers and fathers and all others who use our products and services." James Burke, then CEO, explained the company's actions by simply stating, "We owe it to customers."[36] Public reaction to the company's proactive response was extremely positive. Customers appreciated the way the company took responsibility for protecting them, and within one year Tylenol's market share was back at 35 percent. When a similar poisoning occurred four years later in New York state, Johnson & Johnson again recalled all Extra-Strength Tylenol capsules and offered customers refunds. However, this time the executives decided not to reintroduce the product because, given this second poisoning, they realized they could not guarantee the safety of the capsules from further contamination. This decision was also costly as the company was expected to lose between $100 and $150 million. Again, Johnson & Johnson's actions met with public favor and within months, Tylenol's market share (now in the form of tablets and caplets) was back at 32 percent.

Clearly, Johnson & Johnson acted in accord with the principles of CST. Its actions demonstrated a great concern for the dignity of its customers as well as for the societal common good. Its voluntary recall was an act of social solidarity, directed toward the good of stakeholders rather than the corporate bottom line. Johnson & Johnson was not responsible for the poisonings, but it did take responsibility for protecting the public from the terrible misuse of its product.

In the end, acting ethically is in the best interest of any corporation. Morally it is the right thing to do, and studies have demonstrated that acting ethically does not adversely affect the long-term bottom line.[37] The principles of CST have much to add to corporate decision-making processes as well as to the study of business ethics as a whole. The focus on the human person continually challenges executives to recognize that profit is not the most important aspect of business. Instead, corporations are called to commit themselves to meeting the needs of all they serve.

Review Questions

1. How does the Second Vatican Council's *Pastoral Constitution on the Church in the Modern World* and the United States Catholic bishops' *Economic Justice for All* link faith with business?

2. For what three reasons does CST maintain that human work has an inherent dignity? What specific implications does this teaching have for American corporations?

3. How has CST traditionally viewed labor unions? What are the rights and duties involved with union membership?

4. How did Pope John XXIII and Pope John Paul II uphold the principle of community in speaking about business activity?

5. Concerning stewardship of resources, what two implications follow from the teaching that no one owns resources absolutely?

6. What is the difference between having dominion over the created order and having domination over it?

7. In what specific ways can corporations uphold the option for the poor here in the United States? In what ways can they uphold this principle internationally?

8. How, specifically, did McDonnell Douglas and Ford fail to uphold the principles of human dignity, common good, and solidarity in their actions?

9. How did Johnson & Johnson uphold the principles of CST in its actions?

ENDNOTES

1 Second Vatican Council, *Pastoral Constitution on the Church in the Modern World*, in *Catholic Social Thought: The Documentary Heritage* (Maryknoll, NY: Orbis Books, 1995), no. 43.

2 United States Catholic Conference, *Economic Justice for All: Tenth Anniversary Edition* (Washington, DC: USCC, 1997), no. 25.

3 See James Wishloff, "Catholic Social Thought and Business Ethics: The Application of 10 Principles," *Review of Business*, 25, no. 1 (Winter 2004): 22; and Shirley Roels, "Business Goals and Processes," in *On Moral Business: Classical and Contemporary Resources for Ethics in Economic Life*, ed. Max L. Stackhouse et al. (Grand Rapids, MI: Eerdmans, 1995), 912.

4 *Economic Justice for All*, no. 13.

5 Pope Leo XIII, *On the Condition of Labor*, in *Catholic Social Thought*, nos. 15–17.

6 *Economic Justice for All*, no. 13.

7 Pope John Paul II, *On Human Work*, in *Catholic Social Thought*, no. 6. See also *Economic Justice for All*, nos. 72 and 97.

8 Manuel Velasquez, *Business Ethics: Concepts and Cases*, 5th ed. (Upper Saddle River, NJ: Prentice Hall, 2002), 457–58. See also *Economic Justice for All*, no. 73 and nos. 194–95.

9 See Leo XIII, *On the Condition of Labor*, nos. 48, 51; John Paul II, *On Human Work*, no. 20; and the United States bishops, *Economic Justice for All*, nos. 104–6.

10 Pope John XXIII, *Christianity and Social Progress*, in *Catholic Social Thought*, nos. 91–92 and 219.

11 Pope John Paul II, *On the Hundredth Anniversary of Rerum Novarum*, in *Catholic Social Thought*, no. 42.3.

12 *Economic Justice for All*, no. 110.

13 Ibid., no. 111.

14 For a more complete explanation of shareholder and stakeholder theory, including criticisms of each, see John Boatright, *Ethics and the Conduct of Business*, 5th ed. (Upper Saddle River, NJ: Prentice Hall, 2007), 380–88.

15 *Economic Justice for All*, no. 305.

16 Boatright, *Ethics and the Conduct of Business*, 365. For more information on Malden Mills, see Velasquez, *Business Ethics*, 180–82.

17 *Economic Justice for All*, nos. 112–15.

18 Velasquez, *Business Ethics*, 287.

19 Pope John Paul II, "The Ecological Crisis: A Common Responsibility," in *And God Saw That It Was Good: Catholic Theology and the Environment*, ed. Drew Christensen, SJ, and Walter Grazer (Washington, DC: USCC, 1996), 218–19. See also *Economic Justice for All*, no. 12.

20 James Nash, "Ecological Integrity and Christian Political Responsibility," in Stackhouse et al., eds., *On Moral Business*, 846.

21 John Paul II, "The Ecological Crisis," 218.

22 USCC, "Renewing the Earth: An Invitation to Reflection and Action on Environment in Light of Catholic Social Teaching," in Christensen and Grazer, eds., *And God Saw That It Was Good*, 224, 232, 238 and 241.

23 John Rawls, *A Theory of Justice*, cited in Velasquez, *Business Ethics*, 309–10.

24 John Paul II, "The Ecological Crisis," 220–21.

25 USCC, "Renewing the Earth," 235.

26 For a concise list of general moral principles governing international business, see Richard DeGeorge, *Business Ethics*, 6th ed. (Upper Saddle River, NJ: Prentice Hall, 2006), 521–23. For a summary of international codes concerning ethical business practices, see Boatright, *Ethics and the Conduct of Business*, 430–31.

27 "On Social Concern," nos. 38–39.

28 The DC-10 case is taken from Thomas Beauchamp, "The DC-10's Defective Doors," in *Case Studies in Business, Society, and Ethics*, 3rd ed. (Englewood Cliffs, NJ: Prentice Hall, 1993), 34–40; and from various chapters in *The DC-10 Case: A Study in Applied Ethics, Technology, and Science*, eds. John Fielder and Douglas Birsch (Albany, NY: State University of New York Press, 1992). The quote above is taken from "The 1970 Ground Testing Incident," by Paul Eddy, Elaine Potter, and Bruce Page, *The DC-10 Case*, 86.

29 Beauchamp, "The DC-10's Defective Doors," 39. It should be noted that Convair was forbidden by contract to notify the FAA directly about safety concerns with the DC-10.

30 Information for this case is taken from various chapters in *The Ford Pinto Case: A Study in Applied Ethics, Business, and Technology*, eds. Douglas Birsch and John Fiedler (Albany, NY: State University of New York Press, 1994).

31 Birsch and Fiedler, eds., *The Ford Pinto Case*, 44. Emphasis in the original.

32 Further adding to its culpability, in the early 1970s, Ford had knowledge that the federal government was planning to introduce fuel tank standards beginning in 1976. A 1971 internal Ford memo advised not making any changes to the Pinto's fuel tank until the new regulations went into effect, a delay that would save the company $20 million.

33 Manufacturers today are legally bound to do just this. The legal understanding of reckless negligence states that manufacturers have a duty to protect customer safety and they fail in this duty if they do not take sufficient care in their product's design. If a manufacturer knows of a defect in its product that increases risk to the customer but does not correct the defect or inform the customer of it, then the manufacturer is open to a charge of reckless negligence. In addition, the legal doctrine of strict liability states that a manufacturer can be held liable for harm done by its product even if it does not know about the defect or could have anticipated its potential harm. See DeGeorge, 283-284.

34 See Peter French, "What Is Hamlet to McDonnell Douglas or McDonnell Douglas to Hamlet?" in Fielder and Birsch, eds., *The DC-10 Case*, 182.

35 Information for this case is taken from Robert Hartley, *Business Ethics: Mistakes and Successes* (Hoboken, NJ: John Wisley and Sons, 2005), 303–14; and from Kathleen Fearn-Banks, *Crisis Communications* (Mahwah, NJ: Erlbaum Associates, 2002), 86–96.

36 Quoted in *Time* (March 3, 1986), 59. *Credo* excerpt is taken from Hartley, "Johnson & Johnson's Tylenol Scare," 311.

37 Velasquez, *Business Ethics*, 5–6 and 42–43.

5. GLOBAL ECONOMIC ETHICS: DEBT AND STRUCTURAL ADJUSTMENT

Africa makes a fool of our idea of justice; it makes a farce of our idea of equality. It mocks our pieties, it doubts our concern, it questions our commitment. . . . I truly believe that when the history books are written, our age will be remembered for three things: the war on terror, the digital revolution, and what we did—or did not do—to put the fire out in Africa. History, like God, is watching what we do.

— Bono, White House Prayer Breakfast, February 2006

Our second chapter on economic ethics takes a more global focus by examining the effects of Western economic policies on the people of sub-Saharan Africa—without question the poorest region on earth, according to figures published in the United Nations' 2005 *Human Development Report*. According to the United Nations, of the thirty-one nations in the world classified as "low human development," twenty-four were located on the African subcontinent. Average Gross Domestic Product (GDP) per capita for the region was $1856 (U. S.) with a number of nations significantly lower than this. Per capita GDP in Tanzania was $621, in Malawi it was $605, and in Sierra Leone it was $548, the lowest on earth. In comparison, per capita GDP in the United States was $37,562, one of the highest on earth. Life expectancy in sub-Saharan Africa was 46.1 years, the lowest of any region on earth, while the infant mortality rate (105 per 1000 live births) and the under-five mortality rate (179 per 1000 live births) were the highest.[1]

There are many reasons for the poverty and lack of economic development of sub-Saharan Africa. African economies are externally dependent and lack both the capital and the technical know-how to produce a variety of needed goods. They must deal with unfavorable trade relationships in the global marketplace, ill-advised exchange rate policies, wasteful government bureaucracies, political unrest, and the ongoing scourge of HIV/AIDS. Both the scope and the complexity of problems facing sub-Saharan nations today are tremendous. So how did the situation get this way? Why is the African sub-continent the poorest region on earth, and who is to blame? One answer is that Western nations, including the United States, have imposed economic policies on Africa that, while intending to move the continent toward prosperity, have actually mired it deeper in poverty. In this chapter we focus on just two of these external policies, the repayment of foreign debt and the imposition of structural adjustment.[2]

Foreign Debt

To understand the scope and magnitude of the African debt crisis we must go back to the 1960s and the attempts by the newly independent African nations to modernize their economies. The prevailing theory was that if these nations could modernize, they would develop faster and begin to participate in the world economy. However, in the absence of a functional private sector, African political leaders assumed ever-increasing responsibility for the planning and directing of their nations' economic activity. Generally speaking these political leaders were not effective guardians of economic development. As an example, in the late 1960s, inflation began to increase in many African nations. Instead of lowering their exchange rates or enacting other countermeasures, many African governments did nothing. The results were twofold. First, as other countries (particularly European countries) devalued their currency so as to counteract inflation, the prices for their export goods remained relatively inexpensive on the international markets. It was less expensive for African nations to purchase necessary goods on the international markets than to produce them domestically, so they imported increasingly more goods. Second, because African nations did little to control their internal inflation, their exports became very expensive on the international markets, causing many foreign countries to stop buying African goods. The dramatic decrease in exports and increase in imports caused alarming balance-of-trade deficits in many African nations.

Unfortunately, increasing inflation was not the only cause for growing balance-of-trade deficits. Ineffective or corrupt government officials helped fuel deficits by redirecting agricultural earnings away from private farmers and into state-owned industries. They introduced price controls, protective trade policies, and even limited foreign exchange to their "priority" supporters. As balance-of-trade deficits grew even larger, these leaders could either adopt stringent financial strategies to try to narrow the deficits, or borrow money on the international financial markets to finance their continued deficit spending. Many chose the latter. By 1977 Africa's external debt had grown to $27 billion (U. S.).

Another source of foreign debt concerns the development loans taken out by many African nations during the 1970s. Following the OPEC (Organization of Petroleum Exporting Countries) oil price increases in 1973, oil-producing Arab nations deposited millions of dollars into Western commercial bank accounts. Looking for ways to invest these petrodollars, the banks offered loans to nations around the world, ostensibly for development-related projects. These loans were originally issued with low but variable rates of interest that would increase or decrease according to the prevailing rates in the international financial markets. At first, interest rates remained relatively stable and, although debt principal continued to increase, most nations were able to keep up with their interest payments. However, in 1979 OPEC again increased the price of oil, which contributed to a worldwide recession. This recession caused a further decline in demand for African export goods and, in turn, a dramatic drop in the price of these goods on the world markets. The result was decreased income for African producers and decreased revenues for African governments. These revenue reductions forced many governments to borrow even more money on the international financial markets. From 1978 to 1982, the total African external debt increased from $27 billion to $72 billion.

Further compounding this problem was the fact that as the world economy was moving into recession, interest rates in the international financial markets were beginning to rise. Interestingly, this increase was largely fueled by the Reagan administration's massive borrowing in the international markets to finance its domestic tax cuts and increased military spending. The reason these policies had such an effect is a simple function of supply and demand. As the United States increasingly borrowed money on the international market, the amount available for other nations decreased. The law of supply and demand states that as the supply of any good decreases, the price one pays for it (in this case the rate of interest) increases. As a direct result of U.S. borrowing, global interest rates increased even further.

Global interest rate increases were especially harmful for sub-Saharan nations because the rates on their outstanding loans continued to rise. Note that a 1 percent increase in the interest rate on a $1 billion loan represents an increase of $10 million dollars per year in payments. In reality, the outstanding balances totaled well over $1 billion, and interest rates doubled or tripled. Many sub-Saharan nations (as well as others around the world) were forced to borrow even more money simply to pay their increasing interest, plunging them further and further into debt.

Today the debt accumulation figures for African nations are staggering. Of the thirty-eight nations worldwide classified by the World Bank and International Monetary Fund (IMF) as "heavily indebted poor countries," thirty-two are located in Africa. Various sources estimate the total debt to be between $300 – 330 billion. Even more distressing is the impact upon the nations forced to repay such debts. According to figures from the United Nations' 2005 *Human Development Report*, Zambia's yearly debt service was three times its annual health care budget and four times what it spent on education — this despite that two-thirds of its population lived in absolute poverty, 30 percent were illiterate, and the nation's HIV/AIDS infection rate stood at 16.5 percent.[3] During 2003, almost a quarter of a million people in Angola were infected with HIV/AIDS, yet the nation spent $106 per capita on debt service and only $38 per capita on health.[4] In its 1997 *Development Report*, the United Nations reported that six of the seven most heavily indebted nations in Africa paid more in debt service than the sum required to "achieve major progress" against malnutrition, preventable diseases, illiteracy, and child mortality. If their governments had used the money for human development programs, approximately three million more children would have lived beyond their fifth birthday, and one million cases of malnutrition could have been alleviated. In 2005, the United Nations estimated that nineteen thousand children died each day as the result of the social factors directly related to debt.[5]

With these figures in mind, the debt issue raises a number of important ethical questions. First, is it ethical to demand repayment from those who have not benefited from borrowing in any real way? Borrowing money can be a valuable tool in the development process as long as the money is used prudently. However, this generally has not been the case with African nations (and many others around the world). Corrupt government officials stole much of the development loan money and diverted it to arms purchases or projects that aided only their ethnic tribes or political supporters. Foreign lending institutions share blame for the crisis because when the original loans were made there was little, if any, evaluation of specific funding requests and even less monitoring of how the money was actually spent. As such, relatively little of the money from the development loans has actually aided the people of sub-Saharan Africa.

Second, is it ethical to demand repayment for debts when the money used to service them could be better spent on vital social projects? The United Nations has stated that millions of people's lives could be dramatically improved if the money used to service debt could be used to fight malnutrition, disease, and illiteracy. In fact, more money flows out of the continent each year in debt service than comes in through foreign aid. Because many African nations spend more for debt service than for health care and education combined, debt repayment is a fundamentally moral issue. It involves the well-being of families, the survival of the poor, the health of the community, and the future prosperity of millions of African people.

Third, is it ethical to demand repayment for debts that, in reality, have already been repaid? From 1970 to 2002, African nations took out approximately $540 billion in loans. During that same period they repaid $550 billion, yet by the end of 2002 they still owed approximately $300 billion.[6] The debt crisis exists today in large measure because of increases in interest rates, not default on principal. With all the money African nations have been paying to their creditors over the last thirty-plus years, the original loan amounts have been repaid. Compounding interest fuels the continuing cycle of debt.

Before moving on to structural adjustment, we should point out that few economists realistically expect that African debts will ever be repaid. The shear amount of debt, coupled with the fact that African economies cannot generate sufficient revenues to meet their debt obligations, makes repayment practically impossible. Debt is really a symptom of a much greater problem: social control. Western nations use debt, along with structural adjustment and other policies, to maintain a firm grip on developing nations. Because African nations are firmly under the economic, political, and social control of the West, many of them have never developed the skills necessary to direct their own affairs. As a result, many of the policies imposed on them have actually hurt more than they have helped.[7] African nations will not develop until they can begin to chart their own futures, and this will not happen while they remain under the control of the West. The challenge is twofold. The West must rectify the harmful effects that its policies continue to have on Africa, and African nations (particularly their leaders) must demonstrate to the world a much greater ability to manage their own affairs.

Structural Adjustment

A second external reason for the lack of economic development in sub-Saharan Africa is structural adjustment. By the 1980s the cumulative effects of balance-of-trade deficits, rising interest rates, and ever-increasing foreign debt had caused many African economies to stop growing and in some cases to decline. Sub-Saharan nations were experiencing great difficulty securing loans and other sources of financial assistance necessary to generate economic growth. In response to this situation, the World Bank and IMF, the two dominant international financial institutions, decreed that aid would be continued only if the receiving nations accepted fundamental reforms in both their economic and political structures. In other words, financial support would continue only if these nations agreed to structural adjustment.

There were two primary justifications for structural adjustment. The first was that in order for economic policy changes to bear fruit, debtor nations had to reduce drastically the size of their governments. This, in turn, entailed reducing the size of the civil service and selling off unprofitable government-owned businesses. The second justification was the belief that the private sector was "seriously inhibited from recovery" without these reforms. Both the World Bank and IMF believed the private sector, not governments, should play the primary role in African economic life. As long as governments remained dominant, the private sector had little or no chance of assuming this role.

A more detailed rationale for structural adjustment can be found in two reports issued by the World Bank during the 1980s. "Accelerated Development in Sub-Saharan Africa: An Agenda for Action" (1981), claimed that deficient government policies were the primary reason for Africa's lack of economic development. These policies obstructed efficient resource allocation, weakened market functions, and made African economies especially vulnerable to external influences. The World Bank concluded that true and sustained growth could occur only if the role of government was reduced and if the World Bank exerted greater influence over economic policy decisions through the various lending instruments it offered. In "Sub-Saharan Africa: From Crisis to Sustained Growth" (1989), the World Bank claimed that poor governance was the main cause of Africa's continued economic crisis and proposed sweeping political reforms. Among these were multiparty politics, constitutional reform, public-sector transparency, free and fair elections, free speech, a free press, and greater respect for human rights. Political reform was the first step toward ending the crisis and providing an environment where true economic growth could take place.

Specific policies employed by the World Bank and IMF included the following. First, to cut public spending, governments were forced to sell unprofitable state-owned businesses, fire large numbers of public-sector employees, and remove subsidies on consumer goods and services, including food, education, and health care. Second, African governments had to devalue their currencies and repeal both import tariffs and quotas so as to open their markets to greater international trade. Third, governments had to end the practice of setting artificial prices for domestic goods and allow the market to accomplish this task on its own. The overall rationale for structural adjustment was that once spending and inflation were brought under control and budget deficits began to decrease, investment would increase, job creation and income generation would increase, and governments would then be able to generate sufficient resources to service their debts and provide necessary social services.

Although these rationales were positive in the sense that they sought to address undue government influence, the imposition of structural adjustment has raised a number of ethical issues. By forcing governments to end price subsidies for consumer goods and services, the World Bank and IMF have caused a dramatic increase in the cost of living on the African continent, forcing many people to forego food, basic education, and health care services. African governments have had to fire large numbers of civil service employees without offering them retraining or alternative employment opportunities. Also, because a large percentage of a nation's revenues has to go toward debt reduction, less money is available for maintaining infrastructure (including drinking water and sanitation systems), and ecological concerns are largely ignored.

Although virtually every economist and political scientist consulted for this study agrees that major reform is needed in most sub-Saharan nations, most maintain that the adjustment policies of the World Bank and IMF have been ineffective or have done more harm than good. One reason for this is that because the region is so diverse in its economic, political, and social realities, no uniform and centrally determined development plan will work across the board. Without an individual-nation approach, structural adjustment has actually exacerbated suffering by increasing the income gap between rich and poor. Structural adjustment has also caused great harm by focusing attention away from creating the conditions necessary for democracy to take hold. The World Bank and IMF drew a direct link between democracy and economic development and praised the free market as the solution to Africa's economic difficulties. They then imposed political reforms that assumed that historically repressive governments would suddenly demonstrate a respect for human rights. Unfortunately, there is not one example of an African state where structural adjustment has led to greater political stability or democracy.

A third reason structural adjustment has been ineffective is that in many nations it essentially amounted to the reorganization of a bankrupt company. Nondeveloping nations were infused with massive amounts of capital but were then returned to the control of the incompetent managers (political leaders) who ruined them in the first place. Because such an arrangement would never be tolerated in the West, many have asked why the World Bank and IMF believed it would work in Africa.

Finally, structural adjustment did not take into account that terrorism, civil war, environmental degradation, and deteriorating infrastructure undermine development efforts as well. For example, Western financial institutions and some donor countries tried to restructure economies in Angola, Mozambique, Sudan, and Somalia while these nations were engaged in civil war. These efforts failed. In April 1994, a World Bank mission issued a glowing report on the progress of the Rwandan economy, the same month in which over eight hundred thousand Rwandan Tutsis were killed in ethnic genocide. Economic reform is all but useless without true political reform. The World Bank and IMF recognized this in theory, but in practice they failed to adequately incorporate it into their adjustment policies.[8]

Response from Catholic Social Teaching

The injustices of forced debt repayment and structural adjustment have caused many organizations around the world to pressure both creditor governments and the international financial community to bring about change for the African people. The Roman Catholic Church is one of these organizations. Numerous Church officials on the local, national, and international levels have written pastoral letters and other statements to underscore the moral dimensions of these issues. Most of these statements are highly critical of debt repayment and structural adjustment because of the effects of these policies, particularly on the poor. These criticisms are founded, either implicitly or explicitly, on the principles of Catholic Social Teaching (CST).

Debt

The Pontifical Commission for Justice and Peace spoke to the injustices surrounding debt repayment in "An Ethical Approach to the International Debt Question" (1987). The commission insisted that all parties share the responsibility to find a solution to the debt crisis and that each must approach the issue with a spirit of solidarity. Industrialized nations, including the United States, must evaluate the repayment policies in terms of their effect on the international community. They must recognize that policies have a profound effect on people's lives, and adjust them when they "constitute too much of a burden" for poor nations. Possible adjustments include reducing interest rates, working with indebted nations on a case-by-case basis, and adopting fairer trade policies that would allow nations to pay off their debts while moving toward sustained development.[9]

The commission also stated that indebted nations must take responsibility for their actions. In many cases, debt was incurred as the result of poor policy decisions on the part of political leaders or through the theft of funds meant to aid their people. These leaders must take responsibility for their actions for debt relief to occur. They must also improve their management of natural and human resources and implement greater transparency in their decision-making processes. In short, they must commit to promoting the common good of their nation and not simply their own good.

Finally, the commission held that creditors such as the World Bank and IMF also have ethical responsibilities concerning the debt crisis. These creditors must work with indebted nations, not against them, and seek to balance each nation's debt obligations with its social and developmental needs. Concrete measures included lowering interest rates, extending the life of loans, making special arrangements with nations whose populations were most affected by debt repayment, and offering indebted nations a greater voice in the formulation of international financial policies. Overall, the debt crisis must be approached in a spirit of mutual cooperation and solidarity. Debtors and creditors alike must commit to formulating policies that respect the dignity of all people and foster the greatest possible good for all involved.

Pope John Paul II spoke to the ethical challenges of foreign debt in a number of his own writings. In *On Social Concern* (1987), he echoed the Justice and Peace Commission by calling for greater solidarity between developed and less developed nations. In light of this, he condemned the practice of offering new loans to developing nations simply so they can meet their existing interest obligations. Developed nations cannot impose policies that, while advantageous for themselves, actually mire poor nations deeper in poverty.[10] In *On the Hundredth Anniversary of Rerum Novarum* (1991), he stated that while the principle of justice ordinarily demands that we repay our debts, repayment becomes unjust when it results in severe hardship for great numbers of people. When people's fundamental rights to subsistence and progress are threatened by forced repayment, the international community has a moral obligation to reduce, defer, or even cancel the outstanding debts.[11] In *As the Third Millennium Draws Near* (1994), he argued that a renewed commitment to global justice was a "necessary condition" for celebrating the upcoming Jubilee (the year 2000).[12] Christians around the world have a duty to raise their voices in solidarity with the poor and work toward their integral development. One concrete way people can do this is by working to reduce or outright cancel the debts that threaten the future of so many around the world.[13]

The debt crisis has been an important focus of the African bishops as well. The bishops of Zaïre (now the Democratic Republic of Congo) called for the complete remission of foreign debt in their 1988 pastoral *Christians and the Development of Our Nation*. This call was based on human dignity; the African people's dignity was being undermined by the forced acceptance of their creditors' repayment conditions. The bishops argued that just as an overly indebted individual loses his dignity and becomes a slave to his creditor, so also a nation that cannot repay its debts loses both its dignity and its sovereignty. Dignity is lost because creditors regard the debtor nation as irresponsible and incapable of managing its own affairs. Sovereignty is lost because the creditors then impose strict reform measures (structural adjustment) to both manage and control the debtor nation's economy. The bishops' point was that the debt crisis carried with it not only economic consequences but social and psychological consequences as well.[14]

The African bishops as a whole expressed similar sentiments during the 1994 Synod for Africa in Rome. The bishops claimed that external debt and policies imposed by the West rendered African nations "insignificant" in the world community and burdened them with a "regrettable sense of inferiority and indigence." These factors, in turn, undermined the dignity of the African people and militated against true development. In light of this, they appealed to their brothers and sisters around the world to intervene in the economic and political affairs of their own nations to find just solutions for Africa's economic difficulties. They called upon fellow Christians to help resolve the debt crisis, end reform measures that are contrary to human dignity, and create a more just economic order where African nations can participate as full partners in the world community.[15]

The United States Catholic bishops have also addressed the debt question in numerous statements. In their Administrative Board's *A Jubilee Call for Debt Forgiveness* (1999), the bishops explicitly cited the CST principles of human dignity, common good, solidarity, subsidiarity, stewardship, and option for the poor in their call for the world community to comprehensively address the global debt crisis. They argued that the morality of any debt relief program must be evaluated on its direct relief to indebted nations and on whether it made poverty reduction the central goal of the overall program. They also held that debt relief must be integrated into long-term programs of sustainable development and that indebted nations must have a voice in the formulation of relief policies.[16]

Structural Adjustment

Although structural adjustment goes hand in hand with foreign debt, it has not received the same level of attention from the international community. International organizations, including the Catholic Church, tend to focus on debt even though structural adjustment has caused as much, if not more, suffering around the world. This is not to say that the Church as a whole has been silent on this issue, as a number of African bishops' conferences have critically addressed the adjustment policies of the World Bank and IMF. Here are two examples.

In *Reasons for Economic Crisis* (1990), the bishops of Cameroon argued that structural adjustment implemented to help their nation emerge from its debts actually caused more damage. The adjustment policies caused massive unemployment, condemned millions of families to misery, and allowed lender nations to recoup outstanding loans at exorbitant rates of interest. The bishops argued that because it did not conform to the spirit of the Gospel or to the social doctrine of the Church, structural adjustment was contrary to Christian morality. They appealed to the consciences of those in "rich nations" by calling for the cancellation of all foreign debts, an end to structural adjustment, and the creation of a new international marketplace based on solidarity and mutual interdependence.[17]

The Catholic bishops of Zambia spoke directly to the issue of structural adjustment in their 1993 pastoral *Hear the Cry of the Poor*. The bishops pointed out that 20 percent of Zambian children died before the age of five, 40 percent of all children under age five were undersized (a sign of malnutrition), 80 percent of the rural and 50 percent of the urban population lived below the poverty line, and inflation was increasing at a rate of 200 percent per year. These figures translated into what the bishops termed the "moral problems" facing Zambian life: the ever-widening gap between rich and poor, the escalation of crime, the increase in government corruption, and the get-rich-quick mentality whereby people manipulated the prices of necessary commodities for their own benefit without considering the effects of their actions on others.[18]

For the Zambian bishops, the primary reason for their nation's economic and social woes was the forced imposition of structural adjustment. While the World Bank, IMF, and representatives of Western donor nations praised Zambia for following restructuring guidelines, the bishops questioned whether in light of the people's suffering there was really anything to praise. Concerning timing, they asked why government subsidies for food, health care, and education were removed before intermediate programs were introduced to cushion the impact of their removal. Concerning content, they questioned why human capital improvement (including health care and education), job creation programs, small-scale entrepreneurial promotion, and regional cooperation were all missing from the adjustment programs. Concerning direction, they stated that structural adjustment relied on a trickle-down approach to economic growth in that development aid was directed toward the rich and through their spending the benefit was eventually supposed to reach the poor. However, what had actually happened was that the rich were becoming progressively more wealthy while the poor waited endlessly for the supposed benefit. The Zambian people had been continually assured that structural adjustment entailed "short-term pain but long-term gain." The bishops wondered when the gain would be realized and whether anyone would be left to enjoy it when it arrived.[19]

Before closing this section, we must point out that no pope, bishops' conference, or individual bishop has ever disputed the need for serious economic and political reform. To meet the many challenges of sub-Saharan Africa, difficult decisions will have to be made. Nevertheless, because of the way it was imposed and the consequences it has had on the African people, structural adjustment raises serious ethical concerns for both the Church and the international community as a whole.

Recent Developments and Hope for the Future?

In light of the many injustices concerning debt repayment and structural adjustment, the world community has finally begun to take some modest action. Since the mid-1990s, the World Bank, IMF, and creditor nations have taken steps to help alleviate the suffering caused by these programs. But do these steps go far enough? In this section, we consider some recent developments that may—or may not—bring positive change for the people of sub-Saharan Africa.

Debt

In 1996, the World Bank and IMF created the Highly Indebted Poor Country initiative (HIPC) for the purpose of providing debt relief to nations with unsustainable debts. The HIPC initiative offered the promise of relief for nations that completed two three-year stages of structural adjustment reforms and made a commitment to fight poverty and internal corruption. Under HIPC, a country received relief based on the amount needed to bring its debt to a "sustainable level," normally defined as debt payments equaling 20–25 percent of annual export income and an overall debt stock of 200–250 percent of annual export earnings. Unfortunately, even after undergoing significant reform in 1999, the initiative failed to bring about the level of relief it had promised. The problem was that HIPC focused on economic measures aimed at assuring continued debt service rather than on social measures that aimed to alleviate poverty. That is, it tried to determine how much a country could repay without jeopardizing its economic growth, but in doing so it did not adequately consider the human consequences of debt repayment, most notably the effect on the poor. We have already demonstrated what is lost when countries expend scarce resources on debt service instead of on necessary social projects. The World Bank and IMF failed to recognize this reality and thus undermined HIPC's overall effectiveness.[20]

HIPC also had a number of other deficiencies that contributed to its failure. The initiative offered relief to nations that agreed to complete structural adjustment reforms. However, as previously demonstrated, these reforms have caused great hardship for the African people. HIPC actually exacerbated many of the social problems prevailing on the continent. It was created solely by the creditors, with little or no input from debtors, it did not include all debtor nations, and it did not include debts owed to private banks or corporations. Furthermore, HIPC was not designed to cancel a nation's debts, but simply reduce them to a sustainable level. This was problematic because even after they had completed the initiative process, participant nations continued to pay enormous sums to their creditors. In fact, by the end of 2004 only one-fifth of the debt owed by participating nations had been retired and more than half of them still had unsustainable debts according to the World Bank's own criteria.[21]

Pressured by ever-increasing attention from the world community, the leaders of the G-8 nations (France, Germany, Italy, Japan, Canada, Russia, the United Kingdom, and the United States) implemented a new debt relief plan during the summer of 2005. Meeting at Gleneagles, Scotland, the G-8 leaders endorsed what would become the Multilateral Debt Relief Initiative (MDRI), a program that, when fully implemented in the summer of 2006, cancelled 100 percent of debts owed to the World Bank, IMF, and African Development Fund by nations that had completed the HIPC initiative. MDRI was an important first step because it released much of the money that nations would have paid in debt service to be used instead for health, education, and other poverty reduction programs. For example, Zambia's 2006 national budget allowed for the hiring of 4,500 new teachers, the construction and repair of numerous schools, increased funding for HIV/AIDS programs, and the abolishment of health care fees in rural areas. Tanzania used some money from debt service to provide food for approximately 3.7 million people during a severe drought, and Ghana has announced that it will use similar funds to improve infrastructure in rural areas.[22]

As welcome as this debt cancellation news is, there is still a long way to go. Critics contend that the MDRI plan involves only a small number of nations (as of July 2006 the number stood at twenty-one),[23] yet numerous others around the world require immediate, full cancellation to reach the internationally endorsed Millennium Development Goals.[24] Another problem is that the plan continues the adjustment reforms mandated by HIPC for the nations that have already received cancellation and for others that may wish to be eligible for debt relief in the future.

Although structural adjustment has been discredited by many, its policies remain a requirement for any nation that seeks debt relief under MDRI. Further, MDRI does not cancel a recipient nation's debts. World Bank debts incurred after 2003 and both IMF and African Development Fund debts incurred after 2004 are not affected by this program, nor are those owed to bilateral or private creditors. The program does not address the role of Western nations and financial institutions in the debt crisis or the problem of debt incurred as the result of development loan funds stolen by corrupt government officials. Finally, MDRI is designed, controlled, implemented, and monitored by the creditors. As such, they can continue to use debt, and debt cancellation, as a means to reward nations that follow World Bank and IMF policies and punish those that do not.[25]

What can American Catholics do to help find a lasting solution to the international debt crisis? Our first responsibility is to educate ourselves and others. Most Americans do not understand how the debts were incurred or recognize the devastating consequences of debt repayment policies on the poor of Africa and around the world.

One educational resource for American Catholics is the United States bishops' 2001 pastoral *A Call to Solidarity with Africa*. Here the bishops argue that the United States, as a global leader and one of the wealthiest nations on earth, has a moral obligation to help African nations find solutions to the debt crisis and other challenges. We have a duty to adopt policies that "encourage integral human development," are designed for long-term economic growth, and allow Africans to live in peace and dignity. They also declared the contemporary (2001) global response to the debt crisis "inadequate and indefensible," as the World Bank and IMF should not require nations to pay more than 10 percent of their revenues in debt service. The bishops proposed that debt relief be offered in conjunction with health care and other development-related programs, viewing it as one aspect of an overall program of poverty eradication.[26] Unfortunately, *A Call to Solidarity with Africa* received little attention largely due to its timing: it appeared shortly after the 9/11 attacks and just before the first revelations of the clergy sex abuse scandal.

With recent increased global interest in Africa, some local dioceses are working to educate the faithful. The Archdiocese of Cincinnati published *Stand with Africa: Archdiocesan Africa Solidarity Project Study and Action Report* in 2006. Commissioned by the archdiocesan mission office and intended for educational use on the parish level, this document builds upon *A Call to Solidarity with Africa* by detailing the plight of present-day Africa and offering practical suggestions for what people can do.[27] Only when people understand the problem of indebtedness can there be hope for change.

A second, related responsibility for American Catholics is to become more actively involved in existing international efforts to reduce or cancel debt. Ongoing efforts include pressuring the World Bank and IMF to open the G-8 plan to *all* indebted nations, canceling debts owed to *all* creditors, stopping the use of debt relief as a means for imposing crippling adjustment reforms, returning development funds that have been stolen by government officials, and offering future assistance in the form of grants rather than loans.[28] Luckily, we are not alone. Numerous international organizations, religious and secular, are actively working for change in these areas. Bono, lead singer for the Irish rock band U2, founded DATA (**D**ebt, **A**IDS, **T**rade, **A**frica), an activist group that has been calling for full debt relief, fair trade, and increased funding for HIV/AIDS programs on the African continent. Bono's efforts have done much to publicize these causes. DATA welcomes the participation of new members regardless of religious affiliation, as do other organizations such as Action Africa, the Jubilee Debt Campaign, and the ONE Campaign. We can also opt to work with religious-based organizations such as the Jubilee USA Network, Catholic Relief Services, Christian Aid, the Africa Faith and Justice Network, and Bread for the World. Students at Catholic colleges and universities may also find opportunities with groups like the Jesuit Volunteer Corps, the Lasallian Volunteers, the Franciscan Volunteers, or the Maryknoll Lay Missioners.

Foreign debt is a tricky issue, and no one expects ready-made answers. Cries to retire African debt must be balanced by a concern for the economic consequences that such actions would bring.[29] However, this does not mean we should remain silent. CST holds that the human person's well-being is the primary moral consideration of any social policy or program. Should we demand repayment for debts incurred as a result of loans that have not benefited people in any real way? Should we demand repayment when the money used to service debts could be better spent on vital social projects? Should we demand repayment for debts that have been perpetuated by compounding interest, a reality over which the African people have no control? Should we demand repayment when industrialized nations use debt as a means to impose draconian reform measures? In short, the answer to these questions is no. From a moral perspective, debts incurred as a result of these factors should be retired and, in the absence of this, a strong case can be made that there is no moral obligation on the part of African nations to repay them. Foreign debt is an important moral issue facing the world community, one that Christians cannot ignore in efforts to construct a just global economic order that upholds the dignity of all people.

Structural Adjustment

Like foreign debt, structural adjustment has no ready-made answers. Although its long-term goals are commendable, its direct consequences on the African people raise profound ethical concerns. We do not begrudge the World Bank and IMF, because we believe their intent was genuine. African economies do need to be free of undue government influence, and structural adjustment was an attempt to accomplish this. These institutions applied policies that they honestly thought would bring greater prosperity; unfortunately, the policies have not worked.

The World Bank may be slowly coming to this realization. In 2004 it announced a formal change in its method of offering loans to developing nations. Instead of tying loans to specific adjustment conditions, the new policy focuses on projects already underway. Instead of dictating to recipient nations what they need to do to receive funding, the bank now evaluates projects that have been successful and offers assistance to fund their continued implementation.[30] Interestingly, this new lending policy implicitly upholds a number of the principles of CST. Human dignity and the common good are upheld in the acknowledgement that reforms must be enacted that meet the actual needs of the people. Participation, option for the poor, and stewardship are upheld in that project funding must be implemented in consultation with stakeholders and with a clear understanding of the social and environmental impact that will result. Subsidiarity is upheld in the acknowledgement that there is no single model for development and that both government and the people need to take ownership of development programs for them to be successful. Although structural adjustment remains a part of the Gleneagles debt relief program, we hope that this new outlook will eventually lead to a brighter future for the people of Africa.

One of the most important things we can do is to become better educated about structural adjustment, and—just as with debt relief—we are not alone. The Jesuit Center for Theological Reflection (JCTR), located in Lusaka, Zambia, is an excellent example of a Church-based organization that is speaking out on these issues. The JCTR publishes a quarterly bulletin whose stated aim is "to broaden an understanding of the social, economic, political, and cultural issues of the day and promote response to these issues in light of the Church's social teaching." Specifically in terms of structural adjustment, the JCTR seeks to educate the Zambian people and the international community about the effects these programs have had on their country. It runs a monthly feature in the national newspaper where it calculates the cost of basic necessities (food, clothing, health care, etc.) for a typical Zambian family. This feature shows an ever-increasing cost of living as a result of structural adjustment, and demonstrates the virtual impossibility of the average wage earners to meet the needs of their families. It is said that the JCTR is so well respected that other Christian organizations in Zambia do not speak about economic issues without first checking their figures with it.[31]

The JCTR demonstrates the important role that Church-based organizations can play in educating people about the realities of structural adjustment and evaluating the morality of adjustment policies. Once again we see the primary role of the Catholic Church in the economic realm. The magisterium, national bishops' conferences, Church-based organizations, and individual Catholics have a moral obligation to evaluate secular economic policy in light of fundamental principles of the Church's social tradition. The over-arching question concerning structural adjustment is how does it conform to the fundamental demand of human dignity? Is basic human dignity respected by forcing African nations to accept externally imposed reform measures? If the answer is no, then significant changes need to be made. Similarly, does structural adjustment promote the common good? Does it encourage popular participation, respect local initiative, and adequately take into consideration its effects on the most vulnerable of society? Once again, if the answer is no, then significant changes need to be made.

Although foreign debt and structural adjustment are two important challenges facing development efforts in Africa, they are hardly the only ones. In the final section of this chapter we briefly speak of three further topics that need to be addressed to move the African people from poverty to prosperity. These topics are foreign aid, production and trade, and AIDS.

Foreign Aid, Production and Trade, and AIDS

Foreign Aid

African nations need continued financial assistance for their economies to grow. Decades of mismanagement, corruption, and outright despair have left the continent on economic life support. The problem is that although the industrialized world has pledged greater development aid for the continent, it has not delivered. According to the United Nations, total aid to sub-Saharan Africa was actually lower at the end of the 1990s than it was at the beginning of that decade. Today aid is offered by the United States and other industrialized nations primarily for geopolitical reasons, not to meet the needs of the poor. For example, from 2002–2004, the amount of aid the United States offered to Israel, Jordan, Egypt, Iraq, Turkey, and Afghanistan equaled the amount it offered to the rest of the world combined.[32] Apparently if a nation wants to receive aid from the United States, it must be deemed vital to our national interests and security. We do not dispute the need for aid to the nations just listed, but what about the people in nations that we do not consider strategically important? Can we simply disregard them and allow them to remain mired in poverty?

Further compounding the problem is that the aid offered often does not help the recipients in any real way. One reason for this is that foreign nations or nongovernmental organizations (NGOs) provide funding for projects that meet the "needs" of the donor, not the recipient. Donor agencies have their own agendas and have to answer to their own constituencies so they frequently place conditions upon the aid offered, tying it to a variety of noneconomic objectives. If the recipient nation cannot meet these conditions, it runs the risk of losing the aid. In addition, donor organizations will dictate exactly how the money is to be used. For example, 70 percent of aid offered by the United States is given with the condition that it be used to purchase goods and services manufactured in our own country.[33] Because most African nations are so desperate for this aid, they willingly agree to these conditions, even if the project will do little or nothing to meet local needs. The effectiveness of aid programs can be further undermined by lack of cooperation among various organizations. The sheer number of governmental and NGO stand-alone projects on the continent demonstrates this problem. Lack of coordination leads to inconsistencies in policy, overlapping or duplicate projects, and outright waste.[34]

So what do we do? We know it will take billions of dollars to rebuild African economic infrastructure, and most of this funding will have to come from foreign sources. However, this does not mean that foreign donors should have complete control over the aid packages. Foreign aid must focus first on self-determination. In practice, this means that aid packages must be structured to allow Africans the maximum possible freedom to meet their own needs. Notice that we use the words "maximum possible" here. We do not advocate simply donating money to African nations with no direction or oversight. But aid packages are doomed to failure if there is no African input into their formulation and if they do not allow African nations to develop on their own terms. Put simply, the African people must be empowered to take their economic futures into their own hands and must be afforded the freedom to fulfill their individual goods while at the same time contributing to the common good of their nation as a whole.

We Americans must also pressure our elected officials to increase meaningful aid packages for developing nations whenever possible. The United Nations has called upon industrialized nations to deliver .5 percent of their national incomes in aid by 2010, increasing this figure to .75 percent by 2015. The United Nations not only hopes to reduce poverty in these nations, it warns that the economic well-being and security of the industrialized world could be threatened if global poverty continues to be ignored.

To illustrate this latter point, most Americans are unaware that approximately 18 percent of our nation's oil imports presently come from Africa, a figure that is expected to rise to 25 percent in the next ten years. With continued instability in the Middle East and our ever-increasing demand for oil, it is only prudent that our nation focus greater attention on the African continent. In addition to this, in 2004 a congressional advisory panel submitted "Rising U.S. Stakes in Africa," a report demonstrating that in the post-September 11 world, the African continent has become much more strategically important to the United States. Reasons for this include oil, but also the fact that the despair felt by so many serves as a breeding ground for international terrorism. The report concluded that the United States must increase its overall investment on the continent as well as its actual presence on the ground.[35] In light of this information, the United Nations offered a striking moral challenge to us all:

> The aid policies of rich countries reflect how they think about globalization, about their own security and prosperity and about their responsibilities and obligations to the world's most vulnerable people. Ultimately, aid policies are a barometer for measuring the rich world's tolerance for mass poverty in the midst of plenty.[36]

Production and Trade

Another topic that demands greater attention from the world community is economic production and trade. One of the problems with many post-colonial (mid-1960s to the present) African economies is that they are structured to produce export goods while failing to meet the needs of the domestic population. This situation arose largely as a result of the colonial period (1880s to mid-1960s) when European powers exploited their African colonies to produce goods that could not be produced in Europe. The situation continues as a result of World Bank and IMF policies that force African countries to produce goods to be sold on the international markets so they can earn revenues to repay debts. The result is that countries produce export crops such as cotton, but do not produce sufficient food and other necessities for their people.[37]

Although nothing is inherently wrong with producing export goods, Africans must be free to meet their domestic needs first. Once basic domestic needs are met, these countries can then determine what other goods their economies will produce to meet the needs of the international community. This self-direction is necessary as an issue of human dignity and as a means to promote the societal common good. Unfortunately, current Western policies do not allow this to happen. It is imperative that we recognize the moral implications of economic production and work to assure that the global market serves everyone, including the people of Africa.

Closely related to the challenge of economic production is the challenge of international trade. One of the main reasons African producers, particularly agricultural producers, have a difficult time earning sufficient income is that they do not have access to foreign markets. The United States and numerous European nations have set up trade barriers that only allow African products to reach their markets with great difficulty—if at all. Many have charged that the policies of the World Trade Organization (WTO), which is supposed to oversee international trade, favor industrialized nations to the detriment of developing nations. In recent years, the United States has complained to the WTO that although we allow Chinese products to be readily available in our markets, China has not reciprocated. The complaint is ironic, as in many ways the United States is doing exactly this in regard to Africa. If we are going to have a globalized marketplace, it is essential that all players be able to compete on an equal footing.

AIDS

The third important sociopolitical issue is AIDS. Aside from the monumental social and spiritual toll on people's lives, AIDS continues to have profound economic consequences for the African continent. AIDS often strikes people in their twenties and thirties, significantly reducing the continent's human capital and its future potential. When people contract the disease, they tend to save less, invest less, and in general not look toward the long-term future. As the disease progresses, they can no longer provide for themselves and their families. Their children drop out of school to care for them and never go back. When they die, their children become orphans, creating huge strains on extended families and government services. These realities present African nations with economic burdens that they cannot afford.[38]

In response to this pandemic, American Catholics must be willing to step in and take action. Specific measures include supporting AIDS educational programs, promoting sexual abstinence, challenging governments to publicly recognize the reality of HIV/AIDS, and pressuring Western pharmaceutical companies to provide affordable drug therapies. There have been successes. In Uganda, a strong government response has decreased the HIV/AIDS infection rate from 15 percent in the early 1990s to less than 5 percent today. One reason Uganda has been successful is the willingness of its government to engage in open and frank public discussion about the disease. The government has been able to overcome the stigma associated with AIDS and has made the prevention of the disease a top policy issue. A second reason for Uganda's success is the so-called "ABC" approach used to get the message out. This approach (A) encourages sexual abstinence until marriage, (B) advises people who are sexually active to remain faithful to one partner, and (C) recommends that people always use a condom, especially if they have more than one sexual partner. A third reason for the nation's success is the greater availability of antiretroviral drugs. In 1998 Uganda began one of the first programs in Africa to analyze how antiretroviral programs could be established in developing nations. After completion of the study, the Ugandan Ministry of Health used the data gathered to set up its own National Strategic Framework for HIV/AIDS. Overall, the result of these initiatives has been an HIV/AIDS infection rate significantly lower than that of most other African nations.[39]

Two final points need to be made. First, although we call upon American Catholics to critique policies that are detrimental to the African people, we do not claim to have all the solutions. The primary task of determining how African economies will function remains in the hands of economists, political scientists, and elected governmental officials. For our part, we have the duty to critique economic policies through the lens of CST and assure that the welfare of the African people is always upheld. We can speak out about economic issues and can suggest overall goals—such as canceling debt or allowing for greater participation in the global marketplace—but the details of how these goals are to be realized must always remain in the hands of experts in the field.

Second, we emphasize that working for justice is an essential aspect of living our Christian faith. The people of Africa are suffering. Based on the 1971 Synod of Bishops' exhortation that working for justice is a "constitutive dimension" of preaching the Gospel message, we have a moral duty to do what we can to help. Although the issues may be complex and the struggle may seem insurmountable, our efforts are a response to Jesus' message in Matthew 25:31–46, the story of the Last Judgment. There Christ teaches that the ones who will be saved on the last day are those who feed their brothers and sisters when they are hungry, give them drink when they are thirsty, clothe them when they are naked, welcome them when they are strangers, care for them when they are ill, and visit them when they are in prison. The various papal and bishops' conference statements presented in this chapter respond to Christ's words and challenge us to do the same. Working for the temporal development of the African people is a mandate of CST and a concrete response to Christ's teaching that our eternal salvation is dependent, in part, on how we aid our brothers and sisters in need.

Review Questions

1. What three important ethical questions lie at the heart of the African debt crisis?

2. What effects has structural adjustment had on the people of Africa?

3. The Pontifical Commission for Justice and Peace argued that a lasting solution to the debt crisis can only be realized through a commitment to solidarity. In light of this, what are the responsibilities of industrialized nations, debtor nations, and world financial institutions to finding this solution?

4. How did Pope John Paul II apply the principles of solidarity and option for the poor when speaking of the debt crisis?

5. How did the bishops of Zaïre and the Synod for Africa appeal to the principle of human dignity when speaking about the debt crisis?

6. The United States bishops argued that the morality of any debt-relief program must be evaluated on what two criteria?

7. Why did the bishops of Cameroon argue that structural adjustment was "contrary to Christian morality"?

8. What three questions did the bishops of Zambia ask concerning the content, timing, and direction of structural adjustment?

9. What two general responsibilities do Americans have in terms of the debt crisis?

10. Why have foreign aid programs not been effective on the African continent?

11. What problem arises when African economies are forced to produce export goods? Why do many African nations have difficulty participating in international trade?

ENDNOTES

1 United Nations Development Program, 2005 *Human Development Report* (New York: United Nations, 2005), 219–22 and 250–53.

2 Unless otherwise noted, information in the first two sections of this chapter is adapted from Jozef D. Zalot's *The Roman Catholic Church and Economic Development in Sub-Saharan Africa: Voices Yet Unheard in a Listening World* (Lanham, MD: University Press of America, 2002).

3 This information is cited in Jubilee USA Network, *Deadly Delays: How IMF and World Bank Economic Conditions Undermine Debt Cancellation* (Washington, DC: Jubilee USA Network, 2005), 9–14. This essay also describes the devastating effects of forced debt repayment on Cameroon and Malawi.

4 Action Africa, *Statement on 100% Debt Cancellation for Africa* (Washington, DC: Action Africa, 2005).

5 Figures cited in Christian Aid, *What about Us? Debt and the Countries the G-8 Left Behind* (London: Christian Aid, 2005), 2.

6 Debt figures come from *What about Us?* 10–12.

7 Charles M. A. Clarke, "Debt Forgiveness: Moral Imperative and Economic Necessity," *Vincentian Chair of Social Justice* 6 (2001): 25–26.

8 George Ayittey, *Africa in Chaos* (New York: St. Martin's Press, 1999), 271–72.

9 Pontifical Justice and Peace Commission, "An Ethical Approach to the International Debt Question," *Origins* 16, no. 34 (February 5, 1987): 603–10.

10 John Paul II, "On Social Concern," in *Catholic Social Thought: The Documentary Heritage* (Maryknoll, NY: Orbis Books, 1995), nos. 19 and 43.

11 John Paul II, *On the Hundredth Anniversary of Rerum Novarum*, in *Catholic Social Teaching*, no. 35.

12 From Lev. 25:8–12, the Jubilee occurs every fiftieth year; it is a time when debts are forgiven and all property is returned to its original owner.

13 John Paul II, *As the Third Millennium Draws Near, Catholic International* 6 (March 1995): no. 51.

14 Catholic Bishops' Conference of Zaïre, *Christians and the Development of Our Nation* [Le chrétien et le développment de la nation], *La Documentation Catholique* 1992 (1988): nos. 68–82.

15 Synod of Bishops Special Assembly for Africa, *Synod of Resurrection for the Family of God: Final Message of the Synod for Africa*, Catholic International 5 (1994): nos. 32, 40–41.

16 USCC Administrative Board, *A Jubilee Call for Debt Forgiveness* (Washington, DC: USCC, 1999), 8–14. For further statements on debt by the United States Catholic bishops, see the "Social Justice" section of their home page at www.usccb.org.

17 Catholic Bishops' Conference of Cameroon, *Reasons for Economic Crisis* [Les causes de la crise économique], *La Documentation Catholique* 2010 (1990): nos. 8–10.

18 Catholic Bishops' Conference of Zambia, *Hear the Cry of the Poor: A Pastoral Letter on the Current Suffering of the People in Zambia*, Catholic International 4 (October 1993): 474–75. Two years earlier in their pastoral *You Shall Be My Witnesses*, the bishops stated that to find solutions to Zambia's economic woes, all relevant parties must "find guidance" in the principles of CST, particularly option for the poor and respect for fundamental human dignity. See *You Shall Be My Witnesses: A Second Century of Evangelization in Zambia*, Catholic International 2 (October 1991): nos. 28–30.

19 *Hear the Cry of the Poor*, 476.

20 *A Jubilee Call for Debt Forgiveness*, 9.

21 For further information on the HIPC initiative and other debt-related policies of the World Bank, IMF, and creditor nations, see *What about Us?* 5–15. The Jubilee USA Network has also posted various articles concerning the HIPC initiative on its Web site at www.jubileeusa.org.

22 Jubilee Debt Campaign, *The Multilateral Debt Relief Initiative: The Good, the Bad, and the Ugly*, 1–3. This report is available at http://www.jubileedebtcampaign.org.uk.

23 These twenty-one nations are Benin, Bolivia, Burkina Faso, Cambodia, Cameroon, Ethiopia, Ghana, Guyana, Honduras, Madagascar, Mali, Mauritania, Mozambique, Nicaragua, Niger, Rwanda, Senegal, Tajikistan, Tanzania, Uganda, and Zambia.

24 The Millennium Development Goals seek, in part, to cut in half extreme poverty in the developing world by the year 2015.

25 *The Multilateral Debt Relief Initiative*, 2–4. See also *What about Us?* 1–4, 31–33, and *Loose Ends: The G-8 Debt Deal and the Annual Meetings*, a joint statement of the Jubilee USA Network and the Jubilee Debt Campaign (Washington, DC: Jubilee USA Network, 2005), 3–5.

26 USCC, *A Call to Solidarity with Africa* (Washington, DC: USCC, 2001), 3, 7, 10.

27 The full text of *Stand with Africa*, as well as an executive summary, can be found on the mission office Web site at http://www.catholiccincinnati.org/mission.

28 These are specific policy goals of the Jubilee USA Network and the Jubilee Debt Campaign. See *Loose Ends*, 7.

29 See chapter 4 of Nancy Birdsall and John Williamson, *Delivering on Debt Relief: From IMF Gold to a New Aid Architecture* (Washington, DC: Center for Global Development/Institute for International Economics, 2002), 49–66.

30 See *Good Practice Notes for Development Policy Lending* (Washington, DC: World Bank, 2004) and *Good Practice Notes for Development Policy Lending: Results in Development Policy Lending* (Washington, DC: World Bank, 2005). A concise rationale for this shift can be found in "Development Policy Lending Replaces Adjustment Lending" on the World Bank Web site at http://www.worldbank.org.

31 The Jesuit Center for Theological Reflection's Web site can be accessed at http://www.jctr.org.zm.

32 Ann-Louise Colgan, *Africa Policy Outlook 2005* (Washington, DC: Foreign Policy in Focus, 2005), 4–5.

33 Ibid., 4

34 Nicholas Van de Wall and Timothy A. Johnson, *Improving Aid to Africa* (Washington, DC: Overseas Development Council, 1996), 48–70.

35 Dave Schwinghamer, "Africa: Security Threat or Global Partner?" *NewsNotes*, Maryknoll Office for Global Concerns (May/June, 2005), 14.

36 *2005 Human Development Report*, 75–77.

37 The problem is exacerbated by the use of genetically engineered seeds. Western agricultural corporations have devised ways of genetically altering seeds so that they produce increased yields but do not grow back the following year. This requires farmers to purchase new seeds every year. Because the seeds are patented, they must purchase them from the supplier who holds the patent.

38 "How to Make Africa Smile: A Survey of Sub-Saharan Africa," *The Economist* 370 (January 17, 2004): 10–11.

39 See http://www.avert.org/aidsuganda.

6. THE DEATH PENALTY

Marcel is confused. Her state is about to execute a convicted murderer for the first time in thirty years, and she does not know what to do. Her parish's social justice committee is organizing a protest march outside the penitentiary where the execution will take place, and she has been invited to join the group. Her husband, Mike, disagrees with the protest. He is strongly in favor of the death penalty, arguing that if a person takes the life of another then that person deserves to die. Marcel is not so sure. She understands the logic of her husband's argument, but feels there is something "not quite right" about taking the life of another human being, even a convicted murderer. What should Marcel do about the protest? Before making her decision, she knows she needs more information. What exactly does the Catholic Church teach about the death penalty, and is there room for disagreement?

The death penalty is one of the many social issues that divide our nation today. Outside any prison where an execution is taking place you will see one group of people protesting while another is cheering. In high-profile cases our televisions are inundated with sound bites from politicians, lawyers, police officers, psychiatrists, and other "experts," each commenting on the legality and morality of capital punishment. In this chapter we explore the death penalty from the perspective of Catholic Social Teaching (CST). We begin by briefly summarizing how the death penalty has been popularly viewed throughout the history of the United States. Next, we offer an overview of two important twentieth-century Supreme Court cases concerning the death penalty: *Furman v. Georgia* (1972) and *Gregg v. Georgia* (1976). We then explore a number of the philosophical and theological arguments both for and against the death penalty. Finally, we look at the death penalty from the perspective of CST to determine the Church's "official" teaching on the matter.

A Brief History of the Death Penalty in the United States

As with any major social issue with moral and legal ramifications, we need to understand something of the history of the death penalty in the United States before we discuss its ethical implications.[1] From the colonial period to the beginning of the twentieth century the death penalty was legal, and executions were carried out across our nation. The first execution on record occurred in the Jamestown colony in 1608 when Captain George Kendall was executed as a Spanish spy. Thereafter different colonies (and subsequently states) established their own death penalty statutes, and executions continued. However, during the mid-nineteenth century, abolitionist movements began to have an effect on public perceptions of the death penalty as well as on how it was administered. In 1834, Pennsylvania became the first state to end public executions, preferring instead to carry them out within the walls of the state correctional facilities. In 1846, Michigan abolished the death penalty for all crimes except treason. In 1852, Rhode Island abolished it altogether, and Wisconsin followed suit in 1853. Beginning in 1838, several other states began passing laws against mandatory death sentences for particular crimes, holding instead that death sentences could be handed down only at the discretion of the court.

The anti-death penalty movement gained further momentum in the late 1800s and early 1900s as a result of new theories that questioned whether criminals truly could be held responsible for their actions. One popular argument, based in part on the theory of evolution, held that crime was caused not by one's free choices, but by an inherent defect of the brain. Another theory argued that environmental influences caused people to commit crimes; crime was viewed as a disease brought on by poverty or deprivation, requiring treatment, not punishment. Both of these theories then posed essentially the same question: If a criminal does not commit a crime freely, or if this freedom is impaired, how can one justify the retributive nature of capital punishment? Is it really fair to execute a person for a crime that he or she did not freely choose to commit? As a result of these theories and the continuing work of death penalty abolitionists, a number of states outlawed the death penalty during this period, including Maine (1876), Colorado (1897),[2] Kansas (1907), Minnesota (1911), Washington (1913), Oregon (1914), North and South Dakota (1915), Arizona (1916), and Missouri (1917).

Although the anti-death penalty movement did enjoy some success in the early years of the twentieth century, it did not last long. From 1917 to the late 1940s, the number of executions in the United States rose markedly. One reason for this was the perceived threat of communism. Following the 1917 Russian Revolution, many Americans feared that communism would expand from the newly formed Soviet Union and threaten our nation's democratic system. These fears were not completely unfounded, as socialist ideals did begin to gain footholds in American society. In response, support for capital punishment reemerged, and by 1920 Oregon, Arizona, Washington, and Missouri had reinstated the death penalty. Other factors included increased fear of gangster activity and the arrest of Bruno Hauptmann for the Lindbergh baby kidnapping and murder (although many believe Hauptmann was innocent of these crimes). Criminologists also began to argue that the death penalty was a "necessary social measure" in light of the Great Depression and the many other social challenges that faced our nation during the 1930s. Kansas reinstated the death penalty in 1935, as did South Dakota in 1939. During the 1930s the nation averaged 167 executions per year, more than during any other decade, with a peak of 199 in 1935.

During the 1950s and 1960s, public attitudes concerning the death penalty began to change once again. Many wartime allies of the United States abolished capital punishment, and their influence, in part, led to a dramatic decrease in executions in America as well. The average during the 1940s was 129 executions per year. During the 1950s, this average dropped to 72, and by the mid-1960s, it fell to single digits.[3] In 1968, there were no executions while states waited for the Supreme Court to rule in a series of upcoming capital punishment cases. Furthermore, public support for the death penalty was decreasing as evidenced by a 1966 Gallup poll, which found that only 42 percent of Americans supported capital punishment, the lowest percentage up to that time.

The Supreme Court and the Death Penalty

The late 1960s and early 1970s saw important Supreme Court challenges to the death penalty as well as significant revisions to state death penalty statutes. In *U.S. v. Jackson* (1968), the Supreme Court ruled unconstitutional a provision of a federal kidnapping statute that held that the death penalty could only be imposed upon the recommendation of a jury. The problem with this provision was that it acted as an incentive for defendants to waive their right to a trial to assure that they would not receive a death sentence. Authorities would pressure suspects to confess to crimes and avoid a jury trial, and thus avoid a possible death sentence. This tactic amounted to unfair coercion; the Supreme Court ruled the provision unconstitutional.

Other constitutional challenges to the death penalty were based on the argument that it violated the Eighth Amendment.[4] In *Furman v. Georgia* (1972), the plaintiff (Furman) contended that Georgia's death penalty statutes were unconstitutional because the lack of jury guidelines in capital cases resulted in "cruel and unusual punishment." As long as juries were given complete discretion for recommending a sentence of life in prison or death, with no guidance from the court as to how to use this discretion, the decisions they made were arbitrary and capricious. For example, suppose that John and Walter are convicted for similar, although separate, capital crimes. With complete and unguided discretion, the jury in John's trial could recommend a sentence of life in prison while Walter's jury could recommend death. This entailed "cruel and unusual punishment" for Walter because there was no clear criterion for sentencing him to death but not John. The Supreme Court agreed. In a 5–4 vote, it ruled that as a result of complete and unguided jury discretion, Georgia death penalty statutes could result in arbitrary and capricious sentencing and were, therefore, unconstitutional.

Notice that in *Furman* the Supreme Court did not rule the death penalty itself unconstitutional, just the *means* by which Georgia and other states handed down death sentences. This left the door open for states to rewrite their death penalty statutes, and many of them did. Notice also that nine separate opinions were written in the *Furman* case. Normally one Supreme Court justice writes the majority option (the one that "wins"), and another writes the dissenting option (the one that "loses"). In this case, each of the nine justices offered his own opinion for why he voted the way he did, underscoring the legal complexities of the case. The immediate result of *Furman* was that on June 29, 1972, the Supreme Court essentially voided forty states' death penalty statutes and commuted the sentences of 629 death-row inmates to life in prison.[5]

Although death penalty opponents hailed the decision, the Supreme Court's moratorium on executions in the United States did not last long. To overcome the constitutional problems identified in *Furman*, several states immediately began rewriting their death penalty statutes to avoid arbitrariness in capital sentencing. This was done in a number of ways. The first involved bifurcated trials, which simply means there are separate proceedings for the guilt or innocence and sentencing phases of a trial. In the first phase, a defendant's guilt or innocence is determined by a jury of his or her peers. If the defendant is convicted, a second trial occurs where the same jury decides to impose a sentence of life in prison or death. We saw this practice in high-profile capital cases involving Timothy McVeigh (convicted of the 1995 bombing of the Murrah Federal Building in Oklahoma City) and Scott Peterson (convicted of the murders of his wife, Laci, and unborn son, Connor, in California). The basic purpose of bifurcated trials is to allow the defendant to get a fair hearing in both the guilt or innocence and sentencing phases of the trial.

A second procedural reform was the ability to introduce aggravating and mitigating factors in the sentencing phase of the trial. Once a defendant is convicted in the guilt or innocence phase, in the second phase the prosecution can argue factors that aggravate or increase his or her guilt. An example would be a previous conviction for an unrelated violent felony. The defense can also introduce mitigating or lessening factors such as the defendant's age or lack of violent criminal history. The purpose of introducing these aggravating and mitigating factors is to give the jury as much information as possible (including evidence not introduced in the first phase) to make an informed sentencing decision. Introducing aggravating and mitigating evidence allows the jury to take these factors into consideration when recommending a sentence.

A third procedural reform was the introduction of automatic appellate review. This means that if a defendant is convicted of a capital crime and sentenced to death, the case is automatically reviewed by a court of appeals to assure that the defendant's constitutional rights were upheld throughout the entire judicial process. This is important because it offers another line of protection for the defendant. The trial court could have unknowingly (or knowingly) erred in its procedures. Automatic review offers the defendant an opportunity to challenge the constitutionality of the proceedings.

The fourth procedural reform concerned proportionality review. With proportionality review, the appeals courts can compare capital cases to ensure that defendants do not receive disproportionate sentences for essentially similar crimes. This was one of the primary challenges of *Furman*. The introduction of proportionality review helps courts avoid disparities in death sentences, which in turn helps to overcome the problem of arbitrary and capricious jury sentencing.

The constitutionality of these procedural reforms was challenged and upheld by the Supreme Court in 1976 through its decisions in *Gregg v. Georgia*, *Jurek v. Texas*, and *Proffitt v. Florida* (collectively known as the *Gregg* decision). The court held that rewritten death penalty statutes in Georgia, Texas, and Florida provided necessary constitutional protections and could be enforced in those states. However, following *Gregg* all those whose death sentences were commuted by *Furman* did not return to death row. The new guidelines applied only to those who were convicted of capital crimes after the statues had been rewritten. Today, thirty-eight states as well as the federal government and the military have the death penalty.[6]

This brief overview has demonstrated just some of the many legal issues surrounding capital punishment. In the next section, we identify the main ethical arguments, philosophical and theological, both for and against the death penalty.

Arguments For and Against the Death Penalty

The first argument put forth by death penalty supporters is that capital punishment acts as a deterrent to violent crime.[7] Society has a duty to protect its citizens from violent offenders and to do this it must establish the harshest punishments possible. If individuals know that execution is the potential punishment, they might think twice before committing the crime. Supporters also maintain that capital punishment protects the general public from further crime by the offender. They argue that as long as criminals remain alive in prison there is the possibility that they could be paroled or escape and reenter society. Also, if these individuals are incarcerated for life with no possibility of parole, what is there to prevent them from killing guards or other inmates? The death penalty is the only way to assure that society's most heinous offenders will never again commit a violent crime.

Death penalty opponents respond by arguing that capital punishment is not an effective deterrent to crime. According to the Death Penalty Information Center, 84 percent of criminology society presidents surveyed said that the death penalty does not prevent violent crime, and figures from the Federal Bureau of Investigation would seem to bear this out. According to the FBI's 2003 "Uniform Crime Report," the South had a murder rate of 6.9 per 100,000 people, the highest in the nation, even though southern states (particularly Texas, Virginia, and Oklahoma) led the nation in the number of executions. Conversely, in the Northeast where a majority of states do not have the death penalty, the murder rate in 2003 was 4.2 per 100,000 people, the lowest in the nation. In fact, since the early 1990s, states without the death penalty have actually done a better job of reducing their overall murder rates. Citing these figures as well as the results of numerous scientific studies, opponents hold that there is no definitive evidence that the death penalty acts as an effective deterrent to crime.

Death penalty proponents also invoke economics, arguing that executing convicted murderers is less expensive than keeping them alive in a maximum-security prison for the rest of their lives. Assume it costs $50,000 per year to maintain an individual in a maximum security prison. If the individual is relatively young, say 35 years old, he has on average another 40 years to live. Multiply 40 years by $50,000 and you get a $2,000,000 "bill" that taxpayers must absorb. This per-year cost is only an estimate. Prison operating costs are continually increasing, and many violent offenders commit capital crimes in their teens and twenties. All factors taken together, the cost of a life sentence can be high indeed.

Death penalty opponents dispute the claim that it is less expensive to execute convicted violent offenders. A 2003 review of capital case expenses in Kansas revealed that the median cost for a non-death penalty trial was $740,000 while that for a death penalty trial was $1.26 million or 70 percent more. There are a number of reasons for this. In a death penalty trial, significantly more pretrial preparation is needed and more motions are filed, necessitating more attorneys. The bifurcated trial and the need to question jurors about their views on the death penalty add both time and expense. Furthermore, when a death sentence is handed down, the defendant is entitled to an automatic appeal, adding to the expense. The study in Kansas demonstrated that appeal costs in death sentence cases were approximately twenty times higher than those for cases where the sentence was life in prison.[8]

Figures from other states bear the same results. In 2000 the *Palm Beach Post* reported that the state of Florida would save $51 million per year if it pursued life sentences for its violent offenders rather than death. A 1993 Duke University report showed that in North Carolina the cost of the death penalty per actual execution was $2.16 million higher than the cost of a non-death penalty trial. In 2004 the Tennessee State Comptroller's Office revealed that not only did death penalty trials cost the state 48 percent more than non-death penalty trials but even when a defendant was sentenced to death, the Court of Criminal Appeals overturned these sentences 29 percent of the time.

These findings demonstrate a further financial difficulty with maintaining the death penalty. States spend hundreds of thousands of dollars to win a death sentence, but in many cases these sentences are overturned on appeal, necessitating a repeat of at least the sentencing phase of the trial.[9]

The state of New York has spent over $100 million in death penalty cases since capital punishment was reestablished in 1995, without executing a single person.[10] The irony here is obvious: in pursuing death sentences, states often end up paying twice. They pay high costs to pursue a death sentence, but often end up with the costs of a life sentence anyway.

A third argument concerns justice. Justice is commonly defined as "rendering to each what is owed to her or him" or "rendering to each her or his due." Death penalty supporters argue that if an individual intentionally takes the life of another, then this individual must be punished in the same way. Just as when one person steals from another and justice demands that the offender return what was taken or make proportionate restitution, so also when one intentionally takes the life of another, justice demands that the perpetrator make restitution with her or his life. This argument is often expressed by the families of murder victims. They believe that as a matter of justice, the one who took their loved one's life must die in turn.

Death penalty opponents counter this argument by asking whether executing a violent offender is really an act of justice. Do we put a person to death because we believe it is a just response to what he or she has done, or are we doing it primarily out of a sense of vengeance? Lloyd Steffen offers a poignant challenge on this point:

> Vengeance is not justice. . . . Vengeance can seek justice, but justice is not to be had. Vengeance only serves the illusion that the loss resulting from death can be put right by the death of another. Such a view is folly, sad folly. An irreplaceable loss cannot be replaced, an irretrievable loss cannot be retrieved.[11]

Bud Walsh, whose daughter Julie died in the 1995 Oklahoma City bombing, concurs. He opposed the execution of Timothy McVeigh, claiming it was an act of vengeance, not justice, on the part of the federal government. He argued that because his daughter could not be brought back to life, McVeigh's execution could never be considered an act of justice. He added that although vengeance is a natural and powerful emotion, it has no place in our justice system. These challenges from Steffen and Walsh should force us to ask ourselves exactly what our motivation is for executing violent offenders. Are we seeking justice or vengeance? The line between them is not always clear.

Death penalty opponents also raise questions concerning procedural justice. Since execution is the most final punishment one can receive, the state must assure that the defendant's due process rights have been upheld at all stages (trial, sentencing, appeal) before putting the person to death. Did the defendant receive an adequate defense? Was all testimony from both the prosecution and defense presented at trial? Was the judge impartial? Was the jury impartial, and did it consist of the defendant's peers? We would expect all these requirements to be met in a capital trial, but we know that this has not always been the case. Defendants have been convicted and executed for capital crimes even when there were serious problems of due process.[12] Since 1973, more than one hundred individuals have been taken off death row after new evidence arose in their cases. Examples include witnesses who admit they were pressured into lying at the original trial, the confession of the actual killer, and more reliable forms of forensic testing (including DNA). The new evidence either proved the person convicted had not committed the crime or raised reasonable doubt. This begs an important question: if more than one hundred people convicted of violent crimes have been exonerated since just 1973, how many innocent people have we put to death?[13]

Death penalty opponents also argue that as a matter of procedural justice, capital punishment is unfairly applied to the poor. Simply put, rich people do not go to death row. Defendants who can afford high-powered attorneys are less likely to be convicted or, on the prudent advice of counsel, can plea-bargain for a lighter sentence. A large percentage of today's death-row inmates were represented by court-appointed attorneys (public defenders) who simply were not qualified to take on a capital case or who, because of heavy caseloads, did not have the time or resources to mount an adequate defense. No matter what one believes about the death penalty itself, there is little debate that financial status is a determining factor in whether one receives a sentence of life in prison or death.

Further questions concern racial bias. The Death Penalty Information Center reports that 58 percent of all defendants executed since 1976 were white, while 34 percent were black. At present, 46 percent of death-row inmates awaiting execution are white, and 42 percent are black. Although some question whether these figures demonstrate a racial bias,[14] bias is clearly evident in respect to the race of the *victim* in death penalty cases. Of all the murder cases since 1976 that resulted in an execution, more than

80 percent of the time the victim was white, although whites accounted for only 50 percent of all murder victims. Blacks accounted for about 14 percent of victims in cases resulting in execution, Hispanics only 4 percent. In effect, defendants (regardless of their own race) have a significantly greater chance of receiving a death sentence if the victim is white. In addition, while 212 black defendants have been executed since 1976 for killing a white, only 12 white defendants have been executed for killing a black. Can capital punishment be a just response to violent crime when the processes demonstrate racial bias?

Turning to more theological arguments, death penalty supporters cite the Bible as justification for capital punishment. The "eye for eye" passage (Exod. 21:23) is interpreted to mean that if one person takes the life of another, society may extract the same price from the offender. The problem with this widely held interpretation is it is taken out of context. The passage actually reads:

> When men have a fight and hurt a pregnant woman, so that she suffers a miscarriage, but no further injury, the guilty one shall be fined as much as the woman's husband demands of him, and he shall pay in the presence of the judges. But if injury ensues, you shall give life for life, eye for eye, tooth for tooth, hand for hand, foot for foot, burn for burn, wound for wound, stripe for stripe. (Exod. 21:22–25)

When read in context, we see that the "eye for eye" passage was not necessarily intended as a justification for capital punishment. Its real purpose was restraint: it was meant to assure that an offender's punishment was proportionate to the crime committed, not to justify absolutely the taking of the offender's life.[15]

Another difficulty with using the Bible to justify capital punishment is the large number of offenses punishable by death, including blasphemy, idolatry, witchcraft, adultery, homosexuality, profaning the Sabbath, and cursing a parent. If we were to follow the scriptural teaching strictly and execute every adulterer, homosexual, and all who have worked on the Sabbath or cursed their parents, we would have exponentially more executions! In reality, many biblical scholars believe that capital punishment was never common in Hebrew society.

Death penalty supporters also cite the Christian Scriptures (New Testament) to justify capital punishment, particularly Romans, chapter 13, where Saint Paul teaches that all people, Christians included, are subject to governmental authority. Paul warns, "But if you do evil, be afraid, for it [civil authority] does not bear the sword without purpose; it is the servant of God to inflict wrath on the evildoer" (Rom. 13:4). Supporters argue that as Saint Paul taught that civil authority legitimately bears the sword and can use it to inflict wrath, then capital punishment is morally justified. But "bear the sword" is vague: does it mean that civil authority has the power to execute, or simply that it has a mandate to punish offenders? Joseph Fitzmyer, SJ, an eminent Catholic biblical scholar, maintains that the sword represents "the symbol of penal authority, of the power legitimately possessed by a civil authority to coerce recalcitrant citizens to maintain order and strive for the common good by obeying the law of the society." However, Fitzmyer does not specify what form(s) of punishment this authority can legitimately impose. He notes that the phrase could be interpreted as a symbol for capital punishment, but during Paul's lifetime the authority to impose such a punishment was limited to Roman provincial governors and only toward soldiers under their command. Paul's use of the phrase more likely had a broader scope, referring to the authority of law enforcement officials, civil guards, or even those who enforced taxation policies.[16] In the end it simply is not clear whether Romans, chapter 13, can be used to justify capital punishment.

Death penalty opponents also cite biblical passages to justify their position. They cite the words of Jesus —"You have heard that it was said, 'An eye for an eye and tooth for a tooth.' But I say to you, offer no resistance to one that is evil" (Matt. 5:38 – 39) — as a call to renounce violence and retribution. In Luke 23:34, Jesus asked the Father to forgive those who were crucifying him; why would he do this if his Crucifixion was morally justified? In John 8:1–11, Jesus prevented the execution of an adulterous woman by asking the would-be executioners if they themselves were without sin. While Jesus' teaching concerning the adulterous woman was not a direct prohibition against capital punishment, he did "disqualify" the would-be executioners from imposing an absolute punishment for her crime — this prerogative belonged to God alone.[17] Overall, it is difficult to claim that the Bible offers a single, consistent teaching on the issue of capital punishment.

The question of legitimate authority continues to play an important role in the theological debate over capital punishment. Do we, either as individuals or state, have the authority to take the life of a human being who has committed a capital crime? Most moral systems (including the Catholic Church) hold that it can be morally permissible to use lethal force in self-defense. If Craig is directly threatening Mick's life or is imminently intending him great physical harm, then it is morally permissible for Mick to use deadly force to prevent Craig from inflicting this harm, assuming that Mick has no nonlethal alternative. Death penalty opponents point out that when the state is putting a criminal to death, it is difficult to see how the condemned poses a direct and imminent threat to anyone.

Death penalty supporters respond by arguing that the state's authority to execute comes from its duty to defend the common good. A primary function of the state is to promote the overall good of its citizens; one of the ways it does so is by protecting citizens from those who would cause them harm. This understanding actually forms the foundation of the Catholic Church's historical support of capital punishment during the patristic period. Tertullian (d. 220) taught that putting offenders to death was one of civil authority's just punishments, although he did instruct Christians to refrain from holding positions within this authority that would force them to make judgments over others' lives. Clement of Alexandria (d. 215) held that although reform of the offender was a "higher" purpose of punishment, imposing death was permissible if the individual in question was deemed "incurable" and if the possibility existed that others in the community could be "affected" by him. Clement used the image of a medical amputation to demonstrate his point. If you have a diseased limb, you amputate it to save the rest of your body. Similarly, if a society has a "diseased" member, this member could be "cut away" to save the rest of the community. Origen (d. 254) agreed in principle with both Tertullian and Clement of Alexandria, but added that capital punishment could also act as a form of expiation for sin. Origen believed that the execution itself was the offender's "final" punishment. In other words, through execution the offender is absolved from his sin, and after being put to death God will not punish him any further for his offense. Capital punishment, therefore, should not be viewed as cruel (or unusual), but "full of mercy" because the one put to death is purged of his sin rather than condemned to hell for all eternity.[18]

During the medieval period as well, the Church recognized that, although regrettable, capital punishment (as well as war) was sometimes necessary to maintain peace and stability within the community.[19] Saint Thomas Aquinas taught that legitimate authority — understood as those responsible for maintaining public order — could legitimately put an offender to death if the offender posed a serious threat to the community. He justified this position, in part, by citing the relationship between the whole and the part. The whole is always greater than and prior to any of the individual parts, and the good of the whole supersedes that of its individual members. In the case of an individual posing a grave threat to the community, the greater good of the community always outweighs the good of the individual, and capital punishment can be morally justified.[20]

The legitimate authority argument states that if an offender's threat is so great that the *only* means to protect society is through his execution, then capital punishment is morally permissible. Some extend this argument: even if an offender does not pose an imminent threat at the moment of his execution, he still could be legitimately put to death if his continued existence would pose a serious, ongoing threat to the life and well-being of those around him. As an act of self-defense and as a service to the societal common good, the state maintains the legitimate authority (and right) to inflict capital punishment.[21]

Finally, and perhaps most important, both supporters and opponents of the death penalty have to address the issue of human dignity. Life is the greatest gift we have. It is given to us by God, it is sacred in God's eyes, it is of infinite value, and we only have one chance at it. As we debate the morality of capital punishment, we must constantly remind ourselves that we are talking about a human life. We are debating the morality of taking God's greatest gift from one of God's children. Once taken away, human life can never be given back; that fact should make us think long and hard about our stance on the death penalty.

We must also remember that the Church teaches that all individuals, no matter what sins they have committed, always retain their dignity, and their lives always remain sacred in God's eyes. Our society tends to diminish the value of those who have committed horrendous crimes, as if to say that such people no longer deserve to be considered human persons. The book *Dead Man Walking* powerfully portrayed this sentiment when Vernon Harvey, father of Faith Harvey who had been brutally raped and murdered by Robert Lee Willie, angrily chastised Sr. Helen Prejean for agreeing to act as Willie's spiritual advisor:

> He's an animal. No, I take that back. Animals don't rape and kill their own kind. Robert Lee Willie is God's mistake. Frying in the electric chair is the least of the frying he's going to do when God sends him to hell where he belongs.[22]

Christianity cannot tolerate this line of thinking. God loves Robert Lee Willie as much as Faith Harvey, Timothy McVeigh as much as the 168 people he murdered in Oklahoma City, and Osama bin Laden as much as the 3,000+ people who died in the 9/11 attacks. As difficult as it may be to comprehend, God loves the murderer as much as his victims, and the murderer's life retains the same value and dignity that it had before the murder took place.

With these teachings in mind, we must now ask, do we uphold human dignity when we execute capital offenders, or does respect for dignity demand that we refrain from putting them to death? Once again, there is more than one response to this question. Death penalty opponents will argue that because these offenders maintain their dignity as human persons and their lives remain sacred in God's eyes, the state is never morally justified in putting them to death. When the state does execute, it infringes upon God's rightful lordship over human life and, in fact, "plays God." Death penalty supporters counter by claiming that executing capital offenders does uphold human dignity because the offender's forfeiture of his own life serves to enhance the overall value of life in society as a whole. Although on the surface this position may seem to be a contradiction, the argument is that executions actually demonstrate how valuable human life is. Life is of so great a value that if you take the life of another, the price you will have to pay is your own.[23] This argument is intriguing because it refocuses the object of human dignity. Here the focus is not on the dignity of the offender, but on that of the victim. It is morally justified to execute Robert Lee Willie, Timothy McVeigh, or any other murderer because the forfeiture of their lives underscores the value and dignity of those who died by their hands.

What does the Catholic Church teach about the death penalty? Is it morally permissible to execute capital offenders, or are we bound to preserve their lives no matter what heinous crime they may have committed? There is a wide variety of opinion on this question, and people of faith hold compelling positions on both sides of the aisle, so what should we believe? Is there a truly "Catholic" response to capital punishment? Although much has been written on the subject from the Catholic perspective, in the final section of this chapter we focus on just three documents that together present the Church's contemporary perspective. We first explore the United States Catholic bishops' *Statement on Capital Punishment* (1980) to get the American perspective. We then focus on Pope John Paul II's *The Gospel of Life* and the *Catechism of the Catholic Church* to gain the perspective of the universal Church.

Catholic Social Teaching and the Death Penalty

The most comprehensive teaching on the death penalty from the perspective of the American Church is the United States Catholic bishops *Statement on Capital Punishment*. The document begins:

> In 1974, out of a commitment to the value and dignity of human life, the U. S. Catholic Conference, by a substantial majority, voted to declare its opposition to capital punishment.[24]

From the outset, the bishops identify the value and dignity of human life as the theological foundation for the entire document. In doing this, they underscore that all people are deserving of dignity and respect, including the convicted criminal. As a matter of justice, violent offenders must be punished for their crimes. But in administering punishment we must always remember that the offender is loved by God and remains one of God's precious children. The implication of this understanding is that no one, the state included, has an absolute right to take the life of another human being.

We should note that the statement was endorsed "by a substantial majority," not unanimously. Some bishops maintain that the death penalty is a morally legitimate means of dealing with society's most violent offenders. In fact, 145 bishops voted in favor of the statement, 31 opposed, and 41 abstained.[25] These numbers are significant because the bishops essentially leave the death penalty question open, in contrast to their unanimity on issues such as abortion. They recognize that faithful Catholics can have differences of opinion, differences that are reflected in American society as a whole. This recognition is repeated in the third paragraph of the introduction, where the bishops admit that the debate over capital punishment often involves competing moral values. How do we balance our respect for the dignity of the human person with our duty to protect society from violent offenders? How do we balance this dignity with our duty to preserve order within society or with our duty to achieve justice through the law? These are difficult questions. In the document's conclusion the bishops acknowledge that many Catholics believe capital punishment should remain an integral part of our nation's response to violent crime, a position that is compatible with the Church's historical tradition.

In part 2 of the statement the bishops argue that abolishing the death penalty would promote four important Christian values. The first value concerns peace. The bishops maintain that abolition of capital punishment would be an important first step in breaking the cycle of violence so prevalent in American society. Without a doubt, violence is engrained in our culture. Our movies, music, television programs, and video games have glamorized violence and desensitized us to its effects. One need only observe American society to recognize this reality. We have higher murder and violent crime rates than practically any nation in the developed world, and our prisons are bursting at the seams. The bishops assert that abolishing the death penalty would be a first step in reversing this cycle of violence and bringing about a more peaceful society. The bishops are not naïvely stating that abolishing the death penalty would cure society of violence. They recognize that this is only one of the many steps that need to be taken. Abolishing the death penalty would challenge us as a nation to develop more humane, hopeful, and effective responses to violent crime and to deal with criminals intelligently and compassionately, not simply with power and vengeance.

The second Christian value that abolition of the death penalty would promote is the unique dignity and worth of every human person. As noted, the dignity and value of human life is the theological heart of the entire document. The bishops claim that the dignity and worth of all people "impels" the Church to minister to the needs of outcasts and those whom society has rejected, including violent offenders. All people, no matter what crimes they may have committed, are still children of God and deserve to be treated as such. That is not to say that violent offenders should be absolved, but we cannot view these people's lives as expendable. God's grace is available to all people no matter what they may have done. If God believes the criminal's life has infinite value and worth, then so should we.

In a closely related point, the bishops claim that abolition of the death penalty would underscore the Christian belief that God is the Lord of life. As life is given to us by God, only God has the absolute right to take it away. Joseph Cardinal Bernardin spoke of the "consistent ethic of life." In brief, this ethic held that if you claim to be pro-life, then you have to defend *all* human life at *every* stage of its existence. It is logically inconsistent to oppose abortion on the grounds that it is the direct taking of a human life while at the same time supporting capital punishment. The United States bishops similarly argue that abolishing the death penalty would be a welcome step in the overall defense of human life.

Finally, the bishops maintain that abolition of the death penalty would be "most consonant" with Jesus' call to forgiveness. Throughout the Gospels, Jesus encountered individuals who had sinned, including some who were "deserving" of death. In each case, Jesus' response was one of forgiveness. He forgave people of their sins, often reinforcing his declaration by performing a miracle. Not once did he condemn anyone, including the Roman soldiers who crucified him, or call for anyone to be put to death. How do we understand Jesus' example of forgiveness in terms of our response to violent offenders? Are we willing to forgive? Are we willing to recognize that although people commit terrible crimes and need to be segregated from society, we can forgive in the sense that we will refrain from taking their lives?

Some will argue that a murderer deserves death, not forgiveness. This is a natural and understandable sentiment, but what does it say about those who hold it? Rand Richards Cooper points out that forgiveness is not something to be "earned" by the offender. Rather, forgiveness is a "dynamic encounter" between the offender and the offended. The way that we (the offended) respond to the offender says a lot about who we are. When presented with the challenge of the offender's crime, do we wish vengeance, justice, or compassion? Our responses to these questions have important ramifications for the kind of persons we choose to be.[26] Forgiveness means being open to the contrition of the offender, but it also includes our compassionate and Christ-like response to the offender when this contrition is not forthcoming.

In part 3 of the *Statement on Capital Punishment*, the United States bishops identify a number of "difficulties" inherent with the death penalty, many of which echo the points previously argued by death penalty opponents. Capital punishment involves bias in that death sentences are disproportionately imposed on the poor. It involves the possibility of error in that innocent people can be executed — a reality that the bishops regard "with a special horror"— and its process involves long and unavoidable delays, which work to undermine its deterrence factor. Executions cause anguish for the families of both the condemned and victim(s), not to mention the prison officials who have to carry out the death sentences. Executions also attract "unhealthy" publicity in that the media tend to focus on the conflict between death penalty supporters and opponents, undermining serious and respectful public dialogue. Finally, execution ends any possibility for the criminal to reform, to make restitution, to be rehabilitated, or to grow as a moral being.

We now turn to teachings of the Church as a whole. In *The Gospel of Life* (*Evangelium vitae*, 1995), Pope John Paul II restates the Church's traditional teaching concerning the sacredness of human life. All human life is sacred because it is created by God and because it exists in a "special relationship" with its Creator. God is the Lord of life, and under no circumstances can any individual claim the right to directly destroy an innocent human being. The pope then goes on to assert that the primary purpose of punishment is to "redress the disorder caused by the offence." If an individual commits a crime, civil authority has the duty to redress the violation by imposing on the offender a punishment adequate to fit the nature of the crime. The *Catechism of the Catholic Church* restates John Paul II's teaching by holding that in accord with its duty to promote the societal common good, the state has a moral obligation to protect its citizens from those who would cause them harm. This obligation justifies the right of the state to use force to protect the citizenry as well as inflict punishment that is proportionate to the seriousness of the offense committed. Both John Paul II and the *Catechism* uphold the responsibility of the state to maintain public order as well as its right to administer just and appropriate punishments.[27]

Are there any limits to the punishments that civil authorities can impose? Can capital punishment ever be justified and, if so, under what conditions? Both the *Catechism* and John Paul II tackle these questions directly. According to the *Catechism*, as long as the offender's guilt is clearly established, the Church does not rule out the possibility of execution if that is the *only* possible means of protecting society from the aggressor. This statement is vital. Civil authority has the authority to execute violent offenders, but only if it has no other means to safeguard those whom it has a duty to protect. John Paul II is also clear on this point:

> The nature and extent of the punishment must be carefully evaluated and decided upon, and ought not go to the extreme of executing the offender except in cases of absolute necessity: in other words, when it would not be possible otherwise to defend society. Today however, as a result of steady improvements in the organization of the penal system, such cases are rare, if not practically non-existent.[28]

The Church's position is one of give and take. If civil authority does not possess the means to protect the citizenry, then capital punishment can be morally justified. Executing a violent offender then becomes an act of legitimate self-defense—a position consistent with the Church's tradition. However, if civil authority does have the ability to segregate violent offenders (normally through the prison system) and can protect the citizenry from aggressors through nonlethal means (such as life imprisonment), then executions cannot be morally justified. By stating that situations where society cannot protect itself are now "rare, if not practically non-existent," John Paul II and the *Catechism* indicate that the death penalty must not be viewed as an ordinary means of dealing with violent offenders. Under ordinary circumstances the imprisoned offender is segregated from society and poses no direct threat. Only under extraordinary circumstances, when a society does not have a penal system adequate to protect itself, may an offender be justifiably put to death.

Here, in a nutshell, is the Catholic Church's teaching on the death penalty. It upholds human dignity while recognizing the duty of civil authority to protect its citizens from violent offenders. With this understanding in mind, we can now return to Marcel's dilemma. After careful study and prayer, she decides that she is going to attend the protest. She certainly does not condone the actions of the condemned murderer and believes that he should be punished for his actions. But she also reasons that he should not be put to death because her state has the ability to segregate him from society. When Mike, her husband, questions her on this decision, she informs him that she understands and respects his opinion, but she cannot support it. The condemned person has done a terrible wrong; however, he is still a human being created in the image and likeness of God. God still loves him and still respects his dignity as a human person. She believes that she is called to do the same.

Review Questions

1. During the late 1800s and early 1900s, what factors led to the abolition of the death penalty in many states?

2. During the 1920s and 1930s, what factors caused states to reinstate the death penalty?

3. What specifically did the Supreme Court rule unconstitutional in *Furman v. Georgia*? What was the immediate effect of this decision on death-row inmates?

4. What are the arguments, both pro and con, regarding the value of the death penalty as a deterrent to violent crime?

5. What are the arguments, both pro and con, regarding capital punishment as an act of justice?

6. What "procedural justice" issues must be taken into consideration when speaking about the death penalty?

7. What are the arguments, both pro and con, regarding capital punishment as consistent with the "eye for eye" passage in Exodus?

8. What is the "legitimate authority" argument in favor of the state's ability to put an offender to death? How did the patristic scholars Tertullian, Clement of Alexandria, and Origen, and the medieval scholar Thomas Aquinas explain this teaching?

9. In what ways do death penalty opponents and supporters cite human dignity in support of their argument?

10. Why is it significant that in their *Statement on Capital Punishment*, the United States Catholic bishops were not unanimous in their opposition to the death penalty?

11. In part 2 of their *Statement on Capital Punishment*, the United States bishops argued that abolition of the death penalty would promote four important moral values. What are these values?

12. What did Pope John Paul II and the *Catechism of the Catholic Church* say about government's ability to inflict just punishment? How did John Paul II and the *Catechism* address the morality of capital punishment?

ENDNOTES

1 This brief overview is taken from chapters 8–10 of Stuart Banner, *The Death Penalty: An American History* (Cambridge, MA: Harvard University Press, 2002) and from the Death Penalty Information Center at death penaltyinfo.org.

2 Maine restored the death penalty in 1883 but re-abolished it in 1887. Colorado restored it in 1901.

3 In 1960 there were 56 actual executions, in 1963 there were 21, and in 1965 only 7.

4 "Excessive bail shall not be required, nor excessive fines imposed, nor cruel and unusual punishments inflicted."

5 For more background on the Furman case as well as other death penalty cases heard by the Supreme Court during the 1960s and 1970s, see chapter 9 of Banner, *The Death Penalty*.

6 Five death penalty states (Kansas, New Hampshire, New Jersey, New York, and South Dakota) have not had an execution since 1976. In 2004 the death penalty statutes in Kansas and New York were declared unconstitutional.

7 Unless otherwise noted, these arguments are taken from "The Death Penalty: Arguments For and Against" available at http://teacher.deathpenalty curriculum.org

8 See also Richard Dieter, "Costs of the Death Penalty and Related Issues." This was Dieter's testimony before the New York State Assembly's Committee on Codes, Judiciary, and Corrections (January 25, 2005), 4. It is available at http://www.death penaltyinfo.org.

9 A Columbia University Law School study found that approximately 68 percent of all death sentences were overturned on appeal. When the sentencing phases were retried, 82 percent resulted in the defendant receiving a life sentence.

10 Dieter, "Costs of the Death Penalty," 4–5.

11 Lloyd Steffen, *Executing Justice: The Moral Meaning of the Death Penalty* (Cleveland, OH: The Pilgrim Press, 1998), 100.

12 The Willie Darden case is an excellent example of how procedural justice (and due process) may have been ignored. See Steffen, *Executing Justice*, 9–18.

13 The authors would like to thank Kimberly Moore, one of our undergraduate students, for her research and critical analysis of this issue.

14 Some people do argue this point, stating that the 42 percent figure is significantly higher than the overall percentage of African Americans in the United States.

15 See commentaries on this passage from *The Catholic Study Bible*, ed. Donald Senior (New York: Oxford University Press, 1990), 85, and *The New Jerome Biblical Commentary*, ed. Raymond E. Brown et al. (Englewood Cliffs, NJ: Prentice Hall, 1990), 53.

16 Joseph Fitzmyer, SJ, *Romans*, Anchor Bible 33 (New York: Doubleday, 1993), 668.

17 Steffen, *Executing Justice*, 152.

18 Cited in E. Christian Brugger, *Capital Punishment and the Roman Catholic Moral Tradition* (Notre Dame, IN: University of Notre Dame Press, 2003), 76–82. For a comprehensive history of Church teachings on the death penalty, see James Megivern, *The Death Penalty: An Historical and Theological Survey* (New York: Paulist Press, 1997).

19 Although Christians were "forbidden" to pass judgment or carry out executions during the patristic period, in the medieval period these restrictions applied only to the clergy. During the medieval period the laity was permitted to participate in the execution process.

20 *Summa Theologiae*, II–II, q. 64 a. 2–4. See also Brugger, *Capital Punishment*, 96–99, 108–11.

21 Steffen, *Executing Justice*, 99.

22 Sr. Helen Prejean, *Dead Man Walking* (New York: Vintage Books, 1994), 138.

23 Steffen, *Executing Justice*, 103.

24 USCC, *Statement on Capital Punishment*, Origins 10, no. 24 (November 27, 1980): 373–77. Although the American bishops have published a number of more recent statements on both the state and national level, the foundation for these statements is this document. For links to more recent statements concerning capital punishment, see http://usccb.org/sdwp/national/deathpenalty.

25 Megivern, *The Death Penalty*, 367.

26 Rand Richards Cooper, "Basic Instinct," *Commonweal* (June 3, 2005): 39.

27 Pope John Paul II, *The Gospel of Life* (Boston, MA: Pauline Publications, 1995), nos. 53, 56. See also *Catechism of the Catholic Church*, rev. ed. (Washington, DC: USCC, 1997), nos. 2265–66.

28 John Paul II, *The Gospel of Life*, no. 56.

7. JUST WAR AND THE PRESUMPTION OF PEACE

Peacemaking is not an optional commitment. It is a requirement of our faith. We are called to be peacemakers, not by some movement of the moment, but by our Lord Jesus.

— United States Catholic Bishops, *The Challenge of Peace*, 1983

Dan, a twenty-year-old Catholic college student, is having difficulty paying his tuition. One day at a school-sponsored employment fair, an army recruiter urges him to join the Reserve Officers' Training Corps (ROTC). Dan's tuition would be paid, but in return Dan would have to participate in the ROTC program on campus and, upon graduation, serve in the active military for a period of time. It would be nice to have his tuition paid, but Dan worries he might be sent into combat. His parents are troubled because they do not believe in war as a solution to problems, and they fear that the ROTC will force their son to engage in actions they believe to be unjust. Dan wonders what his Church teaches about war. He knows that Jesus preached peace, but is not war justified in times of international terrorism? Does the Church agree, or is it pacifist? Can one be a good Catholic and a good soldier at the same time?

The dilemma facing Dan is not unique. Students on many college campuses face the question of joining ROTC as a way to complete their studies. This question is arguably more challenging on Catholic college campuses because of ongoing disputes concerning the moral duties of Catholics in times of war. In this chapter we address the question facing Dan by focusing on the issues of war and peace within the context of the Church's social tradition. What does the Catholic Church teach about war? Does it always seek peace, or does it recognize times where a nation can legitimately resort to military force? If force can be used, what conditions govern its use, and how much room is there for dissenting opinion? These questions have taken on greater urgency in recent years as we debate the morality of our nation's actions in the war on terror. Although no one wishes war, our nation's military engagements in Afghanistan and Iraq offer a challenging context for discussing the Church's teachings. As such, much of the chapter deals with ethical questions raised by the war on terror — without bias for one particular position, we hope!

This chapter cannot cover every aspect of this matter. We will, however, present some biblical understandings of peace, offer an overview of how justified war and the conditions necessary for peace have been understood within Catholic Social Teaching (CST), and explore two important documents of the United States Catholic bishops: *The Challenge of Peace: God's Promise and Our Response* (1983) and *The Harvest of Justice Is Sown in Peace* (1993).[1] We will explore the morality of United States' actions in the war on terror and identify some of the conditions necessary for peace to exist in our world today.

Biblical Understandings of Peace

Conflict is a recurring theme in the Bible, particularly in the Hebrew Scriptures. The Israelites had to defeat numerous enemies to hold the promised land, and God is often portrayed as a great warrior leading his people to victory. The ravages of war are also discussed, and the crushing defeat and exile at the hands of the Assyrians and Babylonians is used to demonstrate what happens when the people are not faithful to God. While images of war are prevalent in the Hebrew Scriptures, the theme of peace is also prominent. The Bible portrays God as desiring his people to live in peace. The people, however, had to be "worthy" of receiving it.

> If you live in accordance with my precepts and are careful to observe my commandments. . . . I will establish peace in the

land, that you may lie down to rest without anxiety. I will rid the country of ravenous beasts, and keep the sword of war from sweeping across your land. (Lev. 26:3, 6)

Throughout the Hebrew Scriptures, peace is closely related to living in right relationship with God. If the people are faithful to God and obey God's commandments, they will be rewarded with peace and prosperity in their land. Having escaped the slavery of Pharaoh in Egypt, the Israelites were staking claim to the land that God had given to them; they had not experienced much in the way of peace. Now God was telling them that if they would have faith in him, he would grant them peace. This message must have brought them great hope—it still rings true for us today. True peace involves a reciprocal, or two-way, relationship between God and humanity. God desires humanity to live in peace and is more than willing to grant it to us, but we cannot experience this peace apart from faith and obedience to God.

This reciprocal understanding of peace can also be found in the Book of Isaiah:

A strong city have we; he sets up walls and ramparts to protect us. Open up the gates to let in a nation that is just, one that keeps faith. (Isa. 26:1–2)

Justice will bring about peace; right will produce calm and security. (Isa. 32:17)

Isaiah again links peace to right relationship with God and identifies another factor necessary for the attainment of peace: justice. For true peace to exist, the people have to practice justice (giving to others their due). Many of our present-day armed conflicts result from the fact, or at least the perception, that one group is being treated unjustly by another. The biblical message is that justice is a necessary component of peace, and peace is only possible when people live in right relationship with God and with one another.

Another way to explain the concept is to see what happens to the Israelite people when justice is lacking.

You who oppress the weak and abuse the needy; who say to your lords, "Bring drink for us!" The Lord GOD has sworn by his holiness: Truly the days are coming upon you when they shall drag you away with hooks, the last of you with fishhooks; You shall go out through the breached walls each by the most direct way, and shall be cast into the mire, says the LORD. (Amos 4:1b – 3)

Hear this, you leaders of the house of Jacob, you rulers of the house of Israel. You who abhor what is just, and pervert all that is right. . . . Because of you Zion shall be plowed like a field, and Jerusalem reduced to rubble, and the mount of the temple to forest ridge. (Micah 3:9, 12)

These are a sample of numerous prophetic passages that warn the Israelite people what will happen to them if they fail to practice justice. The lesson from the Hebrew Scriptures is that if we desire peace, we have to place our faith in God and practice justice toward our neighbor. Where faith and justice are practiced, peace and security will follow. Psalm 85 ties these themes together nicely:

I will listen for the word of God; surely the LORD will proclaim peace to his people, to the faithful, to those who trust in him. Near indeed is salvation for the loyal; prosperity will fill our land. Love and truth will meet; justice and peace will kiss. . . . The LORD will surely grant abundance; our land will yield its increase. Prosperity will march before the LORD, and good fortune will fall behind. (Ps. 85:9 –14)

The theme of peace is also prevalent in the Christian Scriptures. In the Beatitudes Jesus proclaims, "Blessed are the peacemakers" (Matt. 5:9). Jesus' use of "peacemaker" is relevant for our discussion because the term is understood in light of the Hebrew word *shalom*. *Shalom* includes peace, but encompasses a person's total well-being. Jesus is praising those who work to bring about the overall good of others, those who practice justice in the community. As such, Jesus' teaching coheres with the teachings on peace in the Hebrew Scriptures and his command to love one's neighbor (Matt. 22:37– 39).[2]

Jesus also speaks of peace in his teaching on retaliation:

You have heard that it was said, "An eye for an eye and a tooth for a tooth." But I say to you, offer no resistance to one who is evil. When someone strikes you on your right cheek, turn the other one to him as well. If anyone wants to go to law with you over your tunic, hand him your cloak as well. Should anyone press you into service for one mile, go with him for two miles. . . . You have heard that it was said, "You shall love your neighbor and hate your enemy." But I say to you, love your enemies, and pray for those who persecute you. (Matt. 5:38–44)

Jesus' teaching here is countercultural. Conventional wisdom holds that we should protect our friends and combat our enemies, but Jesus tells his disciples, and us, to act with love toward all people no matter what they may have done. Jesus' message is one of nonviolence, but it actually provides a strategy for victory because through nonviolent responses we can shame our enemies into a change of heart.[3] This was the strategy used by Gandhi to gain India's independence from Britain, by Martin Luther King Jr. to gain civil rights for African Americans in the United States, and by the Solidarity labor movement in Poland to gain freedom from Soviet oppression. In each of these instances people refrained from violence even though they had suffered much at the hands of their oppressors. Jesus offers his followers a nonviolent means of responding to oppression.

The United States Catholic bishops cite a number of scriptural teachings on peace in *The Challenge of Peace* and *The Harvest of Justice Is Sown in Peace*. In *The Challenge of Peace*, they emphasize the Hebrew Scripture teaching that peace is a gift from God, the "fruit of God's saving activity" that can only be realized when humans live in covenantal solidarity with God and one another. They point to the Israelite people's belief that God's fidelity to the covenant means that in the future there will be a final salvation in which all of creation will come together in a community of justice and peace. This eschatological ("end of time") peace is still the Hebrew people's hope, a hope that can only be realized with the coming of God's messiah.[4]

The United States bishops claim that we can only understand Jesus' message of peace within the context of the Reign of God that Jesus proclaimed and inaugurated. Jesus challenges all people to recognize in him the manifestation of God's Reign and to "give themselves over" to it. In this sense, Jesus does bring the sword (Matt. 10:34) because he is the cause of much division. However, the sword he brings is not one of violence. Jesus teaches that one who lives under God's Reign must be willing to love and forgive the other. This person does not seek revenge but demonstrates mercy, the same mercy that God continually bestows on us. The bishops specifically state that Christian discipleship "implies continual conversion in one's own life as one seeks to act in ways that are consonant with the justice, forgiveness, and love of God's reign." They claim that Jesus' gift of peace is really the "fullness of salvation," the gift that fulfills the Hebrew Scripture's eschatological promise and is the sign of God's reconciliation with humanity.[5]

Ten years later in *The Harvest of Justice Is Sown in Peace*, the bishops again cite New Testament texts as they address the need for a greater "spirituality of peacemaking." At the heart of our faith we discover a God who desires peace for all people. Christ "fulfilled" this desire by redeeming and reconciling us to God through his Passion and death. The Holy Spirit continues this desire by calling each of us to prepare for God's Reign by working for peace. Christians are called to manifest God's love by living in peace with one another.[6] This is not always easy. True peacemaking necessitates a conversion of mind, heart, and word. We must imitate the humility, gentleness, and patience of Christ in our peacemaking efforts while never forgetting the necessity of prayer or that peace is a gift from God.[7] The challenge for all Christians is to create a peaceful social order that recognizes the dignity of all people and promotes justice for all.

War and Peace in Catholic Social Teaching

Since the biblical message is one of peace, can war ever be justified? We will begin our discussion of the Church's just war position with some brief remarks from Saint Augustine and Saint Thomas Aquinas. Then we will focus on specific twentieth-century CST documents that have addressed war and the establishment of peace in our own time.

Ambrose of Milan (d. 397), a Church father and mentor of Saint Augustine, taught that war can be justified if its purpose is to defend the weak and oppressed. Ambrose, who was influenced by the Roman philosopher Cicero, also held that war must be legally declared, innocent people must never be killed, and the defeated party must always be treated with justice following the cessation of hostilities.[8] Saint Augustine (d. 430) built upon Ambrose and taught that the purpose of waging war is to bring about peace. For Augustine, the goal of any society is to establish and maintain the *tranquilitas ordinis* ("tranquility of order"). The purpose of any military action must be to establish *tranquilitas ordinis* within society; thus war can be waged only out of necessity. Augustine taught that war can be declared only by a lawful authority and that it can be waged only for a just cause. Examples of just cause include protecting the innocent from harm or avenging an injury suffered at the hands of an aggressor. Injury for Augustine is specifically understood to be a situation where one nation refuses to return property it has unjustly taken from another, or when it refuses to rectify injustices perpetrated by its citizens. In cases such as these, the victimized nation has just cause to wage war—but in doing so its motivation must remain the restoration of the *tranquilitas ordinis*. Finally, Augustine spoke of "right" intention. The decision to go to war must not be motivated by cruelty, bloodlust, or a desire for vengeance. Correct intention must be grounded in justice and the pursuit of *tranquilitas ordinis*.[9]

Thomas Aquinas (d. 1274) identified three criteria necessary for justified war. First, war must be declared by a sovereign authority, for the sovereign is entrusted with promoting the common good of society and protecting society from aggressors. Fulfilling these duties can mean waging war against those who would do society harm. Aquinas was careful to point out that individual citizens cannot engage their nation in war with another nation even if there is just cause for doing so. Only the sovereign has ultimate responsibility for promoting societal good, and so only the sovereign can legitimately declare war. The second criterion is just cause, meaning that one nation can legitimately attack another "on account of some fault" that the perpetrating nation has committed. Aquinas here cited Augustine's teaching that recourse to war is morally justified to avenge a wrong. A nation may legitimately punish another if the offending nation refuses to "make amends" for its injustices or if it fails to restore what it has "seized injuriously." The third criterion is right intention. The purpose for waging war must be to repress evil and promote the good of society as a whole. Right intention cannot involve a "lust to dominate," a "craving to hurt people," or any "cruel thirst for revenge."[10]

Augustine and Aquinas are often regarded as the "architects" of the Church's just war tradition, but they are not the only ones who have contributed to its development. Bartholomew de Las Casas (d. 1566) forcefully argued against the practice of using military force to "convert" people to the Christian faith, a teaching formulated in response to the actions of the Spanish conquistadors in the Americas. Tommaso Cajetan (d. 1534) distinguished between offensive and defensive war, and spoke about "justice after war" or the need to make restitution to one's enemy after hostilities have ended. Francisco de Vitoria (d. 1546) offered the most comprehensive treatment of justified war, stating, in part, that war is not justified when waged due to differences in religion, the desire to enlarge an empire, or for the personal glory of the sovereign. Instead, the sole just cause for war is to redress a harm that has been unjustly inflicted by an aggressor. De Vitoria further maintained that legitimate authority must carefully examine the reasons why it goes to war, and that it must be willing to negotiate in good faith. In addition, he stressed the importance of non-combatant immunity and insisted that armed forces not inflict more damage than is necessary to achieve victory.

In light of these historical teachings, we now examine how the topics of war and peace are addressed in various CST documents of the twentieth century. Pope John XXIII focuses on the establishment of peace in *Christianity and Social Progress* (1961). Speaking about the gap between wealthy nations and those in the "process of development," he maintains that "economically advantaged" nations must not ignore the poverty, hunger, and lack of human rights experienced by so many others around the world. He points out that all people belong to one human family, the world is becoming increasingly interdependent, and it is difficult to maintain peace in nations where "excessive imbalances" exist in the economic and social structures.

> Whatever the progress in technology and economic life, there can be neither justice nor peace in the world so long as men fail to realize how great is their dignity; for they have been created by God and are his children. . . .
>
> Separated from God, man becomes monstrous to himself and others. Consequently, mutual relationships absolutely require a right ordering of the human conscience in relation to God, the source of all truth, justice and love.[11]

Here the pope demonstrates several conditions necessary to achieve and maintain peace: nations have to act with justice in their dealings with one another, particularly wealthy nations in relation to poorer ones; human dignity has to be respected; and a sense of global community and solidarity must be maintained. Today we see people in Africa, Asia, the Middle East, and Latin America living in abject poverty. These people have not been treated with justice, their dignity has been ignored, and they are not recognized as equal members of the global community. These factors translate into a lack of hope that fosters hostility and international terrorism. The pope's warning to remain in right relationship with God is equally valid as our culture becomes ever more secularized. Even within the Catholic Church we see individuals who, in the name of political correctness, are willing to abandon any notion of faith when debating public policy issues. This is a mistake. Although one certainly should not impose one's beliefs on another, it is perfectly legitimate — and constitutional — to draw upon one's faith tradition in order to meet the challenges of the contemporary world.

In *Peace on Earth* (1963), John XXIII reiterates and expands upon *Christianity and Social Progress*. He argues that international relations must be governed by the norms of justice. Every nation has the right to exist, develop according to its own devices, procure the resources necessary for development, and defend its "good name and honor."[12] Justice demands that these rights be recognized by the world community, as their recognition lays the foundation for peace. John XXIII then discusses what justice means in practice. He argues that "true and solid peace" can occur only though a renewed spirit of mutual trust, and "right relations" between nations requires truth, justice, and active participation on the part of all people.[13]

The bishops of the world address the issue of peace in two important documents from the mid-1960s and early 1970s. The Second Vatican Council's *Pastoral Constitution on the Church in the Modern World* (1965) claims the world cannot become "genuinely human" until all people commit themselves to fostering a peace based on justice and love. For the council bishops, peace is an "enterprise of justice" (Isa. 32:17). Peace can only be realized through social harmony — itself a gift from God — and can only be put in practice through the actions of those who "thirst after ever greater justice." As such, a "firm determination" to respect the dignity of others and an active "practice of brotherhood" (love for neighbor) are essential elements in the establishment of peace.[14] In *Justice in the World*

(1971) the bishops expanded on this theme by intimately linking Christian love with the establishment of peace. In light of the Gospel message they argue that Christians must recognize that their relationships with one another are intertwined with their relationship with God. Our response to God's offer of love is most clearly manifested in our love and service of one another. In other words, Christian love for neighbor cannot be separated from justice. Love implies an absolute demand for justice, which "attains its inner fullness" only in love. Christians are called to recognize God in all people and to embody justice and love in their dealings with one another. Only through this dual practice of justice and love can true peace be realized.[15]

Pope Paul VI speaks to the relationship between justice and peace in two well-known social documents. In *On the Development of Peoples* (1967), he reiterates the words of John XIII by stating that the excessive economic, social, and cultural inequalities among nations foster tensions that pose a "danger to peace." Then, echoing the Second Vatican Council, he states that peace must not be limited to the absence of war. Instead, peace needs to be "built up" every day and it needs to pursue the "order intended by God, [one that] implies a more perfect form of justice among men."[16] Four years later, in *A Call to Action* (1971), Paul VI offered a stern warning:

> In international relations there is a need to go beyond relationship based on force, in order to arrive at agreements reached with the good of all in mind. Relationships based on force have never in fact established justice in a true and lasting manner. . . . The use of force moreover leads to the setting in motion of opposing forces, and from this springs a climate of struggle which opens the way to situations of extreme violence and to abuses.[17]

As we work for peace through the establishment of justice, we must also recognize that peace cannot be brought about by force. The use of force by one party simply breeds in the other a corresponding "need" for force, leading to further conflict.

Finally, Pope John Paul II focuses on the need for greater international solidarity. In *On Social Concern* (1987), he echoes his predecessors by claiming that developed nations have a moral obligation to aid their less-fortunate neighbors and to establish an international system that recognizes the fundamental equality of all people. These actions will lead to increased solidarity among all nations, rich and poor alike. For the pope, solidarity is "the path to peace and at the same time to development," and world peace is impossible without it. Solidarity further demands that we tear down all political blocs, end all forms of economic, military, and political imperialism, and transform our mutual distrust into collaboration. John Paul II firmly believed that world peace could only be achieved through the establishment of international justice, and international justice could only be achieved through solidarity.[18]

In *On the Hundredth Anniversary of Rerum Novarum* (1991), John Paul II makes an even more impassioned plea for an end to armed conflict. Writing in the immediate aftermath of the Persian Gulf War, he implores:

Never again war! No, never again war, which destroys the lives of innocent people, teaches how to kill, throws into upheaval even the lives of those who do the killing and leaves behind a trail of resentment and hatred, thus making it all the more difficult to find a just solution to the very problems which provoked the war.[19]

Several important truths are embedded within this statement. War destroys innocent people, those caught up in a conflict they do not desire. War causes great stress on those who are fighting, both at the time and when they come home. War also leads to resentment on the part of those who "lose," militating against efforts at reconciliation. Following this impassioned plea for an end to warfare, the pope reiterates that true development is another name for peace. Peace will be possible only when all people have the opportunity to share equitably in the world's resources and when world economic structures are directed toward the common good. These are responsibilities of the world community as a whole. Just as there is a collective responsibility to avoid war, there is a reciprocal responsibility to promote the integral development of all people — the pathway to true peace in the world.[20]

Turning now to the United States Catholic bishops, we find in particular two statements published during the latter years of the twentieth century, *The Challenge of Peace: God's Promise and Our Response* (1983) and *The Harvest of Justice Is Sown in Peace* (1993). In these documents, the bishops offer informed and measured responses to questions such as,

"Under what conditions can war be justified?" "What are the 'rules' in war?" "Can one legitimately oppose war?" and, "How are we to work for peace?" Although *The Challenge of Peace* and *The Harvest of Justice* are the most important documents concerning war and peace from the United States Catholic bishops, they are not the only ones. The bishops have built a large body of teachings that encompass almost all of our nation's twentieth-century military conflicts. These teachings are important because they set the context for the two documents we explore, and they demonstrate an ongoing development in the bishops' thinking. The teachings on war and peace are influenced by the concrete situations that faced our nation at different times and the bishops' understanding of the Church's role in society. Because of this, variation exists in the bishops' statements, in recognition that there are no definitive answers to questions concerning the morality of war or the establishment of peace.[21]

The Challenge of Peace

The Challenge of Peace: God's Promise and Our Response was published in a context somewhat different from ours today, but its lessons are still relevant. Written during the height of the Cold War, its primary focus was the nuclear arms race between the United States and the Soviet Union. Because the Soviet Union no longer exists, we will not focus on nuclear weapons as such, although we recognize that nuclear proliferation remains a grave concern for our world. Rather, we will focus on the philosophical and theological foundations underlying the bishops' teachings on justified war and their overall just war doctrine.

Foundations for Justified War

The Challenge of Peace opens with the recognition that people hold differing points of view concerning armed conflict. The bishops acknowledge that the Church's tradition concerning war is "long and complex," and that its teachings "seldom give a simple answer to complex questions" (no. 7). There is no single Catholic response to war. People can and do have differing perspectives, which must be dealt with honestly and with respect.

The bishops acknowledge this diversity by noting that their contributions in this pastoral should not be taken as the "last word." The principles of CST embody universal truths (human dignity, common good, solidarity, etc.), but the actual application of these principles can differ depending on particular circumstances. Consequently, the bishops insist, their teachings on warfare do not carry the same moral authority as do their teachings concerning universal moral principles or formal Church teaching. They clearly state that not every teaching in the document carries the same moral "weight," and that people "of good will" can disagree about how their conclusions should be applied. However, they also caution that while not always binding in conscience, their moral judgments should be given "serious attention and consideration" by all Catholics as they seek to determine whether their own moral judgments are consistent with the Gospel message (nos. 9–10).

Having delineated the "limits" of the pastoral, the bishops identify two important foundations essential for understanding their teachings concerning war. The first is human dignity:

> At the center of the Church's teaching on peace and at the center of all Catholic social teaching are the transcendence of God and the dignity of the human person. The human person is the clearest reflection of God's presence in the world; all of the Church's work in pursuit of both justice and peace is designed to protect and promote the dignity of every person. (no. 15)

Stressing the dignity of human life and repeating the claim that all people have a duty to promote this dignity by working for justice and peace, the bishops quote the following warning from the Second Vatican Council:

> Men of this generation should realize that they will have to render an account for their warlike behavior; the destiny of generations to come depends largely on the decisions they make today.[22]

War is not something to be taken lightly. When we speak about war we are, by definition, speaking about the ending of the lives of others through violent means. As such, Christians should approach any discussion of war with a sense of "fear and reverence" because we are speaking about the taking from another human being God's preeminent gift: life.

The second foundation concerns the two audiences that the document seeks to reach: the Catholic faithful and the wider civil community. Catholics are called to form their consciences in accord with Scripture and the universal moral principles held by the Church. This formation is to be done in faith and, in light of the 1971 Synod of Bishops' exhortation that "action on behalf of justice and participation in the transformation of the world" are a "constitutive dimension" of preaching the gospel message, its implications are to be lived out in the secular world. As the bishops are entrusted with conveying Church teachings to the faithful, *The Challenge of Peace* intends to help Catholics form their consciences in light of the Church's message concerning war and peace.

The second audience — the wider civil community — encompasses people of diverse religions, races, and national origins. The bishops speak to this wider audience as well because the moral principles they cite are binding on all people.

> The wider civil community, although it does not share the same vision of faith, is equally bound by certain key moral principles. For all men and women find in the depth of their consciences a law written on the human heart by God. From this law, reason draws moral norms. These norms do not exhaust the gospel vision, but they speak to critical questions affecting . . . the limits of acceptable action by individuals and nations on issues of war and peace. (nos. 16–17)

The bishops hold that "certain key moral principles" are binding on all people because of their capacity to "reason." Recall from chapter 2 that we are to conform our actions to what we "know" to be correct moral behavior as revealed to us through a rightly formed conscience. We can "know" correct moral behavior through the natural law, the "law written on the human heart by God." Natural law is understood by the Church to be open to all people — it is not reserved for Christians alone. Natural law refers to the fact that through our capacity to reason we can understand and apply moral norms that offer us a guide for how we are to act. The moral principles that underlie the bishops' statement on justified war are based in human reason; therefore they apply to, and are morally binding upon, all people — regardless of their religious tradition.

The Just War Doctrine

The United States bishops begin their explanation of just war doctrine by claiming a "presumption in favor of peace." This presumption can be summarized as follows. (1) We should do no harm to our neighbors. (2) How we treat our enemy is the "key test" of how we love our neighbor. And (3) the taking of even one life is a prospect that we should consider "with fear and trembling" (no. 80). When faced with a serious international crisis, our first inclination should be to seek a peaceful resolution, not immediately go to war. The bishops argue that the decision to go to war "requires extraordinarily strong reasons" for overriding the presumption in favor of peace and that even a justifiable defensive war should be accepted only "as a sad necessity" (no. 83).

With this "presumption in favor of peace," the question remains, "Can war ever be justified?" The bishops, drawing upon the Church's historical just war teachings, go on to state that although regrettable, war legitimately can be waged with the express purpose of restraining evil and protecting society from those who seek to do it harm. They cite Saint Augustine's "classic case" of war being justified when it is fought to protect the innocent,[23] as well as the Second Vatican Council's claim that "as long as the danger of war persists and there is no international authority with the necessary competence and power, governments cannot be denied the right of lawful self-defense, once all peace efforts have failed" (no. 81).[24] Thus, although the U.S. bishops maintain a presumption against war, they acknowledge situations where recourse to war can be morally justified.

Assuming that war can be justified, what moral principles must we consider in the decision to go to war, and what principles must govern its conduct? The bishops here speak of the *jus ad bellum*—the law for going to war—and the *jus in bello*—the law in war.[25] In the following pages we explain these principles and, in order to ground them more concretely in our world, we examine them in light of the war on terror. Our purpose is not to make a political statement but to seek to uphold what the United States bishops maintain in *The Harvest of Justice*:

> The just war tradition is not a weapon to be used to justify a political conclusion or a set of mechanical criteria that automatically yields a simple answer, but a way of moral reasoning to discern the ethical limits of action. Policy-makers, advocates, and opponents

of the use of force need to be careful not to apply the tradition selectively, simply to justify their own positions.[26]

Principles of *Jus ad Bellum*

Just Cause

The United States bishops claim that war is justified only when it is used to confront a "real and certain danger" to the innocent, when it is used to preserve the conditions necessary for a decent human existence, or when it is used to protect human rights. Force may be employed to "correct a grave, public evil," understood primarily as "aggression or massive violation of the basic rights of whole populations."[27]

Depending on how we interpret the just cause principle, we can come to very different conclusions about how it has been applied in the war on terror. Few would dispute that the United States faced a "real and certain" danger in the wake of the 9/11 attack. More than three thousand innocent lives were lost that day, and the terrorists made it clear that they were planning further attacks. Therefore our government had the right and the duty to strike Al Qaeda and the Taliban government that supported it in Afghanistan. Al Qaeda and the Taliban posed a grave threat to our rights and freedoms, and our government went to war to protect us.

Iraq is a different story. While Afghanistan offered a pretty clear example of a "real and certain threat," it is more difficult to make this claim about Iraq. Certainly Saddam Hussein posed a grave threat to the people of Iraq as he was directly responsible for the deaths of many Kurds, Shiites, and even members of his own political party. He also posed a threat to Iraq's neighbors; he fought a decade-long war with Iran in the 1980s, invaded Kuwait in 1990, and continually hinted at hostility toward Saudi Arabia. A just cause argument could have been made on the part of the people of Iraq and the neighboring countries.

But did Iraq pose a "real and certain danger" to the United States? Unfortunately, even to this day we do not have a definitive answer to this question. The primary threat claimed by President George W. Bush and others was the existence of weapons of mass destruction (WMDs). Now, contrary to the claims of the president's critics, there was reason to believe that these weapons existed in pre-war Iraq. Saddam Hussein had used chemical weapons in the past—most notably against innocent Kurds in Halabja (March 1988)—so he clearly did possess such weapons at some time. When the 1991 Gulf War ended with a cease-fire (not a surrender), one of the conditions of the cease-fire was that United Nations inspectors would have full access to Iraq's weapons factories and stockpiles. However, during the 1990s and up until the weeks before the 2003 invasion, this access was repeatedly denied. During this period, the United Nations passed numerous resolutions requiring Iraq to open itself to weapons inspections; Saddam Hussein simply ignored them. In the months leading up to the March 2003 invasion, most members of the United States Congress (both Democrats and Republicans), the international community, and the press believed these weapons existed. In this sense, one could argue that Iraq did indeed pose a "real and certain danger" to the United States and its interests in the region.

Now, years after the invasion, comprehensive searches have yet to turn up any WMDs. This has led many to ask whether President Bush and his administration "hyped" prewar intelligence to make Saddam Hussein appear to be more of a threat than he actually was. The present text cannot hope to answer this question; we simply note that the existence or nonexistence of WMDs in Iraq poses serious questions in terms of the just cause principle. Primary among them is "can we ever know for sure whether our cause for going to war is truly just?" Other, related questions follow: "What happens to the just cause principle when intelligence is flawed?" "What happens to it when a rogue government thumbs its nose at the world community and leads everyone to believe that it has WMDs—regardless of whether it does or not?" "What happens to it when there are serious questions about the motives of those who make the decision to go to war?" Each of these questions underlies the overall question of whether the U.S. and coalition nations had just cause to invade Iraq. It also begs the question of whether a war can be justified even if, unbeknown to political leaders, the reasons offered for it may not be.

Competent Authority

The second *jus ad bellum* principle deals with the question of who may legitimately declare war. The United States bishops teach that war can only be declared by competent authority, those individuals entrusted with the responsibility of protecting the common good of society. In the United States, this duty lies primarily with the president and the Congress. Constitutionally, Congress holds the power to declare war.[28]

In *The Challenge of Peace* the United States bishops point out that while the Constitution clearly mandates how our nation may legitimately declare war, the decision to do so is often controversial. They cite Vietnam and state that some of our nation's "bitterest divisions" have occurred over the question of whether a president acted legally by involving our nation in a "de-facto" war, one that was never formally declared. Similarly, critics have argued that President Bush's decision to invade Iraq was unconstitutional because Congress never formally declared war on Iraq, or because it violated the War Powers Resolution of 1973. But in fact President Bush was legally authorized to order the invasion of Iraq when the House and Senate jointly passed Public Law 107–243, *Authorization for Use of Military Force against Iraq*, on October 16, 2002. Section 3 of the document specifically states:

> The President is authorized to use the Armed Forces of the United States as he determines to be necessary and appropriate to (1) defend the national security of the United States against the continuing threat posed by Iraq; and (2) enforce all relevant United Nations Security Council resolutions regarding Iraq.[29]

Although critics may legitimately oppose the war on other grounds, competent authority is not one of them. President Bush did act constitutionally when he ordered the invasion of Iraq.

Comparative Justice

The third *jus ad bellum* principle, comparative justice, is arguably the most difficult one to apply. Comparative justice asks which side is sufficiently "right" in a dispute, and are the values at stake critical enough to override the presumption against war? Posed differently, this principle asks whether the values involved with a potential conflict can ever justify the taking of human life. From the perspective of the United States bishops, the basis for this principle is human dignity. As stated at various points throughout this text, the Catholic Church always seeks to uphold the dignity and sacredness of human life. Any decision to go to war must be weighed against the recognition that war necessarily entails the loss of life.

Comparative justice asks, "How exactly do we compare the values we are seeking to achieve through the use of military force against the value of human life?" At the onset of the war in Iraq, supporters argued that the invasion was intended to protect our own interests and bring democracy to the Iraqi people — certainly good values to pursue. Opponents countered by questioning whether these perceived values were worth the lives of American soldiers and innocent Iraqis. This was a very difficult question at the time and one that has taken on even greater significance as we look back on what has happened in Iraq since March 2003. The Iraq example points out two difficulties: (1) as is often the case, we recognize viable arguments on both sides of the dispute, and (2) even if we are correct in what we are trying to achieve, how do we determine whether the value of our "correctness" is greater than the value of human life? Although the principle of comparative justice may be fairly simple to understand, it is extremely difficult to apply. Every competent authority has the moral obligation to consider seriously all values inherent in a conflict before making the decision to go to war.

Further adding to the difficulty of applying this principle, the United States bishops point out that comparative justice means that no nation can act as if it has "absolute justice" (God) on its side. Christianity maintains that God's will for humanity incorporates peace, freedom, and the well-being of all people. However, even if we believe our nation is upholding these values in a conflict, this does not mean that God is absolutely on our side. All too often we see people in our country making this claim, and it should make us uneasy. Certainly there are situations where our nation and its allies held the moral high ground, for example World War II. However, there have been other conflicts where we did not. The bishops caution that comparative justice should "relativize" any absolute claim that a party would make, while also "restraining the use of force" even when there is a legitimate justification for entering into conflict.

It is important to clarify that the caution against claiming "absolute justice" does not apply solely to the United States. It applies to everyone, including Islamic fundamentalists who wage campaigns of terror across the globe. Al Qaeda members and their affiliates think they are doing Allah's (God's) will when they attack military and civilian targets, but in fact they are not. Christianity has learned through the Crusades, the Inquisition, and the various "religious wars" following the Protestant Reformation that you cannot force another to accept your religious beliefs through coercion or the threat of violence. Most Muslims recognize this, but there is a minority who believe they have a mandate from Allah to "convert" the world to their understanding of Islam by any means possible—or die trying. This is wrong. No matter what our beliefs, we can never justify using God's name to murder innocent people.

Right Intention

The fourth *jus ad bellum* principle is right intention. The United States bishops explain that right intention is closely related to just-cause because a nation may only engage in war for reasons stated under the just cause principle: to protect innocent life, to preserve the conditions necessary for life, and to protect human rights. They add that while right intention is most often understood in terms of the decision to go to war, it also applies once conflict has begun *(jus in bello)*. During hostilities, it means the parties must seek reconciliation and a peaceful resolution to the conflict. It also means they should refrain from "unnecessarily destructive acts" and from imposing "unreasonable conditions" on the opponent. Right intention means that the goal of any military conflict should be to reestablish peace *(tranquilitas ordinis)*, a peace which is more substantial than what would have existed had the war not been fought.

In debates leading up to the invasion of Iraq, "right intention" was cited by many on both sides of the issue. Opponents questioned President Bush's, as well as British Prime Minister Tony Blair's, motivations for authorizing the invasion. Was protection of the people of the United States really the primary intention, or were there ulterior motives? For example, was the real intention of the invasion to protect oil supplies? Was it really intended as a "slap in the face" to the United Nations and in particular to those nations (France, Germany, and Russia) that consistently opposed military intervention in Iraq? Was it intended to promote the interests of the "military-industrial complex" or to take care of "unfinished business" from the first Bush administration? Supporters of the president argued that the proposed war was necessary to protect our national interests. Should our nation stand by and do nothing while Saddam Hussein threatened our allies in the Middle East? Should we condone the continued oppression of the Iraqi people or should we offer them the opportunity to live in freedom? In the aftermath of September 11, could we simply stand by and let Saddam Hussein aid and abet international terrorists? Was this not a battle of "good against evil," as our president had repeatedly stated? Although there is no evidence that Saddam Hussein was directly involved in the September 11 attacks, there is evidence that known international terrorists were living in Iraq, that terrorist organizations had established training camps in the country, and that Saddam Hussein was paying money to the families of Palestinian suicide bombers.

Again, our reason for identifying these questions is not to support or criticize President Bush or to claim that his motivations were justified or not. It is simply to state that in the months before the Iraq invasion numerous "right intention" questions were asked on both sides of the aisle, many of which still have not been answered. So what do we do? How are we to approach questions of right intention? As Catholic Christians we are called to evaluate each of them and, to the best of our ability, make prudential judgments in light of the information we have at the time. We must be careful in doing this, however, because we rarely have "all the facts." The U.S. bishops prophetically allude to this reality in *The Harvest of Justice* when they state that application of the just war tradition is dependent upon the availability of accurate information—information that is "not easily obtained in the pressured political context in which such decisions must be made."[30] One of the unfortunate results of the debate over Iraq is the tendency on the part of some to condemn not only the decisions of our president and his advisors, but also to condemn them as people. As we stated in chapter 2, we must refrain from this practice for the simple reason that we cannot read the hearts and consciences of others. This ability is reserved for God alone.

Last Resort

The United States bishops hold that war can be legitimately waged only as a last resort or only after all efforts at peace have been tried and failed. As with the other principles, last resort is not as simple as it appears. The bishops admit there are "formidable problems" with applying the principle in a concrete context because there is no international body with the authority to mediate international disputes effectively or to prevent the spread of conflict through the use of peacekeeping troops. Since *Peace on Earth* (1963) CST has looked to the United Nations to assume this mediating and preventive role. Unfortunately, the United Nations has repeatedly proved unable to fulfill this important function, as genocides in Rwanda, Congo, Sudan, and the former Yugoslavia demonstrate. Until some international body can effectively mediate conflict between nations, "formidable problems" concerning the application of this principle will remain.

Some of the concrete difficulties with applying the principle of last resort can be seen in the ongoing war on terror. Most Americans recognize the moral legitimacy of invading Afghanistan. The United States, along with its allies, knew that Afghanistan's Taliban government had been aiding, funding, and protecting Al Qaeda terrorists and that the Taliban was complicit in numerous Al Qaeda attacks, including 9/11. Following 9/11 President Bush issued an ultimatum to the Taliban: turn over the Al Qaeda leadership, particularly Osama bin Laden, or face serious repercussions. The president even gave the Taliban a period of time within which to comply. When the Taliban refused, the United States and its allies invaded Afghanistan, and the Taliban was forcibly removed from power.

Iraq is a different story. As we previously noted, President Bush, the United States Congress, and much of the world community believed that Saddam Hussein had stockpiled WMDs. The United Nations had drafted numerous resolutions demanding that Iraq open itself to inspections, resolutions that Iraq simply ignored, and there were fears that Saddam Hussein was trying to procure nuclear weapons as well. However, in the weeks before the invasion, Iraq bowed to international pressure and allowed UN weapons inspectors back into the country. The inspectors did not find anything in the short time they had to search, but they continually asked their superiors to give them more time. President Bush effectively said no. He set a date for the inspectors to leave Iraq and did not back down even when informed that the inspectors had not completed their investigations.

President Bush's decision to go to war when he did appears to be, at least on the surface, a violation of the principle of last resort. Saddam Hussein had repeatedly ignored United Nations resolutions, and he posed a threat to stability in the region, but the fact that weapons inspections were taking place almost to the day the bombs started falling renders highly problematic the claim that the invasion was an act of last resort. It seems that the president could have pursued other options, such as continuing the inspections. Assuming these options did exist, it is difficult to argue that the invasion was morally justified in terms of the principle of last resort, and thus it should not have overridden the presumption in favor of peace.

Probability of Success

The principle of the probability of success states that war can only be justified if there is a reasonable probability that the military operation will be successful in bringing about its intended result. For example, Cuba could invade the United States with the hope of establishing a socialist society. However, because there is little probability the effort would be successful, the invasion would not be morally justified. The principle seeks to prevent an "irrational resort to force" or a "hopeless resistance" when the outcome of a potential conflict is already known.

Relative to the war in Iraq, probability of success takes on several meanings. The initial invasion of Iraq was extremely successful in terms of the rapid defeat of the Iraqi military and the fall of Saddam Hussein's regime. However, due to miscalculations and outright mistakes, the post-invasion situation has been a mess. In light of what we've seen in Iraq, it is appropriate to expand the question to include the probability that our overall objective will be successful after the military operation has ended. The intent of President Bush and his administration was to create a democracy in Iraq, bringing peace and prosperity to the region as a whole. At the time of this writing, this goal is far from realization. Many have stated that the administration overestimated the response of the Iraqi people and underestimated the resolve of the insurgency. Others have stated that our nation did not invest enough assets to "win" the peace, and that the Iraqi people were never even capable of sustaining a free society.

All of these are astute observations, and each begs the question of whether the overall goal of bringing democracy to Iraq was achievable in the first place. In early 2003 the Bush administration, and probably a majority of the American people, believed that it was achievable, but was that a reasoned probability or naïve optimism? Granted, there is still the possibility that Iraq could become a stable democracy. But if nothing else, our nation's experiences in Iraq should give us pause. In the future we need to ask ourselves exactly what are we trying to achieve through our use of military force and, even following a military "victory," what is the reasonable probability that our overall efforts will be successful.

Proportionality

The principle of proportionality holds that in contemplating the decision to go to war, the competent authorities must determine to the best of their ability whether the costs involved in engaging in conflict are proportionate to the good the war is expected to achieve. Say, for example, there is a rogue state that is threatening to attack the United States or our interests around the world. In contemplating military action, our leaders would have to determine the "good" they are seeking to achieve and then use only proportionate military means to achieve it. Afghanistan provides a good example of this. In the weeks immediately following 9/11, some Americans argued that we should "nuke" Afghanistan in response to the Taliban's support for Al Qaeda. Although the anger and frustration that many people felt toward the Taliban was understandable, a nuclear strike on Afghanistan would not have been a proportionate response. A nation is permitted to do only "what is necessary" to achieve its military goal and in this particular case, the "evil" consequences of nuclear weapons certainly would have outweighed any "good" that could have come from their use.

The United States bishops recognize there are many challenges to applying the principle of proportionality in a concrete military situation. We know that before making the decision to go to war, officials and their advisors have to calculate what it would cost our nation to engage in a military conflict. The problem here is determining exactly what is meant by "cost." Cost certainly includes money. It is expensive to wage war and the financial burden must be borne by taxpayers. It is also important to keep in mind, as the bishops rightly point out, that when financial resources are dedicated to waging war, less is available to aid the poor and those in need. In fact, it has been often stated that in times of war those who bear the heaviest financial burden—those who "pay" the most—are the poor and most vulnerable members of society.[31]

The principle of proportionality also demands that we examine "cost" in nonmonetary ways. Certainly the greatest cost in war is the loss of human life. War means death, the death of soldiers and of innocent civilians. Moreover, who determines when the cost of human life is too high? Our president? Congress? High-level military officers? On what criteria should they base the decision? Are one thousand casualties acceptable to meet a goal? Five thousand? One hundred thousand? As the Church seeks to uphold the dignity of all people, the cost of human life is the single most important factor to be considered in any decision to go to war. As the bishops repeatedly warn, the decision to take human life should be approached with "fear and trembling."

War also involves damage to the environment. No one can deny the profound effects that World Wars I and II had on the landscape of Europe, or the environmental degradation experienced by Korea and Vietnam as a result of wars waged there. Saddam Hussein ordered oil wells to be set ablaze as his army retreated from Kuwait in 1991. These fires took months to extinguish and wreaked untold environmental damage. In addition we do not always know the long-term effects that environmental damage inflicted by war may have on human life. How many Japanese were diagnosed with cancer and other illnesses following the atomic bombings of Hiroshima and Nagasaki? What have been the long-term effects? We simply do not know for sure. Nor do we know for sure how many Americans and Vietnamese suffer from the lingering effects of chemicals employed by our military in Vietnam. These environmental realities are not negligible costs of war. Although it may be difficult, if not impossible, to predict them all, they must be considered in any decision to engage in military conflict.

Finally, the United States bishops point to the fact that war involves many intangible costs as well. Before engaging in a military conflict, a nation must determine how its actions will affect people in other nations as well as its standing in the world community. The war on terror has certainly affected many people around the world, and it is no exaggeration to say that the war in Iraq has cost the United States considerable international respect. The bishops further claim that there are also spiritual costs to war. Every person killed or injured, every home destroyed, and every life forever changed by war has a profound effect on people's spiritual lives.

Overall, do the financial, human, environmental, psychological, spiritual, and other social costs make war worthwhile? The principle of proportionality demands that we consider this question seriously before deciding to go to war.

Jus in Bello

Assuming that each of the above conditions is met so that armed conflict is at least morally permissible, what moral principles govern conduct while actively engaged in war? These are the *jus in bello* principles.

Proportionality

The first *jus in bello* principle is proportionality. The United States bishops explain proportionality *in bello* — much as they explained proportionality *ad bellum* — by insisting that a nation's "response to aggression must not exceed the nature of the aggression" (no. 103). In other words, the tactics employed by a military force during war must be proportionate to the injury that it, or its nation, suffered at the hands of the aggressor. These tactics must never exceed "what is necessary" to achieve victory.

> When confronting choices among specific military options, the question asked by proportionality is: once we take into account not only the military advantages that will be achieved by using the means but also all the harms reasonably expected to follow from using it, can its use still be justified?[32]

The classic example of the principle of proportionality is the use of nuclear weapons. Say, once again, that Cuba attacks the United States using conventional tactics. Our military would certainly be justified in using force to defend us; it could even launch a counter-attack to neutralize the threat. However, the use of nuclear weapons in response to Cuba's attack would be disproportionate because (1) it would exceed the nature of the injury suffered, and (2) it would have devastating consequences for Cuba (not to mention Florida!) far beyond that which would be necessary to achieve victory.

Many would argue that this example is absurd. However, during the height of the Cuban missile crisis in 1962, it was not so far-fetched. President John F. Kennedy faced a potentially daunting decision about what to do if the Soviet Union went ahead with its plan to place nuclear missiles less than 100 miles off the coast of the United States. Luckily, the Soviet Union backed down.

Unfortunately, President Harry Truman was not so lucky. In 1945, as World War II was drawing to a close, Truman made the *in bello* decision to drop atomic bombs on the Japanese cities of Hiroshima and Nagaski. People have debated the morality of his decision ever since, largely on the principle of proportionality. Supporters of Truman's decision argue that if the atomic bombs had not been dropped, our nation would have been forced to invade the Japanese mainland, costing the lives of many thousands of American (and Japanese) soldiers. Thus, the decision to drop the bombs was proportionate. Critics argue that the act was disproportionate (and immoral) because the bombs not only destroyed military installations, but also killed tens of thousands of noncombatants. They also argue that the nature of the threat posed by Japan at the time did not rise to the level of using atomic weapons, because by the summer of 1945 Japan was clearly nearing defeat.

Although it is one thing to look back on a situation after sixty or more years and make moral pronouncements, the decision of whether or not to drop the bombs was precisely what faced Truman and his advisors. They had to weigh the perceived consequences of using atomic weapons (preserving American lives, ending the war, loss of innocent Japanese lives) against those of not using them (loss of American lives, continuing the war, preserving innocent Japanese lives), and they had to make this decision "in the moment" without the benefit of hindsight. The reality that faced Truman illustrates well the difficulty in applying the principle of proportionality in a concrete context.

Before continuing, we must note that the disproportionately destructive power of modern-day nuclear weapons has caused the Catholic Church to speak out very strongly against their use. Some of the most pointed comments come from the bishops of the Second Vatican Council who—while never condemning Truman's decision—state that nuclear weapons inflict a level of destruction "far exceeding the bounds of legitimate defense," and that "any act of war aimed indiscriminately at the destruction of entire cities or of extensive areas along with their population is a crime against God and man [meriting] unequivocal and unhesitating condemnation."[33] In *The Challenge of Peace*, the United States bishops restate this condemnation but offer tacit acceptance of these weapons for deterrence purposes. Nations may legitimately possess nuclear weapons, but they may only posses as many "as are necessary" to prevent other nations from using them, and this deterrence must always be viewed as a first step toward disarmament.[34]

Discrimination

The second *jus in bello* principle is discrimination. Discrimination in this sense refers to distinguishing who is actually a combatant and who is not. In effect, discrimination is the principle of noncombatant immunity. As the Church's historical tradition and the United States bishops have maintained, war can be waged only against combatants. It is never morally permissible to intentionally attack the innocent.

The principle of discrimination appears clear, don't attack innocent civilians, but with the war on terror we know that its application poses many challenges. For example, during the 2003 invasion of Iraq, United States bombs targeted Iraqi infrastructure with the intent of crippling the military. However, this targeting also affected the well-being of civilians because military targets such as bridges, highways, electrical generating stations, and water treatment plants serve civilians as well. Further complicating the issue was that some combatants used civilian buildings to camouflage military activities. In the war in Iraq, terrorists and insurgents have located military production facilities in urban areas and have used schools, hospitals, and private homes to stockpile weapons and plan attacks. Then, when these stockpiles and safehouses are hit, the insurgents provoke mass demonstrations by claiming that our military specifically targeted innocent men, women and children. Insurgents have also fired upon United States troops from mosques, knowing that the rules of engagement will not allow our soldiers to pursue them or fire back. The question that must be asked is what distinguishes a military target from a civilian one. Are we morally permitted to destroy a military target even if we know that innocent civilians likely will be killed?

Another issue involves the direct targeting of civilians by insurgents. Suicide (or homicide) bombers in Iraq have continually targeted markets, mosques, restaurants, and even religious pilgrimages, resulting in the deaths of thousands of innocent people. Unfortunately, these activities are not unique to Iraq. Suicide bombings are not infrequent in Israel, and resurgent Taliban fighters in Afghanistan have resorted to the suicide tactics perfected by their counterparts in Iraq. Al Qaeda has targeted weddings in Jordan and dance clubs in Bali — not to mention the twin towers in New York City. In September 2004, Chechen rebels (themselves Islamic extremists) attacked a school in the Russian city of Beslan and held over 1200 people hostage for three days. When Russian special forces stormed the building, almost 350 people were killed, including 186 children. These examples pose serious challenges to our application of the principle of discrimination. What do we do when our enemy has stashed weapons in a school or a hospital? Do we attack it? What do we do in a standoff with terrorists who have surrounded themselves with "human shields"? Do we engage them knowing full well that innocent lives will be lost? What happens if, God forbid, terrorists hijack another passenger plane with the intention of crashing it somewhere in the United States? Do we shoot it down? Again, in any armed conflict, what is our moral obligation when a justifiable military action is likely to cause serious harm to innocent civilians?

Jus post Bellum

As we conclude our discussion of just war principles it is important to point out that since the United States bishops first issued *The Challenge of Peace* in 1983 and *The Harvest of Justice* in 1993 there has been a significant development in the way Catholic ethicists view just war theory. In addition to the *jus ad bellum* and *jus in bello* moral principles, many ethicists today are speaking of the *jus post bellum* or "law after war." Basically the *jus post bellum* asks, "What moral duties does the victorious party have to the defeated party once combat has ceased?" Actually, *jus post bellum* is not new: in the sixteenth century Tommaso Cajetan spoke of the need to make restitution to one's enemy after hostilities have ended. But in light of the development of new weapons systems and the methods of fighting the war on terror, it is gaining new attention. Catholic ethicists and others have used a number of principles to define the *jus post bellum*. Here we will identify three.

Vindication of Rights

The principle of just cause states, in part, that war is justified if its purpose is to reestablish the rights of those who were unjustly deprived of them by an aggressor, and as soon as these rights are reestablished, the conflict must cease. In terms of *jus post bellum*, vindication of rights means that it is unjust for the victorious nation to realize any gains above and beyond the reestablishment of basic human rights. If the victorious nation has seized land, capital, or other benefits from its enemy through the course of battle, these must be returned.

Reconciliation

This principle states that once hostilities have ended, all parties to a conflict must repent of their actions. The nature of war is such that inevitably both sides in any conflict will have done wrong; each party bears varying degrees of culpability for the suffering and death that resulted from actions taken before and during the conflict. One practical application of this principle is that the terms of surrender must be public knowledge to ensure that the settlement is transparent to all parties. Moreover, these terms of surrender must not demean or unnecessarily punish the defeated nation to avoid fostering resentment that could reignite hostilities. Reconciliation also means that individuals on either side who have committed crimes against humanity must be tried and punished as war criminals to ensure that society will know that this person will never again engage the nation in an unjust conflict or otherwise pose a threat to its safety and security.

Restoration

Restoration means that as a matter of justice, the victorious nation has the duty to help return the defeated nation to a functional civil society where all people have the opportunity to live in a dignified and meaningful manner. Here ethicists point to Augustine's *tranquilitas ordinis* as the ultimate goal of any restoration effort. Restoration also means that the victorious party must "clean up" the battlefield once hostilities have ceased. This includes, but is not limited to, removing such weapons as land mines or trip wires, and working to counter the effects of the various weapons systems employed during the conflict, including gas, defoliant agents, and depleted uranium.[35]

Similar to *jus ad bellum* and *jus in bello*, the *jus post bellum* principles are relatively easy to understand in theory, but can be difficult to apply. The development of new and exponentially more deadly weapons systems over the past fifty years and the particular challenges presented by the war on terror make it difficult to pin down exactly how these principles should be put into practice in today's world. Nevertheless, we do know that much good has come from the *jus post bellum* principles when they have been applied. Following World War II the United States and other allied nations helped to rebuild Western Europe to the great benefit of the people living there. It is no coincidence that nations aided by the Marshall Plan over 50 years ago have today become some of the most prosperous on earth. The Japanese people also benefited greatly from massive post-war aid programs offered by the United States, with the result that Japan is now one of our strongest allies. Exactly how the *jus post bellum* principles will play out in the future, particularly in Iraq and Afghanistan, remains to be seen. But as a matter of justice, any nation must accept the moral responsibility for putting them into practice, even before making the decision to go to war.

Before leaving *The Challenge of Peace*, we would like to highlight a final point that has relevance for our just war discussion. It concerns the moral paradox that many Christians face when it comes to questions of war:

> We believe work to develop non-violent means of fending off aggression and resolving conflict best reflects the call of Jesus both to love and to justice. . . . But, on the other hand, the fact of aggression, oppression and injustice in our world also serves to legitimate the resort to weapons and armed force in defense of justice. We must recognize the reality of the paradox we face as Christians living in the context of the world as it presently exists. We must continue to articulate our belief that love is possible and the only real hope for all human relations, and yet accept that force, even deadly force, is sometimes justified and that nations must provide for their defense.[36]

This brief yet powerful passage captures the moral dilemma facing many American Catholics today. No one wants war. However, because there are people in the world whose stated purpose is to kill us or convert us to their understanding of Islam, we must be willing to defend our freedom. The question is, how do we do it? Can we defend our freedom without recourse to arms? Can we maintain our security without going to war? It would seem that at this point the answer to these questions is no. International terrorists have shown no willingness to discuss diplomatic solutions to our differences, and the only practical response seems to be armed conflict. If this is the case, what does it mean to be a believing Catholic in the world of international terrorism? What should be our response? Should we support our nation's actions in the war on terror, actions that we know will bring about the deaths of many people, or should we continue to seek peaceful resolutions? These are difficult questions and there is no single answer to them. The paradox identified by the United States bishops underscores the great moral challenge facing not only Catholics, but all people "of good will."

The Harvest of Justice Is Sown in Peace

In 1993, the United States Catholic bishops commemorated the ten-year anniversary of *The Challenge of Peace* by publishing a follow-up pastoral entitled *The Harvest of Justice Is Sown in Peace*. This pastoral reexamined many of the issues explored in *The Challenge of Peace* in light of changes in the international situation, most notably the fall of the Soviet Union. The bishops highlight concrete ways that the international community, and the United States in particular, can work to bring about peace in the world.

The bishops begin by restating several themes discussed in *The Challenge of Peace*. They assert that diversity of opinion can exist within the Church regarding questions of war, they emphasize the principle of human dignity by observing that at the heart of all violence lies a lack of respect for the other, and they argue that true peace cannot be realized until all people fully protect the dignity of society's most vulnerable and stand up for human life everywhere. This "consistent life ethic" is the essential "starting point" for genuine peacemaking.[37]

The most comprehensive and lasting contribution of *The Harvest of Justice* is its "Agenda for Peacemaking." Here the bishops focus on five specific areas that must be "improved" if the world community is ever to achieve a lasting peace. The first concerns the international political order. CST has always maintained the need for an "integrated international system" that guarantees human rights for all and that fosters the common good by "transforming" economic and political interdependence into a greater sense of international solidarity. One way to achieve this goal is by strengthening the only international political entity that we have on earth today, the United Nations. In *Peace on Earth*, Pope John XXIII effectively "baptized" the United Nations and its *Universal Declaration of*

Human Rights (1948) by stating that the United Nations' "essential" purpose includes maintaining peace in the world while fostering among its people relations built upon equality, mutual respect, and cooperation.[38] The United States bishops share John XXIII's vision but also state that the United Nations' most urgent and complex challenge in the modern world (1993) is improving its ability to reduce conflict. As such, they urge nations, and in particular the United States, to support the United Nations in its overall mission.

It is important to point out, however, that the bishops also call upon the United Nations to reform itself. They specifically identify the organization's waste and bureaucracy that so often renders it ineffective in dealing with international conflict. Again, the various genocides since 1993 demonstrate this ineffectiveness, as does the scandal in its administration of Iraq's "oil for food" program in the years following the first Gulf War. The ongoing challenge for the United Nations is to reexamine its mandate and its operations so that it can effectively foster peace by working toward the common good of all people.[39]

A second area where the bishops claim there "needs to be improvement" is human rights. The bishops hold that the securing of human rights for all people is a moral priority for all nations. They argue that human rights include not only the civil and political rights (such as freedom of speech and freedom of assembly) that we enjoy in the United States, but also economic rights (right to work, right to a just wage, and right to adequate heath care) that we do not. Promoting the "full complement" of human rights is a "central priority" because authentic peace can be realized only when there is a true respect for the rights and dignity of all people.

The third area concerns sustained development. At the time the document was written (1993), the income gap between the world's richest and poorest nations was growing ever wider, despite decades of effort on the part of the United Nations and other organizations to narrow it. In 1960 the richest one-fifth of the world's population controlled two-thirds of the world's wealth. By 1993 their control had increased to more than four-fifths, while almost one billion people lived in absolute poverty. Aside from the moral issues involved, the income gap between wealthy and poor poses a great threat to world peace. When people who possess nothing see great wealth enjoyed by others, they feel resentment. It is no secret that Al Qaeda recruits new members by demonstrating the injustice of a world order that allows the privileged few to gain tremendous wealth while condemning the masses to wallow in poverty.

The United States bishops argue that to counter this ever-increasing income gap and foster world peace, we need to commit ourselves to sustained development. Echoing the teachings of Pope John XXIII and Pope Paul VI, the bishops claim that sustained development entails more than simple economic growth. Sustained development includes (1) addressing rampant poverty, (2) focusing on the "quality" of development in the industrialized world rather than its "quantity," (3) preserving the created order by embracing "environmentally sensitive" technology, and (4) maintaining population growth through programs that respect cultural, religious, and family values. To realize sustained development the international community needs to stop the ongoing flow of wealth from poor nations to rich ones. As discussed in chapter 5, trade policies need to ensure that poor nations receive fair value for their products. Foreign assistance and investment programs need to focus on empowering developing nations rather than on furthering the agendas of donors. And the massive and unpayable debts owed by many nations have to be dealt with in a fair and humane manner. The bishops' point is that there can be no lasting peace in the world without justice, and there can be no true justice as long as abject poverty exists.

The fourth area is the restraint of nationalism and the elimination of ethnic and religious violence. According to the bishops, the most disturbing threat to peace in the post–Cold War world (writing in 1993) is conflict based on national, ethnic, or religious difference. In the years since *The Harvest of Justice* was published, their analysis has proved astute. During April of 1994 in Rwanda, approximately eight hundred thousand people were murdered in an ethnic genocide while the world stood by and did nothing. The world again stood by while an estimated 4 million people died as either the direct or indirect result of long-standing ethnic and nationalistic conflict in the Democratic Republic of Congo. The world did intervene when Yugoslavia broke apart over ethnic and religious divisions in the 1990s, but could not prevent the killing of over one hundred thousand people. As this text goes to print, Sunni and Shiia Muslims are killing each other in Iraq, and hundreds of thousands have been killed, injured, or displaced in the Darfur region of Sudan.

In response to national, ethnic, and religious violence, the United States bishops propose a series of moral "values" that they hope governments will adopt to help quell conflict. The first is self-determination. The bishops maintain that self-determination is necessary because all people have the right to participate in shaping their political, economic, cultural, and religious identities. Examples of how to accomplish this include a greater respect for, and protection of, human rights and a renewed commitment on the part of every nation to create just political structures. Other values include a respect for minority rights whereby governments would protect minorities against injustice while also helping them to foster their own cultural and religious identities. Tolerance and solidarity are also necessary to build "unity out of diversity." Finally, formerly warring parties need to have a greater commitment to dialogue and reconciliation. The bishops admit that these values will be difficult to achieve in light of the many atrocities committed. However, as forgiveness is a central aspect of the Christian message, we must believe that love can overcome the historic cycles of violence and injustice, and that all people can learn to live in peace.

The final necessity for establishing a peaceful global order concerns the strengthening of cooperative international security. This area contains a number of different subtopics, but here we will discuss only one: nuclear proliferation. The bishops rightly point out that although the threat of nuclear annihilation has lessened with the fall of the Soviet Union, nuclear weapons still remain an important concern. In *The Challenge of Peace* they argued that the possession of nuclear weapons was morally legitimate only as a deterrent, and that the deterrence itself should be seen as a step on the path to full disarmament.[40] In *The Harvest of Justice*, they reiterate this teaching and call for deep cuts in our nation's nuclear arsenals. They also support a halt to nuclear testing and warn against the growing threat of nuclear proliferation. They add that the United States must take steps to reduce the threat of nuclear terrorism, and that we have a moral obligation to help prevent the spread of nuclear, chemical, and biological weapons around the world.

The bishops' warning against nuclear proliferation is as relevant today as it was in 1993. In recent years we have seen North Korea testing nuclear weapons and Iran working toward their development. In Pakistan, President Pervez Musharraf has been an "ally" of the United States in the war on terror, but many within his nation would like to overthrow him and seize control of his nation's nuclear arsenal. Intelligence agencies have been warning for years that terrorist organizations such as Al Qaeda have been seeking nuclear, chemical, and biological weapons. Although none were found, it is widely believed that Saddam Hussein was seeking to acquire nuclear weapons for his own arsenal.

As part of their claim that nuclear nonproliferation constitutes an essential aspect of establishing a peaceful international order, the bishops urge that the United States and other developed nations "should make the investments necessary to help ensure the development of stable, democratic governments in nations which have nuclear weapons or might seek to obtain them."[41] What do the bishops mean by "investments," and what do such investments entail? Some will argue that establishing a secure democracy is exactly what the United States seeks to achieve in Iraq, so investments can include military intervention. Others will argue that investments means monetary, political, or technical support, but not military action. Who is right? The bishops never offer a definitive answer so their words are open to interpretation. But if nothing else, they challenge us to ponder exactly how we will work toward nuclear nonproliferation.

The United States bishops conclude *The Harvest of Justice* with a word of caution and a challenge. They caution that although the power of the United States is undisputed, along with this power comes responsibility:

> Building peace, combating poverty and despair, and protecting freedom and human rights are not only moral imperatives, but also wise national priorities. . . . Reasonable international engagement is based on the conviction that our national interests and the interests of the international community, our common good, and the global common good, are intertwined.[42]

Written in 1993, this passage speaks even more directly to the reality of our world today. No one can deny that the world is now more interdependent than ever before, or that events or decisions made in our country have immediate, far-reaching consequences for millions of people around the world. For such reasons, when we as a nation exercise our power we must do so prudently and with a spirit of international solidarity.

The bishops also challenge U.S. Catholics and all people of "good will" by stating that the Christian commitment to peace rests on two separate but closely related ideals: Jesus' beatitude, "Blessed are the peacemakers, for they will be called children of God" and Pope Paul VI's oft-quoted phrase, "If you want peace, work for justice." Placed together, these ideals demonstrate that "to be a Christian is to be a peacemaker and to pursue peace is to work for justice."[43] The challenge is placed before us. As Catholics, we must recognize that peace is only possible when we live in right relationship with God and when we commit ourselves to fostering justice for all God's people. We need to confront violence in all its forms wherever it may exist, we must combat poverty and offer hope to those in despair here and around the globe, and we must work to assure that all of our nation's policies are directed toward the common good of the world community.

In closing, let us return to Dan, the college student thinking about joining ROTC. It should be clear that there is no inherent problem with him joining the military. Every Christian has a duty to defend society against unjust aggression; active military service is a morally legitimate means of doing so. In fact, our nation's best interests are served by having military officers trained to ask difficult moral questions in times of armed conflict. On the other hand, Dan does have to consider other factors in making his decision. His parents' overall objection to the use of force is morally legitimate and his Church, while not pacifist, does uphold the "presumption in favor of peace." The question for Dan is how to reconcile these values with the fact that the primary purpose of the military is to engage in armed conflict. Dan also has to think about what he will do if ordered to engage in an activity that he believes to be immoral, particularly one that violates one of the Church's just war principles. Will he have the strength to approach his commanding officers and seek clarification of the order? Then, assuming he does not receive a satisfactory response, will he have the strength to refuse the order and deal with the resulting repercussions? Each of these questions is very important and, particularly in light of the war on terror, every young person contemplating military service must reflect on them seriously. As a Catholic, Dan now knows that his Church does not offer ready-made answers to every question concerning justified war, but it does provide a moral framework within which his personal decision must be made.

Review Questions

1. Why is the Hebrew word *shalom* important in Jesus' teaching, "Blessed are the peacemakers"? What is Jesus' teaching on retaliation, and how does it provide "a strategy for victory"?

2. In *The Challenge of Peace* the United States bishops claim that Christian disciples — those who "give themselves over" to God's Reign — are called to embody what specific characteristics in their relationships with others?

3. According to Saint Augustine, what is the *tranquilitas ordinis*, and what relevance does it have for the question of justified war? How does Augustine define the principles of just cause and correct intention?

4. How does Saint Thomas Aquinas define the principles of sovereign authority, just cause, and right intention?

5. What important lessons concerning justice, respect for dignity, and living in right relationship with God are found in Pope John XXIII's *Christianity and Social Progress*?

6. In *On the Development of Peoples* and *A Call to Action*, what contribution does Pope Paul VI make to the Church's understanding of the relationship between justice and peace?

7. According to Pope John Paul II in *On Social Concern*, why is solidarity important for international relations?

8. In *The Challenge of Peace*, what two important "foundations" do the United States Catholic bishops identify as essential for understanding their teachings on war?

9. What is the presumption in favor of peace?

10. Under *jus ad bellum*, what are the principles of just cause, competent authority, and comparative justice?

11. What are the principles of right intention and last resort?

12. What is the principle of probability of success? How might the war in Iraq influence the way we view this principle?

13. What is the *jus ad bellum* principle of proportionality? What are the various ways we calculate "cost" in war?

14. What is the *jus in bello* principle of proportionality? Why do nuclear weapons pose such a challenge to this principle? How do the United States Catholic bishops view the use of nuclear weapons? How do they view the possession of nuclear weapons?

15. What is the principle of discrimination? What specific challenge does international terrorism pose to it?

16. In *The Harvest of Justice*, what do the United States bishops teach about civil and economic rights?

17. What moral values do the United States bishops propose to help end national, ethnic, and religious conflict?

ENDNOTES

1 United States Catholic bishops, *The Challenge of Peace: God's Promise and Our Response*, in *Catholic Social Thought: The Documentary Heritage*, ed. David O'Brien and Thomas Shannon (Maryknoll, NY: Orbis, 1995); and *The Harvest of Justice Is Sown in Peace: A Reflection of the National Conference of Bishops on the Tenth Anniversary of* "The Challenge of Peace" (Washington, DC: USCC, 1993).

2 See Benedict Viviano, OP, "The Gospel According to Matthew," in *The New Jerome Biblical Commentary* (Englewood Cliffs, NJ: Prentice Hall, 1990), 640.

3 Viviano, "Matthew," 641–42.

4 *The Challenge of Peace*, nos. 32–38.

5 Ibid., nos. 39–54, at no. 54.

6 The bishops cite Rom. 12:9–21.

7 *The Harvest of Justice*, 2–3.

8 Ambrose is discussed in *The Ethics of War: Classic and Contemporary Readings*, eds. Gregory Reichberg, Henrik Syse, and Endre Begby (Malden, MA: Blackwell Publishing, 2006), 67–68. See also J. Daryl Charles, *Between Pacifism and Jihad: Just War and the Christian Tradition* (Downers Grove, Il: InterVarsity Press, 2005), 37–40; and Joseph Fahey, *War and the Christian Conscience* (Maryknoll, NY: Orbis Books, 2005), 86–87.

9 See Paul Weithman, "Augustine's Political Philosophy," in *The Cambridge Companion to Augustine*, eds. E. Stump and N. Kretzmann (Cambridge: Cambridge University Press, 2001), 245–47. See also Reichberg et al., eds., *Ethics of War*, 70–82; Charles, *Between Pacifism and Jihad*, 40–45; and Fahey, *War and the Christian Conscience*, 88–89.

10 *Summa Theologiae*, II – II, q.40 a.1.

11 Pope John XXIII, *Christianity and Social Progress*, in O'Brien and Shannon, eds., *Catholic Social Thought*, nos. 157, 215.

12 Pope John XXIII, *Peace on Earth*, in O'Brien and Shannon, eds., *Catholic Social Thought*, no. 92.

13 Ibid., nos. 113 – 16. John XXIII's third point here was taken from Pope Pius XII's radio message of August 24, 1939.

14 Second Vatican Council, *Pastoral Constitution on the Church in the Modern World*, in O'Brien and Shannon, eds., *Catholic Social Thought*, nos. 77 – 78, 82.

15 1971 Synod of Bishops, *Justice in the World*.

16 Pope Paul VI, *On the Development of Peoples*, in O'Brien and Shannon, eds., *Catholic Social Thought*, no. 76.

17 Pope Paul VI, *A Call to Action*, in O'Brien and Shannon, eds., *Catholic Social Thought*, no. 43.

18 Pope John Paul II, *On Social Concern*, in O'Brien and Shannon, eds., *Catholic Social Thought*, no. 39.

19 Pope John Paul II, *On the Hundredth Anniversary of Rerum Novarum*, in O'Brien and Shannon, eds., *Catholic Social Thought*, no. 52.

20 *On the Hundredth Anniversary*, no. 52.

21 For an overview of the U.S. bishops' pastoral statements on war and peace, see Todd Whitmore, "The Reception of Catholic Approaches to Peace and War in the United States," in *Modern Catholic Social Teaching: Commentaries and Interpretations*, ed. Kenneth Himes (Washington, DC: Georgetown University Press, 2004).

22 *Pastoral Constitution on the Church in the Modern World*, no. 80.

23 The bishops cite Augustine's *City of God* (Book IV, C15): "War and conquest are a sad necessity in the eyes of men of principle, yet it would be still more unfortunate if wrongdoers should dominate just men."

24 *Pastoral Constitution on the Church in the Modern World*, no. 79.

25 These just war principles can be found in *The Challenge of Peace*, nos. 84 – 110.

26 *The Harvest of Justice*, 6.

27 Ibid., 5.

28 See Article 1, Section 8, of the *U.S. Constitution*.

29 The full text of PL 107– 243, *Authorization for Use of Military Force against Iraq* can be found on the U.S. State Department Web site at http://www.state.gov/r/pa/ei/rls/18714.htm.

30 *The Harvest of Justice*, 6.

31 See also *Peace on Earth*, n. 109 and the *Pastoral Constitution on the Church in the Modern World*, n. 81.

32 *The Challenge of Peace*, no. 105.

33 *Pastoral Constitution on the Church in the Modern World*, n. 80.

34 *The Challenge of Peace*, ns. 187-188.

35 See Mark Allman, "Postwar Justice," *America* (October 17, 2005): 9–13; and Kenneth Himes, "Intervention, Just War, and U.S. National Security," *Theological Studies* 65, no. 1 (March 2004): 141–57.

36 *The Challenge of Peace*, no. 78.

37 *The Harvest of Justice*, 1–2.

38 *Peace on Earth*, nos. 142–43.

39 The full "Agenda for Peacemaking" can be found in *The Harvest of Justice*, 8–18.

40 *The Challenge of Peace*, nos. 186–88.

41 *The Harvest of Justice*, 14.

42 Ibid., 18.

43 Ibid., 21.

8. MEDICAL ETHICS

Each one of us is born, lives, and dies. We are all vulnerable to illness or disease that can erode our well-being on the physical, psychological, spiritual, and even social levels. To deal with these issues, we seek medical care and enter into a relationship with health care professionals. The relationship forged between patient and health care professional brings with it a number of rights and duties that must be respected if medicine is to be practiced ethically.

How do we practice medicine in an ethical way, and what are the rights and duties of both the patient and the health care professional? These questions are very important today in light of the many technical advances in the medical profession. In this chapter, we explore five principles that form the moral foundation for the patient-professional relationship, and focus on two further general moral principles that are essential for the study of medical ethics as a whole. We also consider the practical implications of our discussion by examining ethical issues concerning the beginning of life and the end of life. We will focus on these because they are the times when we are most vulnerable. The notion of vulnerability helps remind us that the purpose of medicine is to serve the good of humanity as a whole. As such, our study of medical ethics from the Catholic perspective is grounded in the recognition of the inherent dignity of every human person and the need to uphold this dignity throughout the spectrum of human life.

Principles Governing the Patient-Professional Relationship

Five basic principles form the moral foundation for the patient-professional relationship. Each one is based on the premise that both the patient and the health care professional are created in the image and likeness of God, as well as that both parties bring to this relationship their own set of moral values and assumptions concerning the nature and purpose of medical care.

The Principle of Self-Determination

The field of medical ethics is grounded in the relationship between a patient and a health care professional (HCP). The patient seeks the help of the HCP in regard to physical or psychological health concerns, but may attach importance to spiritual and social issues as well.

The HCP enters into the relationship respecting the patient as a person and seeking to help the patient achieve health by drawing upon various medical fields. In addition, the HCP must respect the patient's spiritual and social values. In effect, the HCP must respect the patient's quest for health in the widest sense.

Recognition that the patient and HCP are equals in terms of human dignity is the foundation for the principle of self-determination. Self-determination means that individuals possess the right and ability to make decisions for themselves. From the Catholic perspective the principle of self-determination is founded in the belief that all human persons are created in the image and likeness of God and are endowed by God with the capacity to reason. Therefore we have a moral duty to make decisions for ourselves (although always in light of a rightly formed conscience) and to respect (with certain limitations) the free decisions of others. The principle of self-determination means that individuals are ultimately responsible for determining their own welfare. This does not mean that people's free choices are always morally correct, or that others have an absolute duty to carry out their wishes. It simply means that others must respect the free choices made by rational human persons.

In applying the principle of self-determination, tension can arise between restoring physical or psychological health and upholding one's spiritual or social values. For example, aging patients may decide that they would be better off spiritually if life-prolonging therapy were withdrawn, and they were allowed to die. Some might believe that divine law prohibits blood transfusions even when it is medically known that transfusions could save their lives. In such a case the patient must decide, freely and rationally, what treatment best respects his or her values. The patient's right to choose or refuse a given treatment stems from the fact that the patient is equal in dignity to the HCP.

Neither patients nor HCPs surrender their value systems when entering into the healing relationship. The HCP may face difficult ethical decisions as well. For example, should the HCP perform an operation on a patient who refuses a blood transfusion, knowing that without a transfusion the surgery may prove fatal? These challenges become even more difficult when a third party is involved, like a parent who refuses a blood transfusion for his child. If nothing is done, innocent people will die. What do we do in these situations? Should the decision-maker's personal values be allowed to override the HCP's moral (and legal) obligation to provide quality medical care to another autonomous individual?

The Principle of Integrity and Totality

As we have seen, the human person is made up of physical, psychological, spiritual, and social dimensions. The principle of integrity insists that each dimension must be fully differentiated and developed. Saint Paul articulates this principle:

> Now the body is not a single part, but many. If a foot should say, "Because I am not a hand I do not belong to the body," it does not for this reason belong any less to the body. Or if an ear should say, "Because I am not an eye I do not belong to the body," it does not for this reason belong any less to the body. If the whole body were an eye, where would the hearing be? If the whole body were hearing, where would the sense of smell be? But as it is, God placed the parts, each one of them, in the body as he intended. If they were all one part, where would the body be? But as it is, there are parts, yet one body. (1 Cor. 12:14–20)

Paul uses the body as a metaphor for the Christian Church: just as the human body has many different parts that together serve the whole, so too the Christian Church has many parts that, by their various gifts, constitute and serve the Church. His point is that the proper functioning of the whole depends on the ability of each of the parts to work together in an integrated fashion. This means we have a duty to develop every dimension of our being to the greatest extent possible. We cannot neglect any dimension. The principle of integrity insists that each dimension of the human person be fitted into the whole and harmonized with all others through correct interactions and interrelations. The parts must constitute an integrated whole. Integrity is lacking when we suppress the function of any part of our being or when we focus on a particular part to the detriment of others.

What happens when one part of the body becomes ill or diseased and threatens the overall well-being of the person in question? Is it permissible to sacrifice this ill or diseased part for the good of the whole? Yes, because of the principle of totality. Saint Thomas Aquinas succinctly explains this principle:

> Since any member is part of the whole body, it [the member] exists for the sake of the whole. . . . Hence, a member of the human body is to be disposed of according as it may profit the whole . . . e.g., when a diseased member is injurious to the whole body.[1]

According to Aquinas, if a diseased member is threatening the health of the whole body, this member can (and should) be removed. For example, if I have a cancerous kidney, then my kidney can be removed. The diseased part poses a serious threat to my overall health. The principle of totality asserts that we have a duty to promote the good of the whole in our moral decisions. To promote this overall good, we can (and should) remove that which threatens it. This does not mean that the individual part is not important, or that no effort should be made to save it. We should do what we can to treat each part, but when treatment is futile and a part threatens the body's overall good, it can be sacrificed.

Summarizing the principles of integrity and totality, then, we might say: Human health is not primarily a matter of individually functioning organs, but of capacities to function humanly. The fundamental functional capacities that constitute the human person should be preserved, developed, and used for the good of the individual person and of the community and they should never be destroyed except in those specific situations where life itself is in danger.

The Principle of Informed Consent

Respect for persons, the cornerstone of the principle of self-determination, is concretely applied, in part, through the principle of informed consent. To make rational decisions, patients need to understand their medical condition, prognosis, and the perceived benefits and burdens of various treatments. The ethical and legal requirements for informed consent include information, comprehension, and voluntariness.

Information

Specific information that always should be provided to the patient includes the purpose of the medical procedure in question, its anticipated risks and benefits, its probable results, and alternatives. HCPs should never withhold information and should always answer questions truthfully. In the case of certain research projects, information may be withheld provided the subject in question is informed in advance that not all information will be revealed until after the project is completed, and that no direct harm will result from its withholding.

Comprehension

Patients must understand the information conveyed to them. HCPs have a duty to present information in a way that it can be clearly understood by the patient. If the patient cannot comprehend the information due to age, language barrier, or mental capacity, a third party (a family member or someone appointed by the court) should be asked to act in the patient's best interests. This is called proxy consent.

There are two types of proxy consent, the first being substitution judgment. Substitution judgment applies to a situation where a patient was at one time competent but now no longer is—for example, a patient suffering from advanced Alzheimer's disease, or a patient in a persistent vegetative state as the result of trauma. This type of consent can be described as what patients would want if they were able to exercise their own judgment. In effect, substitute judgment is the proxy making an informed decision about another's care based on what the proxy believes the incapacitated person would choose. The second type of proxy consent is termed the best-interest standard. This applies when the patient in question has never been competent — for example, an individual born with a severe mental disability. Here the proxy judges on the basis of what procedure or treatment would best promote the patient's overall good, based on what an average, reasonable person would want in the same situation.

Voluntariness

Voluntariness implies that patients clearly understand their medical situation and are not unduly influenced by the HCP to choose a specific treatment or to act in a specific way. This is not to say that HCPs should remain silent about treatment options. If the HCP truly believes that one treatment option is better than another, the HCP should say so and clearly explain why. The HCP must not, however, seek to coerce or unduly influence the patient as this would violate the principles of dignity and self-determination. Voluntariness does not prevent the HCP from attempting to persuade the patient, but it does rule out undue coercion or manipulation.

The Principle of Truth Telling

One of the most difficult and delicate ethical questions facing the HCP is, "What exactly should I tell the patient?" The principle of truth telling insists that HCPs are morally obligated to tell patients the truth about their conditions so that patients can make appropriate, informed decisions about their care.

Information concerning serious illness must be furnished to the patient even if the patient has not requested it. But in some difficult situations HCPs may hesitate to tell patients about their true condition. Some patients with serious illnesses might become despondent, even suicidal, if they knew the truth about their condition. With this in mind, the "Patient's Bill of Rights" states, "When it is not medically advisable to give such information to the patient, the information should be made available to an appropriate person on his or her behalf." Unfortunately, this statement does not indicate what the "appropriate person" is supposed to do with the information thus provided. Should the "appropriate person" share the information with the patient, or not share it? Does disclosing pertinent information to the "appropriate person" absolve the HCP of further responsibility to inform the patient directly? Perhaps the question is not *whether* the patient should be told, but *how* the patient should be told.

Truth telling, especially in cases of impending death, is important for religious reasons as well. As Christians, we do not believe that our existence ends with death, but that we live on in the next life. All people should be afforded the opportunity to prepare for death in their own way. In a theological sense, death signifies our transition from this world to the next. The health care community has a duty to inform patients of their true condition so that patients can adequately prepare.

The Principle of Confidentiality

The principle of confidentiality refers to keeping sensitive information private. Unauthorized persons must be excluded from obtaining sensitive medical information about a particular patient, and those who have access to this information must never reveal it to outside parties. Confidentiality protects patient dignity and fosters the open communication of important, sometimes intimate, health-related information. Patients need to trust that their HCPs are always acting in their best interests; confidentiality is paramount if trust is to be established and maintained.

Confidentiality becomes more difficult to maintain as more people become involved in a patient's care and have access to the patient's records. The computerization of medical records also increases the possibility for breaches of confidentiality. Unfortunately, no system will ever be 100 percent secure. However, we can minimize the risk of breaches of confidentiality through self-discipline. It is unethical, for example, for HCPs to participate in indiscriminate conversation, even among themselves, that may jeopardize patient confidentiality. When HCPs must consult with one another in a public setting, they must be careful to mask the patient's identity to ensure confidentiality.

Although confidentiality is vital to the patient-professional relationship, it is not a patient's absolute right. Circumstances can and do limit the patient's right of confidentiality. When a patient threatens suicide, for example, the HCP has an obligation to inform family, next of kin, or even a public authority so that the patient will not do irreparable harm to himself or herself. Public health laws also require the breaking of confidentiality to prevent an individual from doing harm to a third party or to society as a whole. Such is the case with suspected child abusers, individuals who have contracted a contagious disease, or people who have directly threatened the lives of others. In certain situations confidentiality can be broken in the best interests of either the patient or the common good of society.

The five principles we have discussed constitute the moral foundation of the patient-professional relationship, and they offer practical ethical guidelines as to how medicine should be practiced within our society. However, before we explore some practical and controversial issues, we need to discuss two further moral principles that are vitally important for any discussion of contemporary medical ethics: the principle of double effect, which helps us determine what we can and cannot do, and the principle of legitimate cooperation, which helps us determine to what extent we can cooperate with a morally evil act.

General Principles Regarding the Provision of Health Care

The Principle of Double Effect

The principle of double effect comes into play when a particular action will have both positive and negative consequences. Suppose that a pregnant woman is diagnosed with uterine cancer. One treatment option would be to abort her unborn child so that treatment for her cancer could begin immediately. The Catholic Church (among others) teaches that this option is never morally permissible because it is always wrong to directly end the life of an innocent human being, regardless of whether this human being is in utero or not. A second option would be to do nothing about the cancer until the child is born, then aggressively treat the cancer. This option is morally permissible because there is nothing intrinsically wrong with postponing the cancer treatment in light of some other good, i.e., preserving the life of the unborn child. However, this option puts the woman's health, and quite possibly her life, at serious risk.

In a third option, the woman could undergo a hysterectomy and have her cancerous uterus removed. "Wait a minute," you say, "the hysterectomy would result in the death of the unborn child; isn't this an abortion?" To understand how this decision does not constitute a direct abortion and is morally permissible, we must examine it in light of a four-part explanation of the principle of double effect.

1. *The action in question is not intrinsically evil.* The choice to undergo a medical procedure to cure oneself of an illness or disease is not intrinsically evil. As noted in regard to the principles of integrity and totality, you are morally permitted to do what is necessary within reason to return yourself to a state of health, even if this means removing a diseased organ. In the case of the pregnant woman, there is nothing intrinsically wrong with removing her uterus if the cancer within it poses a real and imminent threat to her health.

2. *One intends only the good effect of the action in question and does not intend its harmful side effects.* The choice to undergo the hysterectomy does entail a harmful side-effect, the loss of the child, but the woman does not choose the medical procedure with the intention of causing this harm. Instead, she undergoes the procedure to bring about a good effect, namely the cure of her cancer. The death of the unborn child is an unintended, although foreseen, consequence of her decision.

3. *The evil consequence of the action is not the means by which the good consequence is achieved.* This means that one may never choose an act that has an evil consequence with the intent that this evil consequence will bring about a good. Or, stated differently, one must not pursue a good effect that results directly from an action that produces an evil effect. In our example, the woman is cured of her cancer through the removal of her uterus, nothing else. She is not cured as a direct result of her unborn child's death, nor is this death the means by which the cancer is cured.

4. *The harmful consequences of the action do not exceed its good consequences.* The loss of the woman's unborn child (and her uterus) is a harmful consequence, but we may accept it if there is a proportionate reason for doing so. In this case, the woman's life is at stake. The good resulting to the woman is judged to be a proportionate reason for undergoing the removal of her cancerous uterus and enduring the loss of her unborn child. If, however, there is not a proportionate

reason for accepting the harmful consequences—for example, if the woman simply does not want to bear children because doing so will ruin her figure—her decision to undergo the hysterectomy would not be morally permissible.

With the help of the principle of double effect, we see that it is morally permissible for the woman to proceed with the hysterectomy. Her bodily integrity will be violated, but for the sake of bodily totality. A human life will be lost and the woman will no longer be able to bear children, but only as the indirect consequences of an action the good results of which provide a proportionate reason for undergoing the procedure.

The Principle of Legitimate Cooperation

Scenarios involving the principle of legitimate cooperation occur on both macro and micro levels. On the macro level we could consider the issues that arise when a Catholic hospital merges with a secular hospital where medical procedures are performed that are not morally permissible according to Catholic teaching. On a micro level we could consider the issues that arise when a Catholic HCP is working in a secular hospital where such procedures are performed. The principle of legitimate cooperation helps guide us in such scenarios as it helps us evaluate whether it is ever permissible to participate in a morally questionable act and, if so, to what extent.

The first element of the principle of legitimate cooperation concerns formal cooperation. Formal cooperation occurs when one freely commits a morally evil act or assents to the evil intention of a person performing a morally evil act through advice, encouragement, or counsel. Catholic Church teaching here is clear: formal cooperation with an intrinsically evil act is never morally permissible.

The second element of the principle of legitimate cooperation concerns material cooperation. Material cooperation means there is no assent to the intention of the person performing an evil act; in theory you may even be morally opposed to it, yet in practice you cooperate with the act in some way. Material cooperation can be either immediate or mediate. One engages in immediate material cooperation when an evil act could not be performed without one's help. An example would be a surgical nurse handing medical instruments to a doctor who is performing an abortion. Mediate material cooperation occurs when one's cooperation is not needed in the actual performance of an evil act, but one assists it in some less direct way. An example of this may be the anesthesiologist who "puts the patient under" so that he can undergo a vasectomy or other medical procedure that the Church deems to be morally wrong. Mediate material cooperation can be further distinguished into proximate and remote mediate material cooperation. Proximate mediate material cooperation refers to how closely one is connected to an evil action that is being performed. For example, a nurse who prepares the operating room in an abortion clinic is proximately involved in the evil act. Remote mediate material cooperation refers to one's cooperation with an evil act, but only in a very indirect way. An example would be the janitor who cleans the abortion clinic operating room.

According to Catholic ethics it is never morally permissible to engage in either formal or immediate material cooperation with an intrinsically evil act. However, in some cases, mediate material cooperation may be permissible if the individual's cooperation is remote, not proximate, and if the overall good achieved by this cooperation outweighs the degree of evil inherent in the act. In this way, it could be argued that the Catholic janitor could work in an abortion clinic if he does not participate in the abortion procedures or advise, encourage, or counsel the HCPs or patients, *and* if no other reasonable opportunities are available to him through which he can earn a living for himself and his family.

In Catholic ethics a further consideration that must be taken into account is the possibility of scandal. Scandal here is a theological term that refers to one person's actions becoming a stumbling block to the faith of another. For example, what effect would the janitor's work have on members of his parish community? Recall Jesus' teaching that it would be better for a person to have a millstone placed around his neck and be thrown into the sea rather than have him lead one of his followers astray (Matt. 18:6). We must be careful to consider not only how our actions will be viewed by God but also how these actions will affect the faith of our community.

We now turn our attention to some of the contentious medical challenges that confront us today.

Medical Issues at the Beginning of Life

The Status of the Embryo

The fundamental question underlying many of the medical and reproductive issues we face is, "what is the status of the human embryo?" Is the embryo a human being who must be afforded the same dignity and rights as all other human beings, or is it different? The answers you offer to these questions have profound effects on how you view critical issues involving the beginning of life. People have answered these questions in three primary ways.

1. *The embryo is simply a mass of cells, a part of the mother's body.* Here it is argued that the human embryo, although a living organism, cannot be considered a human life because it does not look like, act like, or display the same cognitive functions as "existing" people. Overall, this view holds that the embryo does not have any moral status and is not to be afforded human dignity or basic human rights.

   The Catholic Church rejects this understanding. We know scientifically that the embryo from conception possesses its own unique genetic makeup—its own DNA. This is significant because as all our genetic markers, the determiners of who we are, exist from the earliest moments of our biological existence, it is difficult to argue that an embryo is simply a "mass of cells." In addition, we know that an embryo, if left undisturbed, will one day become a human person and not something else. We also know that the development of the embryo originates within the embryo itself. The embryo does not need to be prompted by some outside force in order to continue to develop; it already has within it all the genetic material it needs to become a human person.

2. *The embryo is a human person from the time of its conception.* According to this line of thinking, the physical body and the spiritual soul can only come into existence at the same moment. The embryo attains its spiritual soul, its status as a person before God, at conception. Many contemporary theologians agree with this position based on findings from the natural sciences. They argue that the embryo could never become a human person if it were not already a human person.

Other theologians question the belief that the embryo is a person from the time of conception, basing their objections on biology and anthropology. The biological objection is that we know the human person is indivisible, yet for about fourteen days after conception the embryo can divide itself, giving rise to twins or other multiples. Because of its ability to divide into multiple beings, we cannot consider the embryo to be an *individual* being from the time of its conception and, by extension, we cannot consider it to be an individual human person.[2] The objection based in anthropology says human persons can be defined as beings-in-relationship with one another. These interrelationships are defined biologically, psychologically, emotionally, spiritually, linguistically, and in other ways. Conception, however, brings about only a biological relationship. The embryo is physically related to its mother, but at first the mother does not even know that she is pregnant. During this time of a lack of any interpersonal relationship, some theologians argue that the embryo, although properly belonging to the human species, cannot yet be considered a full human person.

3. *It is impossible to discern the precise moment when an embryo becomes a person.* Formerly this position was expressed as "ensoulment," the point in the gestation period when the embryo receives its soul from God. Saint Thomas Aquinas held that the rational soul cannot be infused into biological matter until the biological matter has sufficiently organized itself.[3] Various theologians and philosophers continue to try to determine the exact moment when an embryo becomes a human person. Opinions include the moment that the embryo can no longer divide into more than one being, the earliest emergence of the brain or central nervous system, or when the mother becomes willing to enter into relationship with it.

The magisterium has been reluctant to make a definitive pronouncement on when human personhood begins because we simply do not know. Some people may take this lack of precision as a license to hold whatever position they think is best, but the magisterium asks that the faithful adhere to the constant Tradition of the Church.

The fruit of human generation from the first instant of existence, that is, from the formation of the zygote, requires the unconditional respect due to a person in his or her bodily and spiritual totality. The human being must be respected and treated as a person from the moment of conception, and, therefore, from that moment it must be given the rights of a person among which the most important and fundamental is the inviolable right of all innocent persons to life.[4]

The Church is not definitively stating that the embryo *is* a human person from the moment of conception, but that the embryo, as the fruit of human generation, can only be a human reality that should be treated *as* a human person and afforded all the rights owed to a human person—including most fundamentally the right to life. The primary ethical implication of the teaching is that one must respect the embryo as one respects a human person.

Although it may be difficult to qualify the embryo as a "person" because it has not yet attained many of the essential characteristics of human personhood (especially indivisibility and the capacity for interpersonal relations), because the embryo is a self-directing human organism destined to become a functional human being, we propose that we should regard it as having the status of a human person from the time of its conception and afford it all the rights and protections enjoyed by other human persons. For this reason the Church teaches that the intentional and direct destruction of an innocent human embryo is an intrinsic evil and always morally wrong.

Before we conclude this discussion, we would like to address two difficulties surrounding attempts to determine a precise post-conception threshold where the embryo becomes a human person. The first difficulty is that those who seek to define this threshold often do so with the aim of affirming that before it is attained, one need not respect the embryo's dignity. They propose "X" as the point where human personhood begins so they can argue that "up until X" it is morally permissible to have an abortion, dispose of leftover IVF embryos, or extract stem cells. This position is problematic because each stage of embryonic development is continuous and each stage requires time. Let us illustrate through the following example. The coming together of the ovum and the sperm takes place in several stages: the male gamete attaches to the membrane of the egg, which is followed by penetration, which is followed by a facing of the male and female nuclei, which is followed by the fusion of the genetic patrimony of the parents, which is followed by the chemical expression of the composite genetic message . . . and the process continues. The same is true after conception has been completed, and it continues throughout the life of the person. The point here is that the process of human development is continuous in that each successive step is contingent upon what happens before it. If any one of these steps were not to occur, then the whole process would stop. Thus, human development involves a continual series of successive and interrelated processes, not a conglomeration of unrelated, independent events. The reality makes it essentially impossible to define a precise post-conception threshold where human personhood begins.

A second difficulty with trying to establish such a post-conception threshold is the belief that the embryo need not be respected before this threshold is attained. Hypothetically, let us suppose that we could determine within a millisecond when a human embryo actually becomes a human person. One result of this newly found ability would be that we could determine the exact point at which an abortion (or other life-destroying medical procedure) would no longer be morally permissible. But does this really make sense? What we would really be saying is that one millisecond before this threshold is attained there would be no moral problem with destroying the embryo, yet one millisecond later we would be committing a serious crime (not to mention sin)!

Granted, the magisterium does not definitively state when human personhood begins. Nonetheless, the Church's traditional teaching on this matter demonstrates that in a practical sense, moral decision-making always involves respecting the development of human life in all of its various forms (including the embryo), as well as in all of its ambiguous and fluctuating situations.

Reproductive Technology

A second ethical issue concerning the beginning of human life is the use of reproductive technology. More and more couples who are finding it difficult to achieve pregnancy are turning to reproductive technologies in order to become parents. Here we will briefly consider the ethical ramifications of some of the most common forms of reproductive technology available today. [5]

Insemination: Homologous and Heterologous

Insemination refers to any procedure whereby a man's previously collected sperm is introduced into a woman's reproductive tract to achieve pregnancy. The sperm can come from the woman's husband (homologous insemination), or from a known or unknown donor (heterologous insemination). The Church states that insemination is acceptable only if it serves to facilitate or help the act of intercourse in attaining fertilization. It is not acceptable if it substitutes for the sexual act.[6] For example, if there is a blockage in the woman's fallopian tube so that the sperm cannot travel to the egg, it is morally permissible to surgically move the egg past the point of blockage so that fertilization can then occur. However, it would not be morally permissible to undergo a procedure that takes the place of the sexual act itself—such as a procedure whereby the husband's sperm is harvested and then physically injected into the wife's body.[7]

One reason the Church opposes medical procedures that substitute for the sexual act is that these procedures break the "inseparable connection" between the procreative and unitive dimensions of marital sexuality. To be considered morally permissible, any act of marital intercourse must uphold both the procreative dimension (openness to the transmission of life) and the unitive dimension (offering the full gift of oneself). As early as 1951 Pope Pius XII warned that any medical procedure that substituted for the sexual act cannot be morally permissible because these procedures do not constitute an act of total, self-giving love between a husband and wife.[8]

The Church teaches that homologous procedures, involving only the husband's sperm and the wife's egg, are permissible as long as they do not substitute for the sexual act. Heterologous procedures, involving the third-party donation of either sperm or egg, are never morally permitted because (1) the husband and wife have a reciprocal right to become parents only through each other; (2) using sperm or egg from a third party disregards the couple's commitment to, as well as the essential property of, unity within their marriage; (3) children have the right to know and be raised by their biological parents; and (4) heterologous procedures can cause familial conflict, especially when children discover that their father or mother is not their biological parent. In short, the Church views heterologous procedures as the equivalent of introducing "another flesh" into the marital relationship. As such, they are never morally permissible.[9]

In Vitro Fertilization (IVF)

Despite its relatively low success rate (roughly 20 percent) and its high cost (approximately $15,000 for a single cycle), IVF is one of the most popular reproductive technologies today. An egg is removed from the mother's body and combined in a Petri dish with sperm from the donor father. If the egg is fertilized, the resulting embryo is transferred back into the woman's uterus where, it is hoped, it will develop into a healthy child. Like insemination, IVF can be either homologous or heterologous. It is homologous when a husband's sperm and wife's egg are used, and the resulting embryo is placed into the wife's body. It is heterologous when either sperm or egg is donated by a third party, or when a woman other than the wife carries the child to term (surrogate).

The magisterium has consistently opposed all forms of IVF. Opposition to heterologous IVF arises for essentially the reasons given above. Homologous IVF is opposed because it breaks the "inseparable connection" between the procreative and unitive dimensions of marital sexuality, entrusts the transmission of life to the skill of doctors or technicians, and tends to view the embryo as the product of medical technology rather than as the fruit of a loving act between husband and wife. The Church holds that IVF is intrinsically wrong and that no intention on the part of the couple can make it permissible.[10]

The magisterium's opposition to IVF has caused much controversy within the Church, and many have critically questioned its teaching. Space does not permit a detailed treatment of this important and ongoing debate here. We simply note that whether one believes IVF to be intrinsically evil or not, the procedure raises a number of important ethical concerns. First, to increase the chances of achieving at least one fertilized embryo, the woman is given drugs that produce multiple eggs. These drugs can cause high blood pressure and bleeding, and some wonder whether their use is in the best long-term health interests of the mother. Second, more than one egg is fertilized at a time. Fertility clinics create numerous embryos and implant only the ones they believe are most viable. According to Church teaching, any embryo created must be respected as one would respect any other living person. Embryos created in the fertility clinic but not implanted into the woman are either discarded or frozen.

The problem with discarding embryos is that it is the moral equivalent of abortion. Fertility clinics, as well as the biological parents, are directly and intentionally ending the existence of these embryos through their actions, embryos that the Church defines as worthy of dignity and respect. Today there are over four hundred thousand frozen embryos in the United States alone. Some argue that instead of discarding these embryos, they should be donated for scientific research that will benefit humanity as a whole. Today this usually means stem cell research. We speak more about embryonic stem cell research later, but the main moral issue here is that when stem cells are extracted from the human embryo, the embryo dies. Again, this is the moral equivalent of abortion.

A third problem concerns a process euphemistically termed "selective reduction." To increase the odds of achieving pregnancy, fertility clinics implant numerous embryos into the mother, in the hope that one or maybe two of them will actually develop into a child. In some cases more than two embryos succeed, and the parents are then faced with the prospect of multiple fetuses. To avoid complications associated with multiple births, doctors will often "selectively reduce" a multiple pregnancy by identifying fetuses they believe are most viable and destroying the rest within the mother's womb. The procedure constitutes a direct and intentional abortion.

Gamete Intrafallopian Transfer (GIFT)

GIFT is a variation of IVF. In this procedure, a doctor removes an egg from the woman's body and places it, along with sperm from her husband, into a catheter with an air bubble separating them so fertilization won't occur inside the catheter. The egg and sperm are then inserted directly into the woman's fallopian tube with the hope that they will meet and result in the birth of a child. The advantage of this procedure over IVF is that fertilization occurs within the woman's body. There has been much debate among Catholic ethicists concerning the morality of this procedure, the main point of contention revolving around whether or not GIFT is a personal expression of the couple's sexuality. Does it assist the marital act in achieving pregnancy, or substitute for it? Those who argue in favor of GIFT say that it is used in conjunction with marital relations because it can be done either just before or just after a couple has "completed" an act of sexual intercourse. Those who argue against GIFT say that in reality it substitutes for the act of intercourse because the procedure removes egg and sperm from the parents' bodies, and there are simply too many obstacles to make it a truly personal act. The magisterium has not pronounced on the use of GIFT.

Zygote Intrafallopian Transfer (ZIFT)

In ZIFT, eggs are fertilized in a laboratory as in an IVF procedure. Any resulting zygotes (fertilized eggs) are transferred to the woman's fallopian tube. The advantage of ZIFT over IVF is that there are no "spares": all zygotes created are transferred to the woman. However, because the unitive dimension of marital sexuality is separated from the transmission of life, the Church holds that it is not a viable moral option.

Intracytoplasmic Sperm Injection (ICSI)

In this procedure a doctor uses a microscopic pipette to inject a single sperm into an egg. The resulting zygote is then transferred to the woman's fallopian tube. Once again, because conception occurs in a laboratory and because the zygote is not the fruit of an act of mutual love, ICSI is not morally permissible.

General Evaluation of Reproductive Technologies

We have evaluated a number of the most commonly used reproductive technologies. We now offer some general observations about the opportunities and risks associated with them.[11]

Opportunities: Many of the reproductive technologies available today allow otherwise infertile couples to conceive. Many of us know couples who cannot have children, and we see the considerable pain that infertility causes and the hope that these technologies can provide. If you have ever seen the joy of a couple who has given birth to a child through the use of these procedures, you cannot help but wonder whether their decision to use these technologies was, in fact, immoral.

Risks: In spite of the opportunities that reproductive technologies provide, the Church maintains a negative moral judgment regarding most of them. The primary reason is the Church's long-held teaching that one may not perform an evil act with the intent that something good may come of it. In other words, producing a biological offspring is good, but this good must not be achieved by immoral means. We have already seen some of the specific risks associated with reproductive technologies, risks that are both personal and social; however, there are a number of other, more general challenges associated with these technologies as well. Let us examine some of these general risks in more detail.

(1) Reproductive technologies usually are the privilege of the wealthy, those with the means to pay thousands of dollars for these procedures. This raises a question of justice. Are those who cannot afford reproductive technologies thereby excluded from them, or do we as a society have a duty to provide them?

(2) Reproductive technologies utilize scarce medical resources. In a time when many people do not have access to even basic medical care, does it make sense to use finite medical resources to aid only a small percentage of people?

(3) There are health risks associated with reproductive technology. The process of hyper-ovulation can cause hypertension, nausea, vomiting, and increased fluid build-up in the woman's abdomen and chest. In rare cases (estimated at 1–2 percent), women have also experienced kidney and ovary damage as well as blood clotting disorders. Another issue is the possibility of multiple births. IVF pregnancies are ten times more likely to produce multiple births than are "natural" pregnancies, and these multiple births pose significant health risks, including higher rates of tubal pregnancy, the birth of premature and underweight children, and the increased possibility for long-term handicaps. We must also consider the monetary costs these pregnancies impose on society. In 2005, the average cost to deliver a single child was approximately $10,000, for twins it rose to $100,000, and for triplets and other multiples it was even higher. Since the year 2000 alone, American taxpayers have paid approximately $640 million in medical costs for multiple birth pregnancies that resulted from assisted reproductive procedures.

(4) In the United States, few laws regulate reproductive technology. For the most part, fertility clinics and other researchers can do whatever

they want. Interestingly, several European nations have passed laws that regulate the number of embryos that can be created through IVF, and some even require that all embryos created be implanted into the mother. The United States has no such regulations.

(5) For all of the marvels it accomplishes, reproductive technology is a commercial business. Fertility clinics must earn a profit to stay in business, and in order to attract new customers they advertise their "success rates" to infertile couples. In this sense, children born of assisted fertilization procedures can be seen as "products" in that their conceptions become statistics to be used in the clinics' marketing campaigns.

(6) There is the question of technology versus adoption. At the same time Western society is aborting approximately one out of every six pregnancies, thousands of children around the world are waiting to be adopted. We do not wish to make couples who have used these technologies feel guilty, but simply to demonstrate the social inconsistencies at work.

(7) Reproductive technologies allow us to "play God." These technologies separate the procreative and unitive dimensions of marital sexuality and—through recourse to egg donation, sperm donation, and surrogate motherhood—allow us to disregard natural biological processes. Reproductive technologies also offer us virtually unlimited power over the human embryo. We can let the embryo develop into a human person, or destroy it. We can determine its sex, we can split it in two, and someday we will be able to select its genetic traits. Reproductive technologies allow us to wield tremendous power over nascent human life, including the power to choose life or death. Taken to its ultimate end, this power impedes upon God's providence and becomes a form of idolatry.

(8) Reproductive technologies foster the belief that we have the *right* to produce a biological child. Moreover, these technologies take procreation from its proper marital setting and "open the door" to almost anyone who wants to have a child. They aid not only infertile married couples, but also single individuals and those in same-sex relationships who want to produce their own biological children. The problem with this, aside from the fact we know children are most well-adjusted when raised in a stable, loving family with both father and mother present, is that we turn children into "objects" to satisfy our own desires to become parents. A child is not "owed" to a married couple or anyone else. A child

is, rather, a gift from God and the greatest, and the most free, gift that a couple can give to each other in marriage. To believe anything less would be an offense against the dignity of the child.[12] Children exist for their own sake, not for the good of others. Reproductive technologies have blurred this reality.

(9) Closely related to the previous point, reproductive technologies contribute to the belief that a husband and wife are condemned to a life of misery if they cannot produce a biological child. While sterility can be a terrible trial for many couples, experience demonstrates that many of them have been able to find fulfillment through adoption (domestic or international) or, if this is not possible, by allowing one's maternal and paternal instincts to flower in other social, cultural, or apostolic endeavors.

Certainly, there are many more challenges that can and should be considered. These few we have discussed are merely a starting point.

Embryonic Stem Cell Research

One of the most tendentious ethical and legal issues facing our nation today is human embryonic stem cell research. Politicians, celebrities, and religious and other groups speak out on it, resulting in great confusion. In August 2001, President George W. Bush banned federal funding for any scientific research that creates new human embryonic stem cell lines, a ban that, as this text goes to print, many in Congress are actively seeking to overturn. While we cannot devote the space required to thoroughly consider the issue, we will briefly examine a few of the ethical arguments on both sides of this heated and politically charged debate.[13]

Stem cells are master cells, capable of generating many of the different cell types that make up the human body. Because of this ability, they may hold the cure for diseases such as Parkinson's, Alzheimer's, and diabetes, and someday they may be able to grow and replace damaged organs. Because the potential for stem cells is so great, many within the scientific community are pushing for expanded research and development of new stem cell therapies.

Stem cells come from a variety of sources. The first is human embryos; such cells are called *human embryonic stem cells*. The primary source for these cells is the leftover or "spare" embryos created through the IVF process. Many hold that the more than four hundred thousand such embryos currently in cold storage in the United States would be an excellent source for new stem cell lines. They argue that as these embryos are never going to develop into human persons—in fact they will be discarded—why not donate them to science so that they can be used for good? Further strengthening this argument, embryonic stem cells are believed to be "pluripotent," that is, they can develop into any cell within the human body. Assuming this is true, these cells theoretically hold the potential to treat any illness or injury, and scientists want to create more of these lines so that they can move the research forward.

Despite this potential, a number of drawbacks exist to the use of human embryonic stem cells. One is that the freezing process used to preserve IVF embryos may actually make it more difficult to extract stem cells. Ideally, one would want to extract stem cells from a newly created embryo, not one that has been frozen for months or even years. A second drawback is that many of the more than four hundred thousand frozen embryos are "weak." Recall that fertility clinics create numerous embryos and implant only the most viable. The remaining embryos, the weaker ones, are frozen; some wonder about the quality of stem cells these will yield.

In addition to the scientific questions, the most important ethical (and legal) consideration surrounding human embryonic stem cells is, what happens to the embryo once its stem cells have been extracted. Embryos need their stem cells in order to survive, so when these stem cells are extracted, the embryo dies. Recall that although the Catholic Church does not definitively pronounce when an embryo attains personhood, it does hold that this embryo is a human life from the very earliest moments of its existence, and it needs to be respected as such. Thus, from a Catholic perspective, the greatest drawback to the use of embryonic stem cells is that they are harvested at the cost of a human life. The procedure itself is the moral equivalent of homicide.

Adult stem cells are harvested from the tissue of already existing persons, especially from bone marrow. The upside of harvesting these cells is two-fold: it does not involve the destruction of an embryo, and we already know that they work to cure disease. Many people have been aided or even cured of leukemia, non-Hodgkin's lymphoma, and other illnesses through the injection of adult stem cells.[14] The downside to adult stem cells is that they do not appear to be as versatile as embryonic stem cells. Adult stem cells are believed to be "multipotent" in that they can only be used for specific purposes. For example, bone marrow stem cells may be effective in treating leukemia or other blood-related diseases, but they cannot be manipulated to grow into a heart for transplantation or into nerve cells to mend a severed spinal cord. Further difficulties include that adult stem cells are difficult to grow outside the human body and not all bodily organs produce them.

Umbilical cord stem cells function similarly to adult stem cells, but instead of being taken from an individual's body they are extracted from the blood remaining inside the umbilical cord immediately following the birth of a child. Like adult stem cells, umbilical cord stem cells can be obtained without destroying a human life, and there is documented evidence of people being cured of illness through their use. Drawbacks to umbilical cord stem cells include that they are not as versatile as embryonic stem cells, and umbilical cord blood might not always provide enough cells to treat an adult.

Another source of stem cells is a process called Somatic Cell Nuclear Transfer (SCNT), more commonly known as therapeutic cloning. In this procedure, a woman's egg is harvested from her body and all its nuclear material is removed. The nuclear material from a cell (usually a skin cell) of an already existing person is transferred into the egg, which is then stimulated to begin dividing and a new embryo is formed. Stem cells are then extracted from this embryo in the same way they are extracted from an IVF embryo. The advantage of cells produced by SCNT is that they are an exact genetic match to the donor, but harvesting stem cells from this process requires a tremendous amount of fresh human eggs, and the clinical reproductive trials using this procedure in animals have been marked by failure and complications.

Before concluding this discussion, it is important to clarify that the Catholic Church does not oppose stem cell research as such, as is often suggested by the media and other "experts." Using stem cells to cure disease or repair bodily injury is actually a wonderful moral good because it allows sick and disabled people the opportunity to regain their health. In fact, the Church applauds the recent development whereby ordinary skin cells have been converted into what appear to be (but are not) embryonic stem cells. The advantage of this new discovery is that it eliminates the destruction of human embryos while maintaining the pluripotency of embryonic stem cells.[15] Overall, what the Church questions is the source of the stem cells themselves. Exploiting an embryo for its health-giving or life-saving potential is an offense against human dignity. The embryo must be viewed as an end in itself, it must never become the means to some scientific or medical end, no matter how beneficial this perceived end may be.

Medical Issues at the End of Life

What forms of medical care are necessary when people are at or near death? Is it ever morally permissible to refuse this care? Answers to these questions often revolve around three misunderstood concepts: ordinary, extraordinary, and artificial means of care. We explore the meaning of these terms and discuss under what circumstances individuals are — or are not — morally bound to have recourse to such care. We conclude with an examination of care for patients in a permanent vegetative state.

Ordinary and Extraordinary Means of Care

To understand the distinction between ordinary and extraordinary means of care, let us first consider these two cases:[16]

CASE 1

Six months ago, Barbara, an eighty-four-year-old woman, was diagnosed with non-Hodgkin's lymphoma. Two weeks ago, she was informed that the lymphoma had metastasized to her liver and brain, and she does not have much longer to live. Barbara has also developed bacterial pneumonia. Her doctors suggest that they treat the pneumonia with the antibiotic regimen that is normally indicated. Barbara, however, refuses. She tells her doctors and her family that she simply wants to go home to die. The doctors respect her wishes. Barbara returns home, and within a week she slips into a coma. Two days later, surrounded by family and friends, she dies peacefully.

CASE 2

Timothy, a forty-year-old male, is brought to an emergency room where he is also diagnosed with bacterial pneumonia. Timothy is an otherwise healthy man, but he has been clinically depressed since the death of his wife six months ago. The emergency room physician informs Timothy of his condition, prescribes the antibiotic regimen, and tells him that he should be feeling better in about ten days. Much to the doctor's amazement, Timothy refuses treatment. He says he does not want to live; he wishes to let the pneumonia kill him so he can be with his departed wife.

Legally, of course, both Barbara and Timothy have the right to refuse treatment. Their doctors may try to persuade them to take the antibiotics, but they cannot be legally impelled to take them. But is it morally permissible for Barbara and Timothy to refuse the antibiotic treatment? To answer this question we must first understand how the Church differentiates between ordinary and extraordinary means of care.

In one of the earliest articles ever published on the subject, Gerald Kelly, SJ, defined ordinary means of care as "all medicines, treatments, and operations, which offer a reasonable hope of benefit and which can be obtained and used without excessive expense, pain, or other inconveniences." He defined extraordinary means of care as "all medicines, treatments, and operations, which cannot be obtained or used without excessive expense, pain, or other inconveniences, or which, if used, would not offer a reasonable hope of benefit."[17] For Kelly, ordinary and extraordinary means of care differ in regard to reasonable hope, expense, pain, and inconvenience.

A similar teaching can be found in a 1957 allocution of Pope Pius XII to doctors and students of anesthesiology at the Gregory Mendel Institute:

> Natural reason and Christian morality say that man (and whoever is charged with caring for his fellow human beings) has the right and the duty to take necessary care to preserve his life and health in the case of a serious illness. This duty . . . flows from a well-ordered charity, from submission to the Creator, from social justice and even from justice strictly speaking, as well as from respect for his family. *But this duty does not usually oblige except in the use of ordinary means* (according to the circumstances of person,

place, epochs or culture), *that is, means that are not burdensome either for oneself or for another.*[18]

Like Kelly, Pius XII identifies "the right and the duty" one has to preserve life, but he also makes explicit the moral principles that form the foundation for this right and duty: well-ordered charity, submission to God, justice, and respect for family. In other words, because of these principles, we humans have both a right and a duty to do what we reasonably can to preserve our own health and the health of others. We have a moral obligation to do what is necessary to cure ourselves, or those entrusted to our care, of serious illness.

How far does our moral right and duty to preserve our health extend? Must we pursue every possible medical means in every medical situation, even when we are near death? Pius XII replies that we have a moral obligation to use *ordinary* means to preserve our life and health. We are obliged to pursue medical treatments that, in the words of Kelly, hold out a reasonable hope of benefit and that do not entail excessive pain, expense, or other inconvenience. Pius XII expands on this criterion by identifying circumstances of person, place, epoch, or culture as factors that should be considered when weighing the benefits and burdens of any medical treatment. The Church's teaching as presented by Pius XII and Kelly is fairly clear. If the treatment in question promises a reasonable hope of benefit and this benefit outweighs all burdens that may be involved, then the treatment is deemed ordinary and the patient is morally obligated to pursue it.

Neither Pius XII nor Kelly explicitly addresses extraordinary means in their writings, but the Church's traditional stance is that we are not morally obliged to pursue means of care that are deemed extraordinary. Extraordinary means of care include treatments that do not hold out a reasonable hope of benefit for the patient or treatments that in themselves cause the patient or the patient's family excessive pain, expense, or other inconvenience. When the burdens of a treatment outweigh any benefit that may be gained from it, the treatment is considered extraordinary and no longer morally obligatory. We are not morally bound to pursue every possible medical treatment in order to preserve our life and health, we are only morally obliged to pursue those medical treatments that constitute an ordinary means of care.

More recently the United States Catholic bishops clarified ordinary and extraordinary means of care.

> A person has a moral obligation to use ordinary or proportionate means of preserving his or her life. Proportionate means are those that in *the judgment of the patient* offer a reasonable hope of benefit and do not entail an excessive burden or impose excessive expense on the family or the community.
>
> A person may forgo extraordinary or disproportionate means of preserving life. Disproportionate means are those that *in the patient's judgment* do not offer a reasonable hope of benefit or entail an excessive burden or impose excessive expense on the family or the community.[19]

By emphasizing "the judgment of the patient," the bishops clarify that the ordinary or extraordinary nature of a treatment depends on how its benefits and burdens are judged by the patient or the patient's proxy. In other words, the patient or the patient's proxy determines what constitutes ordinary or extraordinary care. The rationale for placing this responsibility on the patient harkens back to the principle of self-determination: as rational creatures created in the image and likeness of God, individuals possess the right and the ability to make decisions for themselves, decisions that affect every aspect of their lives — including health care. Nevertheless, the patient must not make these decisions in isolation. The patient has a duty to consult with doctors, family members, and possibly clergy.[20]

We should also recognize that under differing circumstances the same medical treatment may be deemed ordinary by one person and extraordinary by another, because a particular treatment may hold out a greater hope of benefit for one person rather than another. Therefore it is impossible to say that a particular treatment in itself constitutes an ordinary or extraordinary means of care. The ordinary or extraordinary nature of a particular medical treatment ultimately lies with the reasoned and informed judgment of the patient or the patient's proxy.

Let's return to the cases of Barbara and Timothy and apply what we have learned. Barbara, in the end stages of non-Hodgkin's lymphoma, decides to refuse treatment for her bacterial pneumonia. She weighs the perceived benefits of undergoing the treatment against its burdens. The antibiotics will cure her of the pneumonia and prolong her life. Why might she want to prolong her life? Perhaps she still has to wrap up her temporal affairs—making out a will or assuring that all of her financial and other commitments are complete. Perhaps she has unfinished business with family members, or has to prepare herself spiritually for death, or maybe she is hoping for a miracle cure for the lymphoma. All these would be valid reasons for accepting the treatment even though she believes her death from cancer to be imminent. In these instances, taking the antibiotics would be considered an ordinary means of care because the perceived benefits of the treatment would outweigh its burdens.

Let us assume that Barbara has already taken care of her temporal affairs, made peace with family and friends, prepared herself spiritually for death, and no longer holds out any reasonable hope for a cure. She knows and accepts that she will not live long, and that her remaining days will entail increasing loss of bodily functions and increasing pain. In this case, the burdens of taking the antibiotics outweigh any perceived benefit and, according to Barbara's informed judgment, they would constitute an extraordinary means of care.

Timothy also has contracted bacterial pneumonia, but he is otherwise physically healthy. He is depressed, but that in itself is not life-threatening. The antibiotics will restore Timothy's physical health, and their benefits clearly outweigh any perceived burdens they may bring. One might ask, "Although taking the antibiotics may present little or no physical burden for Timothy, is he not free to choose to refuse treatment?" From an ethical perspective he is not free to choose for two reasons. In Timothy's case no extraordinary factors are associated with taking the antibiotics; the treatment will simply return him to his normal state of health. Timothy perceives a burden—having to continue living without his departed wife—but it should be possible to overcome this burden through time, professional psychiatric care, and possibly recourse to antidepressants. For Timothy the antibiotics constitute an ordinary means of care and, according to Church teaching, an ordinary means of care is always morally obligatory.

A second reason Timothy is morally obligated to accept the antibiotics can be found in directive 59 of the United States bishops' *Ethical and Religious Directives*. The bishops maintain that while the judgment of what constitutes ordinary and extraordinary means of care ultimately lies with the patient, this does not mean that it is ethical to make any kind of judgment one wants.

The free and informed judgment made by a competent adult concerning the use or withdrawal of life-sustaining procedures should always be respected and normally complied with, unless it is contrary to Catholic moral teaching.[21]

Because the antibiotics will cure the pneumonia and because no other biological pathology is involved, Timothy's decision to refuse the treatment is really a form of suicide. His only reason for refusing medical care is to directly bring about his death, an action that, according to Church teaching, is never morally permitted.

Artificial Means of Care

We often hear people say, "I don't want to be kept alive artificially." Statements like this betray a dangerous misunderstanding of what constitutes an artificial means of care and the extent to which these artificial means are morally obligatory.

The word *artificial* comes from the Latin *ars* and *facere*, meaning that which is made by human art as opposed to nature. In health care, *artificial* applies to the entire range of medicines and procedures that are created by human beings and used by HCPs. In the cases of Barbara and Timothy, the antibiotic treatment was an artificial means of care. The drug may have been constituted from naturally occurring elements, but human beings had to discover, research, develop, and ultimately compile these elements into the form of the actual medication. Humans take what God offers and manipulate it into a particular treatment that helps to foster human health. All medicines or medical procedures are intended to aid the patient when nature is deficient. For this reason, they can all be termed artificial means of care.

Now the question becomes, "Are artificial means of care ordinary or extraordinary, and under what conditions is recourse to them morally required?" Appropriate answers depend on the circumstances at hand. Normally the use of artificial means of care is relatively short term and the patient will eventually resume functioning naturally. Artificial medicines or procedures are the normally prescribed means of care because (1) they help to bring our bodies back to a normal, healthy state, or (2) they assume a primary function (such as breathing or circulation) until such time that the body can resume functioning on its own. The artificial medicines or procedures constitute an ordinary means of care and are morally obligatory. However, an artificial means of care can also be deemed extraordinary. Often a medicine or treatment that starts out as an artificial but ordinary means of care eventually becomes an extraordinary means of care. Let's consider another case.

CASE 3

Martha is an eighty-five-year-old grandmother who is brought into the emergency room suffering from acute respiratory failure. Her grandson, Robert, is with her. The doctors inform Robert that without a ventilator, Martha will soon die. Robert asks the doctors if they know the cause of the respiratory failure. They do not. So Robert makes the decision to have his grandmother placed on a ventilator until a diagnosis can be made. This is done, and Martha's condition immediately improves.

As the diagnostic process proceeds, Martha informs Robert in writing that she does not want to continue living if she must remain "hooked up" to the ventilator. Robert reassures her that she will only remain on the ventilator for as much time as it takes to complete the diagnosis, which should not take long. The following day the diagnosis is complete, and doctors inform Robert that Martha will need to remain on the ventilator for the remainder of her life. As such, she will have to be placed in a nursing home. What will happen, Robert asks, if his grandmother is taken off the ventilator? The doctors tell him that her respiratory and circulatory systems will begin to fail and that she will die relatively quickly. Armed with this information, Robert gently informs his grandmother of the doctors' prognosis. She understands that she has two options, remain on the ventilator and live her remaining days in a nursing home, or be taken off it and die within a week. After some further, brief deliberation with Robert and her parish pastor, she decides that she does not want to live the rest of her life dependent on a machine, nor does she want to lose her independence by being placed in a nursing home. She insists that she be taken off the ventilator.

In Martha's situation the initial use of the ventilator constituted an ordinary means of care. The doctors did not know the reason for her respiratory failure and needed to diagnose Martha's condition. Until the diagnosis was made, the ventilator served as the primary means of allowing her to breathe.

Once the diagnosis was made, the situation was different, and Martha's decision to be removed from the ventilator was ethically permissible. What had been an artificial but ordinary means of care when she entered the hospital became artificial and extraordinary. Given her diagnosis, the ventilator became a physical and psychological burden for Martha—she determined that it was her time to die. Martha's decision to have the ventilator removed was permissible not because the ventilator constituted an artificial means of care, but because the artificial means of care had become excessively burdensome and no longer offered her any reasonable hope of recovery. The ventilator had become extraordinary, and Martha's recourse to it was no longer morally obligatory.

Patients Who Are Comatose or in a Persistent Vegetative State

Although advancements in medical technology are generally good, sometimes they force patients or patients' families to make complicated and heart-wrenching decisions. What should we do when a loved one slips into a coma or a persistent vegetative state? Should we maintain medications and other treatments to preserve life, or should we discontinue them and allow death to occur naturally? What do we do when individuals entrusted to our care have not specifically stated what they would like done to them if they become incapacitated? What do we do when family members disagree on the best course of action? As our small contribution to this ongoing discussion, we focus on two philosophical questions that have particular relevance for the issue at hand: (1) Are comatose individuals still human persons, and (2) assuming that they are still persons, what level of care must be afforded to them in terms of nutrition and hydration?

Are comatose individuals still human persons? A patient may be technically alive in the sense that the heart is beating, but if the patient is incapable of interpersonal communication and probably never will be again, can we really say that the patient is a person in the truest sense of the term?

Physicians have established medical criteria for determining when death has occurred. For example, the Harvard Medical School criteria for brain death includes (1) unreceptivity and unresponsivity to externally applied stimuli, including pain; (2) no spontaneous movement or breathing for a period of at least one hour; (3) no reflexes, indicating the central nervous system's failure to function; and (4) two flat electroencephalogram (EEG) tests recorded at six-hour intervals.[22] These criteria are used today to help determine brain death, and some would argue that personhood ceases when these criteria have been met. But what about situations where the criteria have not been met completely? Is this individual still a person? What about those who are unconscious and unreceptive to others but whose higher-order brain functions remain? Keep in mind that most individuals in a coma are not brain-dead; they are, in fact, very much alive. These individuals may be in a coma as the result of some trauma or other illness. The coma can be "light" in the sense that the patient can emerge from it with little or no ill effect, or it may be more profound, lasting for years. From an ethical perspective, comatose individuals are persons. As such, they retain the dignity and respect that is rightfully theirs until death has been determined by reasonably defined clinical criteria.

The second question is, what level of care (in terms of nutrition and hydration) must be afforded to individuals in a persistent vegetative state (PVS)? Once again, we are morally obligated to provide nutrition and hydration when they constitute an ordinary means of medical care, but not when they constitute an extraordinary means of care. One of the most contentious and controversial end-of-life ethical issues today concerns the ordinary or extraordinary nature of artificial nutrition and hydration for PVS patients. Put more bluntly, are feeding tubes for PVS patients morally obligatory and, once put in, can they ever be removed?

The Terri Schiavo case amply illustrates how we as a nation grapple with these questions. Terri Schiavo, a woman in her mid-twenties, collapsed at her Florida home in February 1990 and remained in a permanent vegetative state until her death in March 2005. She did breathe on her own during this period, and she demonstrated some movement, although most medical experts do not believe these movements were controlled. She was not able to swallow, nor was she capable of any form of interpersonal communication. Early on she was given a PEG (percutaneous endoscopic gastronomy) feeding tube for nutrition and hydration, and she remained this way, with some brief exceptions, until 2005.[23] In 1998 her husband, Michael, petitioned the Florida courts to allow for the removal of the tube, but her parents, Robert and Mary Schindler, objected to this and even offered to become Terri's legal guardians so they could oversee her continued care. The courtroom battles between Michael and the Schindlers went on for years. By 2003 the national media had picked up the story. The governor and legislature of Florida got involved in the dispute, as did the United States Congress. In the end, the courts upheld Michael's request and on March 18, 2005, the feeding tube was removed for the final time. Terri Schiavo died thirteen days later, on March 31.

Many people believe that if Terri had made it unequivocally known that she did not want to be kept alive by means of artificial hydration and nutrition, then her wishes should have been respected. This principle (self-determination) was invoked by Terri's husband, Michael, who repeatedly stated that his wife had told him that she did not want to be kept alive by artificial means. For Michael, acting as his wife's proxy, the PEG tube constituted an extraordinary means of care. Terri's parents maintained that Terri would have wanted to continue living no matter what. For them, nutrition and hydration were ordinary means of care, and they should have been continued until Terri died a "natural" death. Once again, we see that the ethical dilemma is not a question of the use of artificial nutrition and hydration as such, but of what decision Terri Schiavo had made prior to falling into a persistent vegetative state.

Is artificial nutrition and hydration an ordinary means of care for a patient in a persistent vegetative state? In Catholic health care circles this is much debated. A 1990 pastoral letter published by the Texas Conference of Catholic Bishops claimed that artificial methods of nutrition and hydration for PVS patients were burdensome, and recourse to them was not morally obligatory.[24] In 1992 the Pennsylvania Conference of Bishops reached the opposite conclusion.[25] Also in 1992 the United States Bishops' Pro-Life Committee reached a conclusion similar to that of the Pennsylvania bishops, although they acknowledged that "legitimate Catholic moral debate continues."[26] Benedict Ashley and Kevin O'Rourke, two highly respected Catholic health care ethicists, interpreted the Vatican *Declaration on Euthanasia*'s statement that "one cannot impose on anyone the obligation to have recourse to a technique which is already in use but which carries a risk or is burdensome" to mean that it is morally legitimate to withdraw nutrition and hydration.[27] Moral theologian William May disagreed with Ashley and O'Rourke, arguing that since life is an intrinsic good and that PVS patients are not suffering from a fatal pathology (they are not actively dying), withdrawing nutrition and hydration from them is never morally legitimate.[28] The United States Catholic bishops as a whole offered tacit acceptance of removing artificial nutrition and hydration in their *Ethical and Religious Directives*:

> There should be a presumption in favor of providing nutrition and hydration to all patients, including patients who require medically assisted nutrition and hydration, *as long as this is of sufficient benefit to outweigh the burdens involved to the patient.*[29]

However, the immediately following directive states:

> The free and informed judgment made by a competent adult patient concerning the use or withdrawal of life-sustaining procedures should always be respected and normally complied with, *unless it is contrary to Catholic moral teaching.*[30]

Obviously, there has been a good measure of disagreement about whether a feeding tube can be legitimately removed from a PVS patient. The general rule of thumb was that the PVS patient's proxy — always in consultation with HCPs, family, and clergy — should make the informed determination of whether the feeding tube constituted an ordinary or extraordinary means of care, and thus whether the feeding tube should be removed or not. Then, in 2004, Pope John Paul II weighed in on the debate by stating:

> I should like particularly to underline how the administration of water and food, even when provided by artificial means, always represents a *natural means* of preserving life, not a *medical act*. Its use, furthermore, should be considered, in principle, *ordinary* and *proportionate*, and as such morally obligatory, insofar as and until it is seen to have attained its proper finality, which in the present case consists in providing nourishment to the patient and alleviation of his suffering.
>
> The obligation to provide the "normal care due to the sick in such cases" includes, in fact, the use of nutrition and hydration. The evaluation of probabilities, founded on waning hopes for recovery when the vegetative state is prolonged beyond a year, cannot ethically justify the cessation or interruption of *minimal care* for the patient, including nutrition and hydration. Death by starvation or dehydration is, in fact, the only possible outcome as a result of

their withdrawal. In this sense it ends up becoming, if done know-ingly and willingly, true and proper euthanasia by omission.[31]

In short, John Paul II held that nutrition and hydration for PVS patients always constitutes an ordinary means of care, and as such is always mor-ally obligatory and can never be interrupted or withdrawn. The numerous responses from Catholic health care ethicists have ranged from complete assent to critical disagreement. So where do we stand? Is it morally permis-sible to withdraw feeding tubes from PVS patients, even in situations where we believe the tube constitutes a greater burden than benefit? In September 2007, the Congregation for the Doctrine of the Faith clarified John Paul II's teaching by reaffirming that artificial nutrition and hydration are ordi-nary means of care and thus morally obligatory for all PVS patients. The only exceptions to this rule are (1) when the patient's body cannot assimi-late food and water and (2) when the means used to deliver nutrition and hydration (for example a PEG tube) cause the patient significant physical discomfort. The CDF also reaffirmed that because of its ordinary nature, artificial nutrition and hydration may not be removed from a PVS patient even in situations where doctors judge that the patient will never regain consciousness.[32] By issuing these clarifications, the CDF confirms John Paul II's teaching that it is never morally permissible to remove a feeding tube from a PVS patient regardless of the patient's previously expressed wishes or the substitute judgment of the patient's proxy.

We would like to close this section, as well as this entire chapter on medical ethics, by recalling the mystery of the Resurrection. All Christians profess that our earthly death is not really "the end" because just as Christ rose from the dead three days after his crucifixion, so also will we be resurrected like him at the Last Judgment. As such, the mystery of the Resurrection reminds us that human life is not the be-all and end-all of our existence, nor should we act as if nothingness awaits us after our death. We have been baptized, after all, into the life, death, and *Resurrection* of Jesus. Earthly life holds great value, but it is not the ultimate value. Eternal life is. We must always keep in mind the truly relative nature of our earthly exis-tence, including the medical means we use to preserve it, while at the same time maintaining our faith and hope in the risen and living Lord.

Review Questions

1. What is the principle of integrity? What is the principle of totality? How are these principles applied in practice?

2. What is the principle of truth telling? What specific challenge do HCPs face in the application of this principle?

3. What is the principle of confidentiality? Why is it essential for the patient-professional relationship? When can it be "violated"?

4. What is the principle of double effect? What four elements make up the principle of double effect?

5. In terms of the principle of legitimate cooperation, what is formal cooperation with evil? What distinguishes immediate material cooperation from mediate material cooperation? What distinguishes proximate mediate material cooperation from remote mediate material cooperation? What does the Catholic Church teach about each?

6. In what three primary ways have people responded to the question, "What is the status of the human embryo?" What is the Catholic Church's teaching concerning when human personhood begins?

7. According to the Catholic Church, what kinds of insemination procedures are morally permissible? What kinds are not? What is the difference between a homologous and heterologous insemination procedure? Why does the Catholic Church teach that heterologous procedures are never morally permissible?

8. Why does the Catholic Church teach that both heterologous and homologous IVF are morally wrong?

9. What scientific moral questions surround human embryonic stem cell research? What is the main ethical (and legal) consideration with human embryonic stem cell research?

10. What is meant by artificial means of care? Under what conditions are artificial means of care deemed ordinary and morally obligatory? Under what conditions do artificial means of care become extraordinary and no longer morally obligatory?

ENDNOTES

1 *Summa Theologiae*, I – II, q. 65, a.1, c.

2 This view is challenged by Robert P. George, JD, DPhil, "A Note on Twinning," *Ethics and Medics* 31, no. 9 (September 2006): 4.

3 *Summa Theologiae*, III, q. 33, a. 2, 2.

4 Congregation for the Doctrine of the Faith, *Gift of Life* (*Donum Vitae*), (1987), I, no. 1. This document is available online at http://www.vatican.va/roman_curia/congregations/cfaith/documents/rc_con_cfaith_doc_19870222_respect_for_human_life_en.html.

5 For concise descriptions of these procedures, see Sharon Begley, "The Baby," *Newsweek* (September 4, 1995): 38 – 41, 43 – 47.

6 *Gift of Life*, II, no. 7.

7 For further discussion on permissible and impermissible methods of assisted fertilization, see William May, *Catholic Bioethics and the Gift of Human Life* (Huntington, IN: Our Sunday Visitor, 2000), 87– 94.

8 Pope Pius XII, *Discourse to the Italian Catholic Union of Midwives*, October 29, 1951 (*Acta Apostolicae Sedis*, 1951), 850.

9 *Gift of Life*, II, no. 1– 2.

10 *Gift of Life*, II, no. 4 – 5.

11 In this section, we draw from Xavier Thévenot, *La bioéthique: Début et fin de vie* (Paris: Le Centurion, 1989); and from Scott Gilbert et al., *Bioethics and the New Embryology: Springboards for Debate* (Sunderland, MA: Sinaur, 2005), 73 –79.

12 The Church's Congregation for the Doctrine of the Faith speaks to this point clearly: "[T]he child has the right… to be the fruit of a specific act of the conjugal love of his parents; and he also has the right to be respected as a person from the moment of his conception." See *Gift of Life*, II, #8.

13 The information in this section comes from Nancy Gibbs, "Stem Cells: The Hope and the Hype," *Time* (August 7, 2006): 40 – 46; and Gilbert et al., *Bioethics and the New Embryology*, 143 –75.

14 For more information on how both adult and umbilical cord stem cells have cured various diseases, see the Web site of the National Catholic Bioethics Center at http://www.ncbcenter.org.

15 Cf. http://www.nytimes.com/2007/11/27/science/27stem.html?_r=1&fta=y&oref=slogin

16 This section is adapted from Benedict Guevin, "Ordinary, Extraordinary and Artificial Care," *The National Catholic Bioethics Quarterly* 5, no. 3 (Autumn 2005): 471–79. Used with permission.

17 Gerald Kelly, SJ, "The Duty to Preserve Life," *Theological Studies* 12 (December 1951): 550 – 56.

18 Pius XII, "Allocution on Reanimation," *Acta Apostolicae Sedis* 49 (November 24, 1957): 1027–33 (emphasis added).

19 United States Conference of Catholic Bishops, *Ethical and Religious Directives for Catholic Health Care Services*, 4th ed. (NCCB/UCCB, June 15, 2001), nos. 56 and 57 (emphasis added). In Directive 56, the bishops refer to the Congregation for the Doctrine of the Faith, *Declaration on Euthanasia* (1980), Part IV.

20 Benedict Ashley, OP, and Kevin O'Rourke, OP, *Health Care Ethics: A Theological Analysis*, 4th ed. (Washington, DC: Georgetown University Press, 1997), 428.

21 *Ethical and Religious Directives*, no. 59. See also the CDF's *Declaration on Euthanasia*, Part II.

22 These criteria are taken from Richard J. Divine, *Good Care Painful Choices*, 3rd ed. (Mahwah, NJ: Paulist Press, 2004), 202–3.

23 During Terri Schiavo's incapacitation there were short periods when the feeding tube was removed, but was subsequently reinserted by order of the various Florida courts.

24 Texas Conference of Catholic Bishops, "On Withholding Artificial Nutrition and Hydration" (May 7, 1990), *Origins* 20 (1990): 53–55.

25 Pennsylvania Conference of Catholic Bishops, "Nutrition and Hydration: Moral Considerations" (January 14, 1992), *Origins* 21 (January 30, 1992): 542–53.

26 United States Catholic Bishops Pro-Life Committee, "Nutrition and Hydration: Moral and Pastoral Reflections" (April 2, 1992), *Origins* 21 (April 19, 1992): 705–12.

27 Ashley and O'Rourke, *Health Care Ethics*, 427.

28 William May, "Tube Feeding and the 'Vegetative State,'" *Ethics and Medics* 23, no. 12 (December 1998): 1–2.

29 United States Conference of Catholic Bishops, *Ethical and Religious Directives for Catholic Health Care Services*, June 2001, no. 58 (emphasis added).

30 Ibid., no. 59 (emphasis added).

31 John Paul II, "Address to the Participants in the International Congress of 'Life-Sustaining Treatments and Vegetative State: Scientific Advances and Ethical Dilemmas,'" (March 20, 2004). For the full text of the pope's address, see *National Catholic Bioethics Quarterly* 4, no. 3 (Autumn 2004): 573–76 (emphasis in the original). For commentary and discussion on the address, see articles by D. O'Brien, J. P. Slosar, A. Tersigni, P. Cataldo, and G. Kopaczynski in the same issue.

32 Congregation for the Doctrine of the Faith, "Responses to Certain Questions of the United States Conference of Catholic Bishops Concerning Artificial Nutrition and Hydration" (September 14, 2007).

9. SEXUAL ETHICS

It has been said that the way to avoid arguments in a social setting is to refrain from talking about politics and religion. Why is this? One reason, we think, is that both politics and religion engage us on a personal level.

In terms of religion, nothing is more personal to us than who we are as sexual beings. Because of the personal nature of our sexuality, we find it difficult to tolerate prying into it from the outside, whether the intrusion is from parents, teachers, or the Church. The general perception today is that the Catholic Church's teachings on sexuality are negative, obsolete, and too focused on its biological aspects rather than on its personal and interpersonal dimensions. Here we challenge these perceptions by demonstrating that what the Church teaches is essentially positive, always timely, and takes seriously the biological, personal, and interpersonal dimensions of human sexuality. Let us begin this exploration by examining the biological and personal dimensions of sex.

Persons Are Embodied and Therefore Sexual Beings

We often hear people say that we *have* bodies: "She has a great body; he has a great body." But what do we mean when we say that we *have* a body? We often mean different things: "I possess my body, this is my body and no one else's, I can do whatever I want with my body, and I can do it with whomever I choose" (usually with the caveat "as long I don't hurt anybody"). I once knew a young woman who was promiscuous. According to her own reckoning, she had had sex with over two hundred different partners. When I asked this bright, articulate, and caring young woman how she dealt with a sexuality that was, by her own admission, out of control, she said: "It's only my body that's rotten; my soul is pure." What this young woman is saying — and in fact what much of society says as well — is that her body and soul are two separate entities and that what she does with one in no way affects the other. As we move through this chapter, we will see that this assumption is incorrect.

Although it may sound awkward, it is more correct to say that I *am* a body. Evidence for this comes directly from the Scriptures. Our original parents recognized their kinship with one another through their bodies, and it was through their bodies that they related to each other as husband and wife.

> So the LORD God cast a deep sleep on the man, and while he was asleep, he took one of his ribs and closed up its place with flesh. The LORD God then built up into a woman the rib that he had taken from the man. When he brought her to the man, the man said: "This one, at last, is bone of my bones and flesh of my flesh; this one shall be called 'woman,' for out of 'her man' this one has been taken. (Gen. 2:21 – 23)

In the language of the creation narratives, there are two ways of being a person: male and female. The unity of human nature includes the duality of masculinity and femininity, each existing as a complement to the other. Through their bodies, men and women are physically present in the world, and as embodied persons they relate to God who created them, to others in general, and to one "other" in particular through the inseparable bond of marriage that makes the two persons "one body." The body, then, is man and woman in the concreteness of their existence and in the multiple, varied relationships that they experience throughout their lives.

It is essential to affirm the goodness of the embodied person and of sexuality. Too often Christianity has been criticized for being opposed to the bodily dimension of our being. Although there is some truth in this observation, the authentic tradition has always upheld the body's inherent dignity. Immediately after stating that humanity is created in the image and likeness of God, the Scriptures state:

> God blessed them, saying to them, "Be fertile and multiply; fill the earth and subdue it. Have dominion over the fish of the sea, the birds of the air, and all the living things that move on the earth." (Gen. 1:28)

And a few verses later:

> God looked at everything he had made, and he found it very good. Evening came, and morning followed — the sixth day. (Gen. 1:31)

From these Scriptures we know that everything God created was good, and the human body shares in this goodness. But the goodness of the human body is not to be understood as the goodness of some "neutral" body. As we have seen, there are two ways of being embodied: male and female. The sexuality that results as a consequence of male and female embodiment needs to be regarded as an essential dimension of who that person is. It is because the man and the woman are created as sexual bodies that God can command them to come together to be fruitful and multiply, and fill the earth and subdue it. The act of intercourse by which the man and woman procreate is in itself good and blessed. It is also through this act that the couple, each of whom is created in the image and likeness of God, shares in God's own creativity.[1]

How do we live as sexual beings? Or perhaps more bluntly, how do we exercise self-mastery over our sexuality? The Catholic Church teaches that no matter who our "neighbor" may be (spouse, friend, parent, sibling, relative, stranger), our relationships are governed by the virtue of chastity, which is a subcategory of the cardinal virtue of temperance.

Temperance

Temperance is one of many virtues we are called to cultivate. A virtue is a disposition (or pattern of behavior) of the will by which an individual willingly and consistently chooses to act in a morally good way. Stated differently, virtues are ongoing patterns of moral behavior that develop through our free and intentional choices. Humans are not born with virtues; virtues develop through the good decisions that we make throughout our lives. For example, we develop the virtue of honesty by freely choosing always to tell the truth. We develop the virtue of justice by consistently seeking to render to others that which is their due. Virtues serve as the foundation for consistent responses to the moral decisions we face.

Temperance is one of the four cardinal virtues, along with prudence, justice, and fortitude. The cardinal virtues are the primary virtues on which all other virtues "hinge" (this is what the term *cardinal* means). Thus any virtue that we cultivate falls under one of these four main categories. In this section we explore the cardinal virtue of temperance; later in the chapter we explore one of temperance's particular sub-virtues: chastity.

Temperance is the virtue that brings reason to bear on what are called the affective emotions. The affective emotions move us to desire certain sensed bodily goods that are important for the maintenance of the individual person (food and drink) and the species as a whole (sex). As expressions of desire for what is pleasurable and aversion to what is painful, the affective emotions are neither good nor bad in themselves. This does not mean that they are contrary to reason or that they cannot be controlled by the human will. Affective emotions can be controlled by the will and thus moral judgment applies to them.[2] When temperance is exercised with respect to the bodily desire for drink, we have the allied virtue of sobriety.[3] When exercised with respect to food, we have the allied virtue of fasting.[4] And when temperance is brought to bear on matters of sex, we are in the realm of chastity.

How does one acquire the virtue of temperance? According to Thomas Aquinas, two passions in particular dispose us to temperance: the feeling of shame[5] and the sense of honor.[6] The feeling of shame is a kind of fear of possible disgrace concerning the thought or use of some bodily good. The fear of possible disgrace arises when something, which by its nature or in view of its purpose ought to be private, passes through the bounds of a person's privacy and becomes public.[7] Most people probably experience sexual shame more acutely than shame over food and drink. There is, on one level, an experience of shame connected to the body, especially to the sexual organs. There is an almost universal tendency to conceal the sexual organs from others, especially from the opposite sex. But nakedness does not always mean shamelessness. In some cultures nakedness is a simple adaptation to climatic conditions. What is, perhaps, a more essential expression of sexual shame is the concealment of the sexual value of the body itself, particularly insofar as it constitutes in the mind of another person a potential object of enjoyment. Young children, for whom sexual values do not yet exist, do not experience shame the way older children and adults do. It is only when children mature that they begin to experience sexual shame, not as an imposition from the outside, but as an interior need of an evolving personality. As persons mature they become aware of their bodily and sexual integrity. Healthy individuals have the sense that no one can or should take possession of a person's physicality unless that person permits it and gives him or herself to the other out of love. This sense of personal inviolability is a healthy expression of sexual shame.[8]

The feeling of shame is present only in those who experience a certain attraction to moral goodness, but who have not yet succeeded in acquiring the virtue of temperance necessary to live according to this attraction in a sustained manner. They may, in fact, be attracted to moral evil as well. The virtuous person and the nonvirtuous person may lack shame, but for opposite reasons. The former lacks shame because he or she has acquired virtue and is, therefore, not disposed to fall into anything dishonorable or can avoid dishonorable deeds more readily. The latter lacks shame because he or she is psychosexually immature, unhealthy, or is so sunk in vice that the perception of having done something shameful is not apprehended.[9] Most of us fall somewhere between these two extremes. We seek to do good in our lives, but we are often attracted to evil. The feeling of shame, then, is experienced neither by the truly virtuous nor by the completely vicious, but by one who is attracted at one and the same time to both good and evil. Now the feeling of shame is morally good,[10] but is not the virtue of temperance. What is lacking in shame is both reason (shame is a feeling) and the freedom that is specific to virtue.

The sense of honor is of the same order as the feeling of shame, but is, in some senses, its opposite. The sense of honor is a feeling of love for what is good. Now a good can be loved because it satisfies the appetite for what is pleasurable or because it is somehow useful for achieving a given end.[11] But a good can also be loved simply because it is worthy to be loved in itself, apart from either the pleasure it procures or its usefulness (although pleasure and utility are not excluded from such a good).[12] This sense of honor prepares a person for the practice of temperance insofar as it is an attraction to what is good and beautiful, and a rejection of what is indecent and ugly. We can generally say that temperance incorporates that which is honorable.[13] But to the extent that a sense of honor remains merely on the level of a general attraction to the good, it is not yet the true virtue of temperance.

Our experiences of shame and honor, while not virtues in themselves, help dispose us to the virtue of temperance. The reason for this is that shame and honor compel us to make concrete choices concerning our affective emotions. If we feel a sense of shame about something, we tend to avoid it. If we feel a sense of honor about something, we tend to act upon it. Over time, as we willingly and consistently choose to act in morally good ways, we develop the virtue of temperance. Recall that the virtue of temperance brings reason to bear on the affective emotions; the temperate person can control his or her passions through the exercise of reason. Our experiences of shame and honor help us to develop this virtue.

Temperance is unlike the other cardinal virtues because it is directed toward an individual's desire for self-preservation.[14] As individuals, we need to eat and drink to live. As a species, we need to reproduce to continue our existence. This desire for self-preservation is good, and those things that contribute to it are not to be disparaged. Yet these powerful and fundamental drives, while good in themselves, also harbor the seeds of personal destruction. Gluttony, or the lack of temperance regarding food, can lead to obesity, heart disease, and death. Drunkenness, or the lack of temperance regarding drink, can lead to personal destruction as well as the destruction of families and friendships. Lust, or the lack of temperance in the area of sexuality, can lead to both personal and social disintegration as well as injustice. Temperance brought to bear in matters of sexuality leads to the virtue of chastity. Let us now take a closer look at this virtue.

Chastity

What is chastity? Most people would probably say, "Not having sex — period," "Being pure," or "No sex before marriage." Although there is a measure of truth in each of these answers, they are inadequate. According to the *Catechism of the Catholic Church*, chastity is "the successful integration of sexuality within the person and thus the inner unity of man in his bodily and spiritual being." It is not a denial of one's sexuality or of one's sexual feelings, but the virtue by which sexuality becomes personal and interpersonal — becomes truly and fully human. "The virtue of chastity therefore involves the integrity of the person and the integrality of the gift."[15]

The integrity of the person and the integrality of the gift of one's sexuality are not assured in our fallen human nature. According to Scripture, the first man and woman chose to act in a way that was at odds with the truth of who they were — creatures who shared in God's creative activity through, among other things, the blessing of the power to procreate. With this choice they began a history of sexuality all too often marked by impersonalism, selfishness, and a lack of integration; in other words, by lust. Pope Benedict XVI captures well the dynamic of lust in his encyclical *God Is Love*:

> Eros, reduced to pure "sex," has become a commodity. This is hardly man's great "yes" to the body. On the contrary, he now considers his body and his sexuality as the purely material part of himself, to be used and exploited at will. Nor does he see it as an arena for the exercise of his freedom, but as a mere object that he attempts, as he pleases, to make both enjoyable and harmless. We are actually dealing with the debasement of the human body: no longer is it integrated into our overall existential freedom; no longer is it a vital expression of our whole being, but it is more or less relegated to the purely biological sphere.[16]

The "matter" of human sexuality, the pope says, is not simply biological. Rather, the "matter" is the reality of the human person, the unity of the body and soul in relationship with God, self, and others. To maintain otherwise by excessively spiritualizing the body — as some Christians have done — would have the effect of emptying the body of its moral meaning. Similarly, viewing the body as simply a physical object — as society tends to do — reduces the person to the level of a beast. The body is as integral to our human nature as is reason. To regard the body as a commodity or as a meaningless physical structure would be to act not only against the body itself, but also against reason's apprehension of the body's special character and the integral place it occupies in human nature.[17]

Pope John Paul II asserted that the essence of chastity "consists in quickness to affirm the value of the person in every situation, and in raising to the personal level all reactions to the value of 'body and sex.'"[18] That is, chastity leads us to treat others as persons and not merely as bodies. Chastity does not simply mean "don't have sex." It means recognizing what sexuality is for and conforming our actions to it. That is why those who take a vow of celibacy—the Catholic clergy and those who have professed vows to a religious order—do not engage in sexual relations. That is also why those who are not married should not engage in sexual relations: they have not made a lifelong commitment to the other person. For married people chastity means remaining faithful to one's spouse. Married people are permitted—and expected—to engage in sexual relations both to express their committed love for one another and to have children. However, within marriage sexuality is exclusive in that the spouses are to experience it only with each other. It is only through this faithfulness and exclusivity that human sexuality becomes the gift that it was meant to be by God's design. When we willingly and consistently act in accord with this understanding of sexuality, we develop the virtue of chastity.

Because integrity in the area of sexuality is not a given, progress in the virtue of chastity is a lifelong process. The *Catechism* states that chastity, or self-mastery in the area of sexuality, is "long and exacting work." In fact, the *Catechism* claims that we never fully acquire the virtue of chastity in our lifetime, but that it requires "renewed effort at all stages of life." It is a process of growth, and the stages are often marked by imperfection and sin.[19] We should accept that imperfection and sin are inevitable—but we should not adopt a cavalier attitude toward them. Rather, amid our imperfection and sin we should continually strive to live ever more perfect lives of chastity.

To conclude, chastity is the virtue by which our sexuality becomes integrated into the whole person, body and soul. This integration leads to a sexuality that values and respects the dignity of the self and others as persons. Chastity leads to a more fully human sexuality, one that is lived as a gift to oneself and others. Paraphrasing Pope Benedict XVI, sexuality can only attain its full human stature when it is lived as an expression of our intimately united body and soul. Only through this intimately united expression of body and soul can human love mature and attain its authentic grandeur.[20]

Issues in Sexuality

In the remainder of this chapter we explore a number of contemporary and controversial issues concerning human sexuality. Based on what we have established so far, chaste human sexuality is both self-giving and life-giving. It involves the full gift of oneself to another, and is open to the creation of new life. Expressions of sexuality are problematic if they involve some deficiency in either the self-giving or the life-giving dimensions. Such deficiencies are found not only in what we do, but also in what we think and how we speak.

Why do we use the word *deficiency* rather than *sin*? Recall from chapter 2 that moral acts do not occur in a vacuum but always within a set of circumstances (Who? What? Where? When? Why? How? How much?). Before deciding whether things like premarital sex, cohabitation, contraception, homosexual activity, and masturbation are sins, one first has to know who is acting (or thinking about acting) and with what level of knowledge and freedom she or he is doing so. When we talk about the sinfulness of certain sexual behaviors, we are talking about the behavior as a known and freely chosen act of the will. The more individuals know and the more they are free to choose their actions, the more they are responsible for their behavior and — if the act is problematic — the more serious the offense. Therefore, as we explore various sexual behaviors it is better to speak of deficiency rather than sin when the behaviors are lacking in regard to the self-giving and life-giving dimensions of human sexuality. Such deficiencies *may* entail sinfulness, but we do not always know to what extent. In any case, these are important matters, as Gerald Coleman, SS, reminds us:

> Sexual expression manifests the *self*, the total person, in a peculiarly intense way. . . . The modern adage that our sexual activities have nothing to do with the kinds of persons we are is profoundly untrue and represents a trivializing of sex which leads to a trivializing of the self.[21]

Premarital Sex

Premarital sex is any sexual act performed before marriage. Behaviors range from "hooking up" with someone you've just met to intercourse with the person to whom you are engaged. This broad range of behaviors reflects a similarly broad range in level of affection and commitment, from "one-night stands" (with no affection or commitment) to long-term but premarital relationships (with greater affection and commitment). Premarital sex also refers to a wide variety of sexual acts, including oral sex, anal sex, mutual masturbation, and full sexual intercourse.

Premarital sex is quite common, and those who engage in it are getting younger. One often hears, "Everyone is doing it, so what's the big deal?" In some circles, to be a virgin after a certain age is considered freakish: "What, you haven't done it yet? What's wrong with you?" Secular society, including the media and many educators, conveys the message that it is all right to have sex "as long as you are responsible." "Responsible" usually means using a condom or other contraceptive device; thus "safe sex" has come to mean responsible (and by extension, moral) sex.

At the same time, a growing number of young people are committed to "saving themselves" for marriage. Some are virgins. Others have committed themselves anew to chaste living after a negative experience or a religious awakening. The truth is that not everyone is "doing it," and there is nothing wrong with a person who chooses not to engage in premarital sex.

Premarital sex, like any sexual behavior, at its most base can be treated as a contact sport, something to do when you're bored or when you want to release sexual energy. It can be exploitative and even commercialized. At a higher level, it can be seen as a sign of love or some level of commitment to another person. Ideally sexual intercourse should not be a *sign* of a couple's love and commitment, but the *sign and the fruit* of a relationship that is permanent, exclusive, faithful, and sealed by public declaration of the couple's love for each other.

When we speak of love, we are not talking about mere affection or physical attraction. Rather, we are talking about the kind of love that is rooted in respect for the other as a person and in willingness (for love is more a matter of the will than natural attraction) to be with this person "for better or for worse, in sickness and in health, for richer or for poorer until death do we part." This kind of love presupposes, and is an expression of, a commitment that is permanent, exclusive, and faithful. It is the kind of love found only within marriage.

An extended discussion of what marriage is and what it requires would be helpful here, but space limitations do not permit it. Instead, we simply note that the key issue is commitment. Marriage is a commitment on the part of a man and a woman to love, honor, and be faithful to each other, made in the eyes of the community, the Church, and God. Sexuality is the physical sign and fruit of this committed relationship. In marriage, a man and woman give themselves completely to each other, body, soul, mind, and heart. Sexual intercourse is the physical sign of this total gift of oneself, it is "the fullest self-disclosure one person can offer to another."[22] That is why the Catholic Church teaches that sexuality is only to be experienced within marriage.

The problem with premarital sexuality is that it is not, nor can it ever be, an expression of the full self-gift of one person to another. Without the free commitment of one's whole self to another given through the marriage vows, it is impossible to experience the fullness of what sexuality entails. *The Code of Canon Law* speaks to this by describing the requirements of a valid marriage. The exchange of vows initiates marriage, intercourse consummates, or completes, it. No matter how many times a couple has intercourse before exchanging vows, the marriage is not consummated until the couple's first act of intercourse after vows have been exchanged. The reason for this is simple: one cannot complete what has not been initiated.[23]

Because it does not embody the commitment, permanency, exclusivity, and faithfulness inherent in marriage, premarital sex brings with it a whole host of serious risks. There are physical risks, including pregnancy, HIV/AIDS, and other sexually transmitted diseases. There are emotional risks, too, for intercourse with another person is not simply a matter of commingling flesh; it is the full giving of one's person with all the physical, emotional, and psychological vulnerabilities this entails.[24] In this sense premarital sex is always in some way flawed. It always involves some lack of love, inability or unwillingness to give oneself away in love, or refusal to commit oneself to another person. This deficiency of love makes it impossible for sex to embody the meaning it was meant to have. By experiencing the expression of full human love without giving of themselves fully, the couple only hurt themselves.

Whatever the level of affection or commitment that a couple may have, one is not capacitated to engage in intercourse outside of marriage. Certainly one is able to engage in it on the biological level, but biology does not qualify or make one capable of engaging in intercourse. Consider the following analogy. Supposing that on the day before my ordination to the priesthood I decided to hear confessions. I may be physically able to hear them, and I am physically capable of saying the words of absolution, but these features do not qualify me to administer the sacrament. I must first be ordained to the priesthood and receive the faculties from the bishop. Without these there is no absolution (forgiveness of sin) because there is no sacrament. In a similar way, there may be intercourse without the exchange of marital vows, but this act is neither the sign nor the fruit of the genuine love that can be found only within the marital union.

Cohabitation

Cohabitation is on the rise. Between 1965 and 1974, 10 percent of marriages were preceded by cohabitation. Between 1990 and 1994, that percentage rose to 60 percent. This trend will most likely continue into the future, and cohabitation will be part of the cultural landscape for years to come. The morality of premarital sex was discussed in the previous section, and we will not repeat it here. Instead, we will focus on the different types of cohabitation and the challenges unique to each.

There are two types of cohabiting couples: those who have no definitive plans to marry and those who do. Scott Stanley and Linda Waite, respected marriage researchers who have studied cohabitating couples, have found that the couples whose relationships are most at risk for damage from cohabitating are those who have not decided for sure that they wish eventually to marry.

> Couples who live together with no definite plans to marry are making a different bargain than couples who marry or than engaged cohabitors.[25] . . . Those on their way to the altar look and act like already-married couples in most ways, and those with no plans to marry look and act different. For engaged cohabitating couples, living together is a step on the path to marriage, not a different road altogether.[26]

Waite concluded from her studies that when compared to marriage, uncommitted cohabitation is "an inferior social arrangement."[27] Based on their findings, these researchers conclude that cohabiting couples who have no definitive plans to marry fare much worse than those who do plan to marry.

Why do cohabiting couples with no plans to marry fare worse than those who do plan to marry? Part of the reason is that those who live together without plans for marriage are, general speaking, less economically and educationally privileged than those who plan to marry, and they also tend to come from families broken by divorce. Those who intend to marry the person with whom they are living, or couples that cohabit after a formal engagement, tend to be better off economically. They also tend to have higher levels of education and come from traditional two-parent families. Another study suggests that pre-engagement cohabitors demonstrate a higher risk for "relationship distress" (including domestic abuse) and that this risk generally does not diminish even if the couple eventually decides to marry. Conversely, there are "few differences in risk" between couples who cohabit only after engagement and those who wait until after marriage to live together.[28] These findings should give pause to those who are contemplating cohabitation absent long-term commitment. These people are often young adults who view cohabitation as "no big deal," it is simply a social arrangement accepted and promoted within our culture. In addition, further studies have indicated that in terms of divorce and domestic violence, engaged cohabitors who plan to marry are at near parity with those who do not live together before marriage. In other words, living together before exchanging vows does not lessen the odds of one's marriage failing. All this should make us think twice about the need for a "trial marriage" before a full commitment is made.

Given the risks for non-engaged cohabiting couples, why do people make the decision to live together without any plans for marriage? Some do not believe in the institution of marriage or that "a piece of paper" (a marriage license) will change how they feel about each other. Others want to have a "trial marriage" to determine their emotional and sexual compatibility, and to find out if they can actually live with one another. Others cohabit for financial reasons, reasoning that it is cheaper to share expenses with another person.

Despite its prevalence in society and the many reasons offered for it, cohabitation is, objectively speaking, morally wrong. This is true not only for cohabitors who do not intend to marry, but also for those who do intend to marry—including those already engaged. Only the sacrament of marriage brings about a marriage, and with it the capacity of the couple to express their love and mutual commitment in a physical way. But we have to be realistic as well. Many couples who present themselves for marriage in the Catholic Church are already living together. This is a reality and it must be acknowledged as such. Nevertheless, the Church must take practical, pastoral steps to avoid the impression that it somehow condones the practice of premarital cohabitation.

Michael Lawler recommends that during the period when an engaged couple is living together, they should undergo a period of intensive marriage preparation that includes a sound and realistic theology of marriage.[29] Kline et al. suggest that the best approach to cohabitation is preventative. The couple's desire to test marriage before committing to it could be addressed through research-based relationship education programs that deal with the religious, social, and legal implications of cohabitation. The purpose of these programs would be to allow the couple to weigh the costs and benefits of cohabitation before they move in together.[30] We strongly encourage the couple to separate until vows are exchanged or, if this is not possible, at least refrain from sexual contact until the marriage is celebrated. We do this because we do not want the couple to receive the sacrament of marriage unworthily, and we do not want sexual issues to cloud their judgment and thus impair their freedom to marry. We want their coming together as husband and wife to maintain something of the gift of new discovery. None of these proposals is perfect, nor will they end the practice of premarital cohabitation. However, they are important first steps in ministering to the special pastoral needs of engaged cohabiting couples.

Overall, the picture for cohabiting couples is not good. Numerous researchers conclude that cohabitation's many negative dimensions outweigh its positives. What will happen in the future is anyone's guess, but with the continuing prevalence of premarital cohabitation, the Church must continue developing positive pastoral programs to meet this ever-growing concern.

Contraception and Birth Control

The question of birth control and contraception is one of the most controversial issues facing the Roman Catholic Church today, at least in the Western world. Surveys indicate that American Catholics are aware that the Church teaches against the use of artificial methods of birth control, but most tend not to follow the Church's teachings. Some argue that the Church's position is outdated or that the magisterium has no business prying into people's private lives. Others assert that the teaching raises serious questions about how magisterial authority is applied, or point out that even the bishops are not unanimous on the issue. And yet most American Catholics are unaware of the reasons the Church teaches what it does.

The *Catechism of the Catholic Church* states, "Fecundity [fertility] is a gift, an *end of marriage*. A child does not come from outside as something added on to the mutual love of the spouses, but springs from the very heart of their mutual self giving, as its fruit and fulfillment."[31] The Church takes the creation and raising of children seriously, but what does this have to do with birth control and contraception?

First, we need to distinguish birth control from contraception. In *Humanae Vitae* ("On Human Life"), Pope Paul VI spoke about the importance of marital love and sexuality. Being responsible parents involves the couple *either* having a large and "numerous" family *or* regulating the number of children they have as long as there are serious reasons for doing so.[32] In other words, married couples can regulate when they have children and how many they have, based on the number they can support or the concrete circumstances of their family life. The Church is not opposed to birth control; the Church is opposed to contraception.

Paul VI went on to assert that God has established an objective moral order that is binding on all human beings. Sexual behavior is included in this moral order, and all people are bound to understand and incorporate it into their lives. Particularly, the Church teaches that "each and every marriage act remain ordered per se to the transmission of life."[33] This means there is an unbroken connection, willed by God and unable to be broken by humanity, between the procreative and unitive meanings of marital intercourse. As such, when a couple is having intercourse and the wife is fertile, the couple must respect this fertility.

Pope John Paul II further explained this inseparable connection between the procreative and unitive aspects of marital sexuality by focusing on the metaphor of "gift":

The conjugal union can be understood and fully explained *only by recourse to the values of the "person" and of "gift."* Every man and every woman fully realizes himself or herself through the sincere gift of self. For spouses, the moment of conjugal union constitutes a particular expression of this. It is then that a man and woman, in the "truth" of their masculinity and femininity, become a mutual gift to each other. . . . In the conjugal act, husband and wife are called to confirm in a responsible way *the mutual gift* of self which they have made to each other in the marriage covenant. The logic of the *total gift of self to the other* involves a potential openness to procreation: in this way the marriage is called to even greater fulfillment as a family. . . . *The intimate truth of this gift* must always be *safeguarded* . . . [and] *the two dimensions of conjugal union*, the unitive and the procreative, *cannot be artificially separated* without damaging the deepest truth of the conjugal act itself.[34]

John Paul II teaches that both the unitive and procreative aspects of marital sexuality involve "gift." The unitive aspect involves the "two-in-oneness" that characterizes marital sexuality. Through the act of intercourse, the husband and wife offer their entire self (body, soul, mind, heart) to their spouse and they become a mutual gift to each other. By offering the gift of their total self to their spouse, the couple together opens themselves to receiving the gift of new life from God. In other words, it is only through the complete giving of themselves that they open themselves to receiving the gift of a child. This is the "intimate connection" between the procreative and unitive aspects of marital sexuality, a connection that is willed by God and can never be broken by humanity.

Why is the separation of the unitive and procreative meanings of the marital act considered deficient? When a couple gets married they respond affirmatively to the following intention, "Have you come here freely and without reservation to give yourselves to each other in marriage?" By this intention, they are agreeing to give themselves to each other in a special way, in a married way. Part of their self-giving is the agreement to become one flesh in marital intercourse. This they do freely. If, afterward, a couple chooses to use a contraceptive, what they in effect are doing is going against the intention they formulated on their wedding day. It is as if they were saying, "Remember that promise I made to you to give myself to you freely and without reservation? Well, I do have one reservation. You cannot have my fertility." In so doing, they deny the procreative aspect of the sexual act, and effectively split the bond of unity and procreation that they had freely pledged to each other on their wedding day. The use of contraception is not only a physical act that impedes procreation, but it is also a deeply personal act that strikes at the heart of the marital meaning of intercourse. For these reasons, having recourse to contraception is always disordered.

It is important to note that the Church's teaching does not mean, as is often thought, that a married couple must intend to conceive a child every time they have intercourse. This is biologically impossible. Some men are infertile, and women are not fertile during the majority of their menstrual cycle, and after menopause they are not fertile at all, so any act of inter-course occurring during these times will not produce a child. The Church's teaching also does not imply that having children is the only purpose for sexual intercourse within a marriage. The Second Vatican Council clearly states that while marital sexuality is "ordained for the procreation and edu-cation of children," this "does not make the other ends of marriage (i.e. the mutual good of the spouses) of less account." Marriage was not instituted by God "solely for procreation."[35] The 1983 *Code of Canon Law* further states that marriage is a covenant "by which a man and woman establish between themselves a partnership of their whole life, and which of its very nature is ordered to the well-being of the spouses and to the procreation and upbringing of children."[36] Procreation is but one purpose for the mari-tal act. An equally important purpose is to demonstrate the mutual affec-tion and support of the couple by expressing their love physically.

Contraception, as opposed to birth control, is any act that intends to impede procreation, "whether it is done in anticipation of marital inter-course, or during it, or while it is having its natural consequences."[37] "In anticipation of marital intercourse" refers to any action that a couple freely chooses to do *before* intercourse that would impede fertility ("mechanical" devices such as condoms, diaphragms, intrauterine devices, cervical caps, sponges, patches, and spermicides; pharmaceuticals such as pills, implants, and shots; and direct surgical sterilization of either the male or the female). "During marital intercourse," refers to an action that is done *during* inter-course that would render fertility impossible (withdrawal of the penis before ejaculation). "While it is having its natural consequences" refers to an action done *after* intercourse that would not allow for fertility to take its course (douching and direct abortion, either through a surgical procedure or by means of prescription birth control pills, Plan B/the "morning after pill," or RU 486).

The Church teaches that each of these methods is problematic because in one way or another each separates the unitive and the procreative aspects of the marital act. They do this either by rendering the act sterile when it would otherwise be fertile or by interfering with the implantation of the ovum after fertilization. Recall from our discussion of health care ethics the Church's teaching that once an egg is fertilized by a sperm there exists a unique human life, one that needs to be respected and protected. Many argue that a fertilized but not-yet-implanted egg does not constitute a human life—the position the media most often takes when reporting about contraceptives. The Church vehemently disagrees with this view and argues that any interference with the implantation of the fertilized ovum constitutes a direct abortion. Contraception, therefore, does not refer solely to preventing a sperm from fertilizing an egg (contra-conception), it also refers to preventing an already fertilized egg from traveling to the uterus and actually implanting in the uterine wall.

What, then, can a couple do if they wish to limit or space their children? One option is the group of methods termed Natural Family Planning (NFP). NFP can be used either to avoid or achieve pregnancy. When used to avoid a pregnancy, NFP requires that a couple abstain from sexual intercourse during times in the woman's menstrual cycle when she is fertile. NFP involves daily fertility awareness, or monitoring of the woman's body, by which it can generally be determined when the woman is fertile. Though cycles can vary from one woman to another and from one cycle to the next, in general a woman begins ovulating on or about the eleventh day of her cycle and continues to be fertile for 3–4 days. Her husband's sperm can live inside her body for about 2–3 days. To avoid pregnancy, a couple should abstain from sexual relations for the 3–4 days that the woman is fertile. To make sure none of the husband's sperm is still able to fertilize an egg once ovulation occurs, they should also abstain for 2–3 days before ovulation.[38]

How do we know for sure when ovulation begins? Through daily fertility awareness, which focuses primarily on the quality of the woman's cervical mucus and her basal body temperature. Normally, when a woman is infertile her cervical mucus tends to be dry and sticky, serving as a natural barrier to the sperm. When a woman is fertile her cervical mucus tends to be clear and more slippery, serving as a natural conduit for the sperm. Similarly, when a woman is infertile her basal temperature will be about 98.6 degrees. However, when she is ovulating her temperature will spike up approximately one-half to one full degree. If a woman charts her temperature every morning over a period of months, she begins to recognize a pattern of when her ovulation periods begin. This charting, along with changes in her cervical mucus, inform her of when she and her husband should abstain from sexual relations.

A number of studies have found NFP to have an excellent effectiveness rate. The Los Angeles Study, conducted at the behest of the United States Department of Health, Education, and Welfare, showed a 100 percent effectiveness rate for couples who followed the method exactly, and a 99 percent effectiveness rate overall. The Fairfield Study also showed a 99 percent effectiveness rate, as did the Roetzer and Vincent studies, while the Doring Temperature-Only Study showed an effectiveness rate of 97 percent. Overall, NFP studies conducted in five nations showed an effectiveness rate of 85 – 99 percent.[39] These rates are comparable to, if not greater than, those for condoms and birth control pills. NFP studies have further demonstrated that the best guarantor of success is open and honest communication between the husband and wife.

Many people do not see much difference between the use of contraception and NFP. After all, they say, couples using either method are doing so to avoid getting pregnant. Although the motive in each instance is the same, the intentional act is different. In the case of the couple using contraception, their intentional act is to prevent pregnancy by rendering either the husband or the wife infertile. This act interferes with the procreative aspect of marital sexuality and thus the choice to do so is morally disordered. In the case of the couple using NFP, their intentional act is different. This couple is choosing to prevent a pregnancy in a way that respects the natural cycle of fertility. In other words, this couple is not working against nature to prevent a pregnancy, but working in accord with it. This is not philosophical hair splitting. It is, rather, the recognition of what constitutes a specifically human act.

Some complain that the Catholic Church is too caught up in the "natural" aspect of sexuality (procreation) and inattentive to its more personal dimensions. Although the Church does draw upon biology, it does not neglect the more personal dimensions of the sexual act. We have already discussed one aspect: the gift of self that the couple makes to each other. However, this gift is not simply the gift of one's body but the gift of one's whole person, including the person's biological fertility. It is through the personal love of the couple for each other, expressed in part through their biology, that the couple is able to bring forth another person who, like them, is created in the image and likeness of God. If we were to focus exclusively on the biological dimensions of marital intercourse, we would reduce ourselves to sub-rational creatures. If we were to focus exclusively on the personal dimensions of marital intercourse, we would reduce ourselves to disembodied creatures for whom the body has no moral value. We must acknowledge and respect both the biological and the personal if we are to understand fully the Church's teaching on marital intercourse and contraception.

Homosexuality

Homosexuality is a hot topic these days, as seen in media coverage of same-sex marriage, homosexual adoption of children, the election of an openly gay bishop in the Episcopalian church, or the "don't ask/don't tell" policy of the U.S. military. While each of these issues merits individual examination, our discussion is limited to a consideration of what homosexuality is, how it expresses itself, and how the Church responds to this sensitive issue.

First, we have to distinguish between a homosexual orientation and homosexual activity. A homosexual orientation is found in those individuals who have a sexual inclination or attraction to members of the same gender. Homosexual activity is sexual behavior: sexual acts performed with a member of the same gender. It is important to point out that just because one has a homosexual orientation, it does not mean that he or she automatically engages in homosexual activity. There are people with a homosexual orientation who choose not to engage in same-sex relations for various reasons. There are also people of a heterosexual orientation who, in certain circumstances (in prison, for example), may be pressured into engaging in homosexual activities.

It is difficult to know for certain what percentage of the population has a homosexual orientation. Statistics range from 4–8 percent of males and 2–4 percent of females.[40] It is also difficult to discover what percentage of the homosexual population leads an openly gay or lesbian lifestyle. Various theorists attribute the homosexual orientation to genetic, hormonal, or prenatal factors. Others posit adult hormonal or other postnatal factors. Still others postulate a psychological origin. At present we simply do not know the origins of the homosexual orientation. We do know that those who have this orientation experience it as an integral aspect of their being; it is as much a part of who they are as the heterosexual orientation is for those who are "straight." Moreover, one does not choose to be homosexual any more than one chooses to be heterosexual. In fact, the inclination is discovered as the person matures, not unlike the discovery of one's heterosexual orientation at puberty. The activities in which one engages and the lifestyle that one adopts are subject to choice, even though the orientation is not.

The *Catechism of the Catholic Church* is clear both with respect to the homosexual orientation and homosexual activity. The homosexual orientation is "objectively disordered,"[41] while homosexual acts are "intrinsically disordered" and contrary to the natural law, thus under no circumstances can they be approved.[42] The wording of the Church's teaching regarding the homosexual orientation and the homosexual act is not well received by many. Because of the close connection between sexuality and personhood, terms like "disordered" are read as an indictment of the homosexual's personhood, that somehow their "being" is objectively disordered. This merits a close reading of the Church's words.

Actually, the Church's choice of terms here derives from natural law. Homosexual acts are considered contrary to natural law in that they go against our understanding of the way men and women were created as sexually differentiated persons. Men and women were created by God to complement each other, as evidenced by their ability to procreate with one another. Thus homosexual acts are "disordered" in that they are essentially sterile acts, incapable of generating new life. The natural law is, in part, the expression of the essential finalities of human nature, and the essential finality of sexual relations is the survival of the species. This procreative understanding of sexuality does not exclude other purposes for sexual relations, but the act of intercourse of a married couple is potentially generative of new life. A homosexual act never is. Homosexual acts are deficient — notice we are talking deficiency, not necessarily sin — in their ability to bring forth new life, and thus they are deemed by the Church to be contrary to natural law.

John Raphael Quinn, former archbishop of San Francisco and one who is sensitive to the challenges facing homosexuals, explained the meaning of "objectively disordered" in these terms:

> This is philosophical language. The inclination is a disorder because it is directed to an object that is disordered. The inclination and the object are in the same order philosophically. But the particular inclination of the homosexual is not a sin. In trying to understand this affirmation, we should advert to two things. First, every person has disordered inclinations. For instance, the inclination to rash judgment is disordered, the inclination to cowardice, the inclination to hypocrisy — these are all disordered inclinations. Consequently, homosexual persons are not the only ones who have disordered inclinations. Second, the letter [*Letter to the Bishops of the Catholic Church on the Pastoral Care of Homosexual Persons*, Vatican Congregation for the Doctrine of the Faith (1986)] does not say that the homosexual person is disordered. The inclination, not the person, is described as disordered. Speaking of the homosexual person, the letter states that the Church "refuses to consider the person as a 'heterosexual' or a 'homosexual' and insists that every person has a fundamental identity: the creature of God and, by grace, His child and heir to eternal life" (no. 16). Consequently, the document affirms the spiritual and human dignity of the homosexual person while placing a negative moral judgment on homosexual acts and a negative philosophical judgment on the homosexual inclination, which it clearly states is not a sin or a moral evil.[43]

Here, Quinn makes some important clarifications. The homosexual orientation is disordered because of its object: members of the same gender. This is a philosophical distinction, not a theological one, so we are not speaking about sin. Rather, the philosophical language expresses that an inclination toward members of the same gender (the object) is not in keeping with the natural order of things. This disordered inclination is not unique to sexual orientation. Philosophically speaking, all of us have disorders of one kind or another—inclinations to cowardice, rash judgment and hypocrisy to name but a few. These inclinations are not evil in and of themselves, but if we were to act on them we then would be committing a moral evil. The same is true with respect to the homosexual orientation. The inclination to have sexual relations with a member of the same sex is not, in itself, sinful. What is sinful is when a person chooses to act on this inclination and has relations with a member of the same sex.

Particularly helpful is Quinn's observation that "the Church refuses to consider the person as a 'heterosexual' or a 'homosexual' and insists that every person has a fundamental identity: a creature of God and, by grace, his child and heir to eternal life." The Church's teaching serves as an important corrective to the tendency of many people who view their orientation as "who they are" as persons. Although it is true that sexuality is an important aspect of ourselves, there is also the danger of reducing personhood to sexuality. To claim that the Church is opposed to homosexual behavior is true; to claim that the Church is unwelcoming of homosexuals is false. The United States Catholic bishops asserted that homosexuals "have a right to be welcomed into the community, to hear the Word of God, and to receive pastoral care." In fact, they held that homosexuals living chaste lives can both serve and hold leadership positions within the worshipping community.[44] To be clear, the Church teaches that homosexual acts are objectively sinful, but the homosexual orientation is not.

The Church offers guidelines to inform our attitudes and behaviors with respect to homosexual persons. We find a clear statement in the *Catechism*:

> Homosexual persons are called to a life of chastity. By the virtue of self-control, which helps to educate their interior freedom, sometimes with the support of disinterested friendships, through prayer and sacramental grace, they can and must grow, gradually and resolutely, toward Christian perfection.[45]

All Christians—heterosexual or homosexual, married or single—are called to a life of chastity. The Church holds that sexual activity is permitted in only one context: marriage. This is not to say that all other people cease to be sexual beings—that would be to deny how God created us. But sexual activity belongs properly and exclusively within the confines of marriage between a man and a woman. Homosexuals are called to recognize this virtue and to act in concert with it throughout their lives.

With respect to our own attitudes toward homosexuality, recall Archbishop Quinn's statement that "the Church refuses to consider the person as a 'heterosexual' or a 'homosexual' and insists that every person has a fundamental identity: the creature of God and, by grace, His child and heir to eternal life." This attitude is repeated, in different ways, throughout all the recent documents on homosexuality issued by the Vatican and the United States Catholic bishops. The *Catechism* well summarizes this attitude when it states:

> A non-negligible number of men and women present deep homosexual tendencies. They do not choose their homosexual condition; for many of them, in fact, it is a real trial. They must be received with respect, compassion and care. All unjust discrimination in their regard must be avoided. These persons are called to experience the love of God in their lives, and if they are Christians, to unite to the sacrifice of the Lord's Cross the difficulties that they can encounter from their condition.[46]

Masturbation

Masturbation is defined as the stimulation of the genital organs to orgasm. Masturbation is practiced by males and females, young and old, married and unmarried. According to a survey first done by Alfred Kinsey over a half century ago, 92 percent of males and 58 percent of females claimed to have masturbated to orgasm at least once in their lives.[47] In the years since this first survey was completed, these figures have increased, especially among women. For example, *The Hite Report* of 1976 stated that the frequency rate for males has jumped from 49 to 52 times per year, while for women it has increased from 21 to 37 times per year.[48] Generally speaking, males masturbate earlier and more frequently than women, but this usually declines with age. Females start masturbating later, but once they start their rate tends to remain constant no matter what their age.[49] These statistics should disabuse us of the notion that only the young or unmarried engage in masturbatory acts. But the question remains, why do people masturbate?

There are several features that make masturbation attractive. It is safe, it relieves the buildup of sexual tension, and it is perceived to combat loneliness. Further reasons include that through masturbation, one gets to know one's body and what gives it pleasure. Within marriage, masturbation also can be a supplemental form of pleasure even when intercourse is satisfying, or it can be practiced when sexual relations cease because of health or other reasons.

Despite the widespread practice and comparative lack of harmful effects of masturbation, however, the Catholic Church teaches that it is always a serious matter.

> Both the Magisterium of the Church . . . and the moral sense of the faithful have declared without hesitation that masturbation is an intrinsically and seriously disordered act. The main reason is that, whatever the motive for acting in this way, the deliberate use of the sexual faculty outside normal [marital] relations essentially contradicts the finality of the faculty. For it lacks the sexual relationship called for by the moral order, namely, the relationship which realizes "the full sense of mutual self-giving and human procreation in the context of true love." All deliberate exercise of sexuality must be reserved to this regular relationship.[50]

The Church teaches that masturbation is deficient for essentially the same reason premarital sex is deficient: it is not the sign and fruit of a loving and committed relationship between two people. There is no procreative aspect, and the fact that one performs the act by oneself demonstrates that there is no unitive aspect. The absence of the procreative and unitive aspects means that the act falls short of, or is deficient in, that which sexuality truly entails. In addition, the Church considers masturbation disordered because it goes against the natural law or because it "contradicts" the finality or end purpose of the human sexual faculty. Masturbation's disorder is seen in its deficiency to function as a fully self-giving and life-giving act.

In making these claims, the Church does not deny the prevalence of masturbation or its frequency.

> [The Church's teaching] is not intended to deny the psychological or sociological data, which indicate that such behavior is common, especially among the young. Modern behavioral sciences provide us with much valid and useful information for formulating better contextual judgments and more sensitive pastoral responses.[51]
>
> Psychology helps us to see how the immaturity of adolescence (which can sometimes persist after that age), psychological imbal-

ance or habit can influence behavior, diminishing the deliberate character of the act and bringing about a situation whereby subjectively there may not always be serious fault. But in general, the absence of serious responsibility must not be presumed.[52]

These statements recognize that there is an objective dimension to the moral seriousness of masturbation such that it always remains a deficient act, but the Church also recognizes a subjective dimension. The masturbatory act may or may not be sinful on the personal level, depending on the person's freedom, knowledge, will, and level of maturity.

Given the frequency and prevalence of masturbation, is there a real hope that this objectively deficient behavior can mature into a self-giving and life-giving behavior? We think so. On the pastoral level, we find most individuals are bothered by their masturbatory behavior. There is inherent within the person a sense of its unworthiness, its incompletion, its sterility, and its immaturity. We encourage people not to pay too much attention to this kind of behavior, for that usually only allows it to continue. Rather, we recommend recourse to prayer, reception of the sacraments, and a refocusing of thoughts outward toward others (e.g., helping the less fortunate). With time and continued prayer, such behavior becomes less important to the person and he or she moves outward to meet both others and the self.

Conclusion

The Church's teachings on sexuality are essentially positive, timely, and always take seriously the biological, personal, and interpersonal dimensions of sex. Sex is a biological reality: without it we could not continue the species. But sexuality is also a constitutive dimension of the human person as created by God. And sex is an interpersonal reality; an embodied person relates to a specific "other" in a way that expresses full self-giving and also (potentially) participates in God's creative activity. Any expression of sexuality that falls short of these biological, personal, and interpersonal dimensions is deficient, lacking in the fullness of who we are meant to be as sexual beings.

Review Questions

1. Why is sexuality understood as an essential dimension of the human person?

2. What are affective emotions? What is the role of temperance in terms of the affective emotions?

3. According to the *Catechism of the Catholic Church*, what is *chastity*?

4. How did Karol Wojtyla (the future Pope John Paul II) define chastity?

5. Why does the text speak about deficiencies and not sins when discussing aspects of sexuality that the Church finds problematic?

6. How is sexual intercourse the "sign and fruit" of a relationship between two people? What are the characteristics of this relationship?

7. What do the authors strongly encourage cohabiting couples to do before a marriage ceremony? Why do they encourage such couples to do this?

8. According to the Church, what is "deficient" when a couple separates the procreative and unitive aspects of marital sexuality?

9. What important clarification did Archbishop Quinn make concerning the *Catechism's* teaching that the homosexual orientation is disordered?

10. How do you feel about homosexuality? What is your attitude toward homosexuals? If you are a homosexual, what do you make of the Church's teaching?

11. Why does the Congregation for the Doctrine of the Faith teach that masturbation is morally wrong?

ENDNOTES

1 Rev. Benedict M. Guevin, OSB, *Christian Anthropology and Sexual Ethics.* (Lanham, MD: University Press of America, 2002), 17.

2 Cf. Saint Thomas Aquinas, *Summa Theologiae*, I–II, q. 24, a. 2, *responsio.*

3 Ibid., q. 149.

4 Ibid., q. 146.

5 Ibid., q. 144.

6 Ibid., q. 145. When honor involves the virtue of chastity, it is called purity.

7 Cf. Karol Wojtyla, *Love and Responsibility*, trans. H. T. Willetts (New York: Farrar, Straus, and Giroux, 1994), 174. A balanced description of healthy shame is in John Cassian's ideal portrait of the monk in Conference 12: "He is found to be the same at night as in day, the same in bed as in prayer, the same alone as when surrounded by a crowd of people, he sees nothing in himself in private that he would be embarrassed for others to see, nor wants anything detected by the omnipresent Eye [of God] to be concealed from human sight" (*Conl.* 12.8.5), quoted in Columba Stewart, *Cassian the Monk* (New York/Oxford: Oxford University Press, 1998), 83.

8 Cf. Wojtyla, *Love and Responsibility*, 175–78.

9 Cf. *ST* II–II, q. 144, a. 4.

10 Ibid., a. 1, *ad* 4.

11 Ibid., q. 145, a. 3.

12 Ibid., Ia, q. 5. a. 6; II–II, q. 143, a. 3.

13 Ibid., II–II, q. 144, a. 4, *ad* 1.

14 Josef Pieper, *Fortitude and Temperance*, trans. Daniel F. Coogan (New York: Pantheon, 1954), 50–52.

15 *Catechism of the Catholic Church*, 2337.

16 Cf. Pope Benedict XVI, *God Is Love* (*Deus caritas est*), 5.

17 For a further discussion of this, cf. Benedict Ashley, *Theologies of the Body: Humanist and Christian* (Washington, DC: The Pope John Center, 1985; repr. 1995), 370; cf. also Benedict M. Guevin, OSB, "Aquinas' use of Ulpian and the question of Physicalism Reexamined," *The Thomist* 63, no. 4 (1999): 613–28.

18 Wojtyla, *Love and Responsibilty*, 171.

19 *CCC*, 2242–2343.

20 Cf. Pope Benedict XVI, *God Is Love*, 5.

21 Gerald D. Coleman, SS, *Human Sexuality: An All-Embracing Gift* (New York: Alba House, 1992), 39.

22 Patrick McCormick and Russell Connors, *Facing Ethical Issues: Dimensions of Character, Choices and Community* (Mahwah, NJ: Paulist Press, 2002), 164.

23 See the commentary on Canon 1061 in *New Commentary on the Code of Canon Law*, ed. John P. Beal et al. (Mahwah, NJ: Canon Law Society of America/Paulist Press, 2000), 1257.

24 See Thomas Lickona's "The Neglected Heart: The Emotional Dangers of Premature Sexual Involvement," in *Perspectives on Marriage: A Reader*, eds. Kieran Scott and Michael Warren, 2d ed. (New York: Oxford University Press, 2001), 158–68.

25 Linda J. Waite, "Cohabitation: A Communitarian Perspective," in *Marriage in America: A Communitarian Perspective*, ed. Martin King Whyte (Lanham, MD: Rowan and Littlefield, 2000), 26. Cited in Michael G. Lawler, "Cohabitation: Past and Present Reality," *Theological Studies* 65, no. 3 (September 2004): 623–29.

26 Ibid., 627.

27 Ibid., 26. Cited in Lawler, 627.

28 Galena H. Kline et al., "Timing Is Everything: Pre-Engagement Cohabitation and Increased Risk for Poor Marriage Outcomes," *The Journal of Family Psychology* 18, no. 2 (June 2004): 311–18, especially 317.

29 Lawler, "Cohabitation," 629.

30 Kline et al., 317.

31 *CCC*, 2366.

32 *Humanae Vitae (On Human Life)*, no. 10.

33 Ibid., no. 11.

34 Pope John Paul II, *Letter to Families on the International Year of the Family*, no. 12 (emphasis in the original).

35 Second Vatican Council, *Gaudium et Spes (Pastoral Constitution on the Church in the Modern World)* (1965), nos. 48–50.

36 *Code of Canon Law* (1981), no. 1055.1.

37 Ibid., no. 14.

38 This section does not claim to offer a complete description of NFP. See the Couple to Couple League Web site at http://www.ccli.org/nfp/index. shtml.

39 Couple to Couple League at http://www.ccli.org /nfp/effect3.shtml.

40 Coleman, *Human Sexuality*, 216.

41 *CCC*, 2358.

42 Ibid., 2357. For "intrinsically disordered," see *On the Human Person (Persona humana)*, 8.

43 "Toward an Understanding of the Letter on the Pastoral Care of Homosexual Persons," in *America* 156 (1987), 92–95 and 116, esp. 94.

44 U. S. Conference of Catholic Bishops, *Always Our Children: A Pastoral Message to Parents of Homosexual Children and Suggestions for Pastoral Ministers* (1997); available online at www.usccb.org/laity/always.shtml.

45 *CCC*, 2359.

46 Ibid., 2358.

47 A.C. Kinsey et al., *Sexual Behavior in the Human Male* (Philadelphia: Saunders Publishing Co., 1948), 502.

48 Shere Hite, *The Hite Report*. N.Y.: Dell Publishing Co., 1976 (cited in Coleman, 307).

49 Coleman, 306–7.

50 Congregation for the Doctrine of the Faith, *Declaration on Certain Questions Concerning Sexual Ethics* (December 29, 1975), no. 9.

51 The United States Catholic Conference, *Human Sexuality* (Washington, DC: USCC, 1990), 62.

52 *Declaration on Certain Questions*, no. 9.

INDEX